Dennis Cometti is one of the best known and most respected sportscasters in Australia, covering everything from Test cricket with the great Alan McGilvray to Commonwealth Games and the Barcelona and Atlanta Olympics. He played football for Footscray in the 1970s before injury forced him to hang up his boots. No longer able to play, Dennis turned his focus and passion for AFL to commentating where he has earned the reputation of being the most distinctive, eloquent and beloved football commentators the game has ever known.

The Age's **Jon Pierik** has been a football fan since he was old enough to see over the boundary fence and a sports journalist for major metropolitan newspapers for more than a decade. He understands what makes the game great—and why it inspires fine journalism. Pierik combines these two ingredients to deliver a must read for AFL fans.

THE GAME

A COLLECTION OF THE BEST AFL STORIES

EDITED BY

DENNIS COMETTI

WITH JON PIERIK

FAIRFAX BOOKS
ALLEN&UNWIN

First published in 2012

Fairfax Books, an imprint of
Allen & Unwin
Sydney, Melbourne, Auckland, London

83 Alexander Street
Crows Nest NSW 2065
Australia
Phone: (61 2) 8425 0100
Email: info@allenandunwin.com
Web: www.allenandunwin.com

Cataloguing-in-Publication details are available
from the National Library of Australia
www.trove.nla.gov.au

ISBN 978 1 74331 317 6

Cover design by Squirt Creative
Set in Electra LT and Bell Gothic by Midland Typesetters, Australia
Printed and bound in Australia by Griffin Press

10 9 8 7 6 5 4 3 2 1

The paper in this book is FSC® certified.
FSC® promotes environmentally responsible,
socially beneficial and economically viable
management of the world's forests.

CONTENTS

CONTENTS

INTRODUCTION

Dennis Cometti

I'M NOT THE NEWSPAPER READER I once was. Things have changed! These days newspapers are fighting for their very existence. But unlike dinosaurs, V8s and Mark Neeld, they have the tools to fight back. This book celebrates that battle and takes us to the frontline. It's all about fine writers telling good stories. But these aren't just any stories, they're AFL stories.

While AFL is an institution, I need to go on record by pointing out that AFL writing is no Roman ruin. It's younger than Alex Turner. If you're wondering who the hell Alex Turner is, read on. That blank look will help me make a point further down the line.

By its nature writing about footy can't always be epic; the need to fill space and meet deadlines, of necessity, means thin gruel can often take the place of rich bouillabaisse. Seems to me, outstanding writing relies on two things—time and topic.

The articles you're about to read on the following pages show just what can be done when both find their way to the right keyboard. Each article will draw you in. Much like an afternoon watching Gary Ablett (the father and the son) running amok or Lance Franklin notching a lazy 13 (13 that left James Brayshaw exploring the vagaries of DIY acupuncture) you'll come away knowing it was time well spent.

I was lucky growing up in Perth. It was the home of Australian Football Hall of Fame journalist Geoff Christian, a man who had a way with words, and people. Geoff was a product of his time. His match reports were just that, succinct analytical reports. But by contrast, given time and a major topic

Geoff Christian wrote with a graceful charm I shall always remember. He was Oscar Madison of *The Odd Couple* long before *The Odd Couple* were odd. A cigarette, a typewriter and a big heart!

Footy sells papers and fills papers in the southern states of Australia, but what I intend here is to roam a little further afield than just footy. Because while footy writing is sports writing, sports writing has been around since before the Colosseum!

I guess the first time I sat up and took notice of a sports writer was reading a best-of collection by Englishman Neville Cardus in the mid-seventies. At the time, cricket was high on my priorities list. I was broadcasting Test cricket on the ABC and Cardus had a style of writing I'd never encountered before. His was a very personal account. He became part of any story. His innermost thoughts were pivotal to every article he wrote.

Cardus (later Sir Neville) worked for numerous newspapers including Sir Keith Murdoch's Melbourne *Herald* and *Sydney Morning Herald*; but it was at his local, the *Manchester Guardian*, that he first won acclaim as England's foremost cricket correspondent. Within a few summers he had been elevated to the standing of a Princeton mathematician!

But perhaps the most unique thing about Cardus was his passion for writing classical musical critiques. He quit more than one paper, including the Melbourne *Herald*, because he felt that his music columns were underappreciated. Often his columns ran just pages apart, music and sport, with a language common to both.

"The elements are cricket's presiding geniuses."

"There ought to be some other means of reckoning quality in the best and loveliest of games; the scoreboard is an ass."

"We remember not the scores and the results in after years; it is the men who remain in our minds."

"In no other game does the law of averages get to work so potently, so mysteriously."

My experience of football journalism had been limited to matter-of-fact stuff. Big Bob Johnson might have been in the goal-square and I was happy to leave it at that. Whether he should be in the goal-square, just why he was in the goal-square and the relationship of both to the cosmos was something I hadn't thought much about. Cardus seemed to think it was important; more to the point, if he thought it was important he intended for me to think so too. I liked that.

I guess I also liked the fact he was a music man like me. Neville Cardus was a guy who refused to be pigeonholed. Okay, our tastes didn't exactly dovetail but on paper, at least, classical and classic rock aren't so dissimilar! What I liked also was his ability to challenge his reader. At times in his autobiography he was like a batsman dancing down the pitch to get on the front foot:

> Such reproductions may not interest the reader; but after all, this is my autobiography, not his; he is under no obligation to read further in it; he was under none to begin. A modest or inhibited autobiography is written without entertainment to the writer and read with distrust by the reader.

That's about as amusing as Cardus got. Then again, I'm sure the prospect of making his readers smile rarely crossed his mind. Almost always it was heady, heavy stuff and when it came to cricket his was the stuff.

Which reminds me, this is my foreword. So just before you immerse yourself in AFL footy I'd like to share with you some of my favourite sports writers. Too bad then if you don't feel inclined to join me! Over the years I have collected many memorable and hard to find articles, mostly from what I like to call my "American period". In fact, as recently as the past week some of those articles have become even harder to find. Experience is teaching me the more things I store in one place (like a foreword) the easier they are to find.

In the early eighties I fell in love with American sport, particularly football and basketball. At the same time I came to know the writing of Hunter S Thompson. Thompson was Sir Neville Cardus on acid. Alongside this new breed it's fair to say the man from Manchester all but put the staid into stadium.

Thompson claimed to be the sports writer for *Rolling Stone* magazine (again that mix of sport and music) and for the most part the magazine played along. It was also the time of his masterpiece, *Fear and Loathing in Las Vegas*. Two hundred and four pages of drug-fuelled laugh-out-loud political incorrectness! I still try to read it annually.

Without putting too fine a point on it I think he rewrote writing. He pioneered a new style (pop culture) of journalism. Thompson worked hard at being offensive, humorous, abrasive and informative. He wanted to be the story and he constantly sought new ways to visit old themes and make them his own.

I think of him often when I hear and read the cliches of sport in general, and the AFL in particular. Perhaps in February 2005, on the day he shot himself, Hunter inadvertently tuned in to an NAB Cup game on cable. Can you imagine? "Judd has shown great vision, he's put his hand up and is leading from the front." Okay, so Judd has never set foot in the NAB Cup but you're missing the point, the player is immaterial. Is it any wonder my man pulled the trigger back in '05? The whole thing sounds like a job description for Hitler's chauffeur. Thompson wanted no part in somebody else's cliches. His trick was to write about the familiar but somehow be unique.

In *Fear and Loathing* the writer and his attorney set out from Los Angeles en route to Las Vegas ostensibly "to cover the richest off-the-road race for motorcycles and dune buggies in the history of organized sport—a fantastic spectacle in honor of some fatback grossero named Del Webb, who owns the luxurious Mint Hotel on the Vegas strip ... at least that's what the press release says". But the sporting connection soon gets lost!

My read on Hunter S Thompson is that his love of sport was more a love of gambling and that his true passion was for the game of politics. Besides *Rolling Stone*, he wrote regular columns for the *San Francisco Examiner* and *ESPN* magazine. At times, particularly in his latter days, the distance between his best and lesser work was substantial, but at his best he remained a force.

Just one question: pardon me for asking, but what are you if you openly admit you admire and aspire to the work of a narcissist? I asked Carlton defender Nick Duigan, a man with a Masters in psychology. He was nothing if not evasive. He said the answer was tricky but thought it could be found in a Freudian paper dealing with "the difficulty of diagnosing senility in extremely stupid people". I must say I found Nick's laugh unsettling.

Almost as unsettling as Hunter S in full rant covering the presidential campaign trail:

One of the things you have to deal with in this business is being whipped on by brainless freaks and special-interest pleaders. It never ends. On some nights they gnaw on your doorknob, and on others they plot rotten lawsuits and fondle themselves like chimpanzees in rooms lit by 25-watt bulbs.

These things happen. Not everybody lives like the Cleavers. Some people are bent like Joe Theisman's leg, but few of them work for the Redskins, and nobody takes them to hospital when their bones erupt through their flesh.

(*Generation of Swine*, 1988)

And:

Kill the body and the head will die. This line appears in my notebook for some reason. Perhaps some connection to Joe Frazier! Is he still alive, still able to talk? I watched the fight in Seattle—horribly twisted about four seats down the aisle from the Governor. A very painful experience in every way, a proper end to the sixties.

Bob Dylan clipping coupons in Greenwich Village, both Kennedys murdered by mutants, Owlsey folding napkins on Terminal Island, and finally Cassius/Ali belted incredibly off his pedestal by a human hamburger, a man on the verge of death.

Joe Frazier, like Richard Nixon, had finally prevailed for reasons that people like me refused to understand—at least out loud.

(*Fear and Loathing in Las Vegas*, 1998)

What a remarkable stew that out-of-control mind could throw together. From *Leave it to Beaver* (the All-American Cleaver family) to Joe Theisman (the famous Redskin quarterback and his infamous broken leg) to Frazier, Ali, JFK and RFK, Dylan, Owlsey (NFI) and Nixon!

No doubting he was a human briar patch, but he knew how to connect. It was pop culture pure and simple. Politics with a sporting bent in a music magazine. Perfect! Mind-changing substances aside, I still find the mix compelling. If Hunter S Thompson didn't inspire a generation of writers he certainly provided them with much food for thought.

In this book you will find many familiar footy themes. They are separated from the pack almost always by the flair and the personality of the writer. What I hope to do in the remainder of *my* foreword is highlight some of those themes for both commonality and tasty writing.

THE PUTDOWN

I met American PJ O'Rourke while he was on assignment for the *Atlantic Monthly* in Perth during the America's Cup. Politically he was the polar opposite of Thompson but he wrote with an edge only slightly less cutting. At our one meeting (albeit brief) he seemed a really good bloke, but weeks later I had difficulty explaining this outburst. In fact I took it personally:

Fremantle is Dayton-on-the Sea. In fact Western Australia is Ohio with one side of its hat brim turned up. As soon as I got on solid ground, I went over to the famed Royal Perth Yacht Club. It looked like a cinder-block drive-through bottle store. (Cinder-block drive-through bottle stores are the main architectural features of the greater Perth–Fremantle metropolitan area.)

Then I visited the Fremantle docks where the twelve-metres are parked. Welcome to Hoboken, circa 1950. I expected Marlon Brando to saunter out at any moment and have the climactic fistfight in *On the Waterfront*.

God knows how the America's Cup race wound up out here. Somebody told me it had to do with Australia cheating in 1983 and putting tail fins on their boat bottom, but that sounds unlikely. I think the International Sailing-boat Racing Politburo, or whatever it's called, got Fremantle confused with Port-de-France and thought they were going to Martinique. Australia was like "Australia Nite" at the Michigan State Phi Delt house.

(Holidays in Hell, 2000)

THE SNEER

Steve Rushin (not to be confused with the Russian judge) is a writer at *Sports Illustrated*. One assumes his job description would include the phrase "sports nut". Apparently, though, in the small print it must suggest to keep one sport free to be your whipping boy. I presume soccer was taken!

The Stanley Cup isn't merely the most fetching trophy in North America, it is also the hardest earned. The action in OT, by which time most players are toothless, drained and darned like socks, is an end-to-end, whistle-free, whiplash-inducing blur: of slap shots ringing off the post, of heads being speedbagged in the corners, of Toronto keeper Curtis Joseph wandering so far from his crease that he sometimes becomes confused and briefly defends his opponent's goal.

On and on and on it goes, until somebody finally lights up the lamp, the goal judge's siren turning as if atop an ambulance. Then when the series ends, the two teams line up to exchange handshakes and pleasantries.

("Sorry about the teeth." "Better get that nose looked at." "Your head will grow back," etc.)

Why, America, have you not embraced this?

(The Caddy Was a Reindeer, 2004)

THE OUTRAGE

Tony Kornheiser was a long-time writer at the *Washington Post*. About a decade ago he joined ESPN, first as co-host of ESPN's *Pardon the Interruption* then as a colour commentator on the network's *Monday Night Football*.

> I haven't been watching the Sydney Olympics that much. It's too anti-climactic. By the time we see the events, the medal winners are eligible for social security.
>
> NBC's announcers say, "Stay tuned and we'll see if the US beat Kuwait in baseball." We'll see? By the time they run tape, it's been so long since the actual game we could have invaded Kuwait! Um, pardon, the US PROTECTS Kuwait, it doesn't invade it.
>
> Whatever. My point is that the Olympics may be reality based, but they're not reality. It's like *Survivor*—but with a bigger torch and lower ratings. If you want to know the truth, I think the Olympics are already over. All the athletes have been flown to Hawaii and sworn to secrecy, and NBC will string out the results over the next three years, or until George Clooney comes back to ER.
>
> (*I'm Back For More Cash*, 2003)

THE INSIGHT

For many years Frank Deford was chief writer for *Sports Illustrated*. He also dabbled in network television. Deford had the innate ability to write almost as conversation.

> I have a horse named after me. I don't mean anything obtuse like Flasher Frank or Frankie's Delight, but just plain Frank Deford, exactly as my name reads above and in the IRS and FBI files.
>
> At last count Frank Deford had made 12 starts and finished somewhat less than first in all of them. In chronological order the *Racing Form* tells us that Frank Deford has: been no factor, weakened, shown early speed, been far back, weakened, been outrun, run gamely, rallied (these last two constituted something of a hot streak), fell back, been no factor, performed evenly and been outrun.
>
> But this magnificently pithy catalogue of futility from the pen of some unknown turf poet does not do Frank Deford's efforts full justice. Take my favourite, the "performed evenly". "Performed evenly" was the time

Frank Deford got beat by 17 lengths. But everything is relative. If a guy met Job along about Chapter 11 of his travails and said, "How's tricks Pal?" Job could have answered that he'd "Performed Evenly" quite accurately.

And there are several things you ought to know before letting anybody name a horse after you. First, you are required to write to the Jockey Club to give your approval. I don't think the reverse is necessary. For example, if you want to call your daughter Clyde Van Dusen (Google him), I don't believe you have to obtain the Jockey Club's permission.

(torn out of a *Sports Illustrated* circa mid-to-late seventies)

THE SLEDGE

Rick Reilly made his name writing on golf in *Sports Illustrated*. He was the first American after a string of Brits to wear the tag of "the doyen". Reilly now writes for *ESPN* magazine where clearly he has been given a roving commission. Here are two fascinating examples of his work.

Michael Jordan's Hall of Fame talk was the Exxon Valdez of speeches. It was, by turns, rude, vindictive, and flammable. And that was just when he was trying to be funny. It was tactless, egotistical and unbecoming. When it was done, nobody wanted to be like Mike.

And yet we couldn't stop watching. Because this was an inside look into the mindset of an icon who'd never let anybody inside before. From what I saw, I'd never want to go back. Here is a man who's won just about everything there is to win—six NBA titles, five MVPs, and two Olympic gold medals. And yet he sounded like a guy screwed out of every trophy ever minted. He's the world's first sore winner!

In the entire 23-minute cringe-a-thon, there were only six thank yous ...

He was like that Japanese World War II soldier they found hiding in a cave in Guam 27 years after the Japanese had surrendered. The only difference is, Jordan won! What good is victory if you never realize the battle is over?

This is how Jordan really is, I just never thought he'd let the world see it ...

But there he was, in Springfield without a filter or a PR guy to cut him off.

(http://sports.espn.go.com/espn/columns/story?columnist=reilly_rick=4477759)

8

And Reilly at the 1986 Masters watching a legend, 46-year-old Jack Nicklaus, defy the odds:

> Just in the Nicklaus of time, too. Who else but Jack could save us from the woeful, doleful bowl full of American Express (do-you-know-me?) golf winners of late?
>
> And who else could play John Wayne, riding to rescue the Yanks from golf's rampaging foreign legion: the dashingly handsome Seve Ballesteros of Spain; the stone-faced Bernhard Langer of West Germany; Australia's Norman, he of the colossal swing and larger-still reputation, more unfulfilled now than ever; and Zimbabwean-South African-Floridian Nick Price, who on Saturday broke the course record that had gone unsurpassed for 46 years, then on Sunday recoiled in the giant shadow of what he had done.
>
> Here had come Nicklaus, an American legend still under warranty, armed with a putter the size of a Hoover attachment, denting the back of Augusta's holes with 25-foot putts at an age when most guys are afraid to take the putter back.
>
> Here had come Nicklaus, sending such a deluge of decibels into the Georgia air that lakes rippled and azaleas blushed; starting such a ruckus that grown men climbed trees, children rode on shoulders, concession-stand operators abandoned their posts, all just to tear off a swatch of history.
>
> Was that Jack in the checked pants and yellow shirt? Hmmmm. Yellow goes nice with green, doesn't it Jack? You devil.
>
> Maybe that was it. Maybe Nicklaus had drawn up a contract with Lucifer for one last major, for that slippery 20th that had eluded him since 1980, for a sixth green blazer. In exchange, Nicklaus would do pro-ams in Hades for the rest of his days.
>
> (*Life of Reilly*, 2003)

Like most things, good sports writing is subjective, but I hope you liked something about my collection of larger than life characters and events.

One person I've saved until last, Alex Turner (remember him, back at the beginning?), to help explain the radically changing face of broadcasting and writing. Turner is lead singer for British rock group the Arctic Monkeys. He underscores the fragmented, diverse nature of today's market place. The internet and social media have sent society in a million different directions.

The Arctic Monkeys remain one of the hottest bands on the planet yet only the devout really know them. It's a bit like being the best centre half-forward in Kazakhstan! A far cry from the Beatles, we knew each of the four by name. Even my mum knew the Beatles by name. The drummer was mum's favourite. She liked Ringo, but how many people have a favourite Arctic Monkey?

There are hardly any more in-jokes or stories—only people who aren't in on the joke or the story. It's a tough gig these days as broadcasters and writers try to keep pace and touch as many of the bases on the way through as they can.

The good thing about this book is it's not trying to be all things to all people. It's footy, which all but guarantees it's in footballing hands. That's reassuring.

COACHES

They are the men in the hot seat, whose fates are ultimately determined by wins and losses. Since 2000, we have bidden farewell to some of the coaching greats—Parkin, Matthews, Malthouse, Sheedy and Blight—before welcoming Sheedy back into the fold with the AFL's newest club, Greater Western Sydney. A new breed has also emerged, led by premiership trio Paul Roos, Chris Scott and Alastair Clarkson, and Collingwood great Nathan Buckley. In his early days in charge, before he would go on and lead the Cats to an unexpected premiership, Scott would say of coaching: "There's so many ups and downs—and I even felt this as a player—a lot of it's not very pleasurable. Like being nervous before a big game. It's not a nice feeling, but at least you feel alive."

Parkin and Matthews would step aside voluntarily, so, too, Roos. The Swans' premiership mentor would be handed a major compliment by columnist Jake Niall when he decided to hand power to assistant John Longmire: "Coaches don't set out to change the game. They want to win games. By achieving the latter Roos also did the former." However, the ruthless nature of the sport doesn't always allow coaches to bow out on their own terms. Just ask Blight. Malthouse would also find it difficult to come to terms with his tenure at Collingwood being over. In 2009, he had agreed to a handover to Buckley after the 2011 season, but as the clock ticked the reality of such a move hit him. "All of a sudden that [coaching] stopped, and it stopped very abruptly. And it was just finished. There were no leftovers," he told Konrad Marshall as he began his new life as a media analyst heading into the 2012 season.

Rodney Eade and Grant Thomas would also be prominent characters through the decade. The pressures coaches face are enormous—witness Mark Williams' exuberant celebrations after Port Adelaide's break-through flag in 2004. "I am the son of a premiership coach and I know that the primary emotion is relief more than anything," Williams would say later. As Parkin commented, there can only be one day a senior coach really enjoys.

499 GAMES COACHED, ONE ENJOYED: DAVID PARKIN

Linda Pearce

DAVID PARKIN MADE THE MISTAKE, a few years back, of arriving late to Mark Maclure's 40th birthday party. By the time he got there, about 20 of his former players had already gathered around the barbecue on the hill.

"What do you see up here?" Parkin was asked. "Twenty Carlton footballers," he replied.

"Have another look."

"Twenty great Carlton footballers."

"Have another look."

"Sorry, 20 premiership players."

"Have another look."

"I give up."

"You sacked the lot of us."

Five hundred games as a coach can do that to you. Stay around long enough and players who helped bring you a premiership or two in your first stint at a club have to be tapped on the shoulder when you return, in Parkin's case, six years later for another 10-year association.

Only four other coaches have lasted longer in the VFL/AFL than Parkin, who has now delegated the match-day responsibilities to his assistant Wayne Brittain—"Everybody thinks I finished at 493," he quipped—but whose 500th game will officially come against Richmond on Monday.

He is friends with all except, obviously, the late and legendary Jock McHale. Parkin succeeded Allan Jeans as Victorian president of the Australian Football Coaches Association and regards Jeans as an enormous contributor to football;

Tom Hafey paid an unsolicited visit briefly to provide reassurance after the incident in which Parkin took a swipe at a spectator as he left the ground; Barassi was one of the idols of his Melbourne-supporting youth and dropped by near the end of Parkin's Fitzroy days.

"I was about to be sacked and didn't know it, Ron came in and spent a couple of hours, slipped in off the street, he must have perceived what was about to happen and he was telling me about life after footy," Parkin recalled. "I didn't understand at that moment but two weeks later I did and I was always thankful for that, and Ron and I have remained pretty good mates. I didn't know Jock, obviously, but the other three I'm pleased to be in that sort of company."

Parkin's journey has encompassed four stints at three clubs, over 22 seasons for four premierships, including 336 games at Carlton. There have been stress and pressure, dismissals and regrets (notably at Fitzroy), and, last year, a debilitating illness that reduced his capacity. The only game of footy he says he truly enjoyed was the 1995 grand final, when he was keen to pop the champagne in the box during the third quarter, only for his focus to be slapped back into place by long-time lieutenant Col Kinnear.

Much in football has altered since Parkin returned from a stint with Perth club Subiaco to inherit a champion Hawthorn team in 1977. He jokes that when he began, teams did endless circle work each night at training to prepare to play straight up and down the ground.

"So the good thing is that footy's now changed: we train up and down the ground and we go round and round when we play, so there's been a massive revolution in footy over the last 40 years and it's basically just summed up in that."

Parkin describes himself as not so much a great innovator as the man unwittingly responsible for introducing a language of footyspeak that others came to adopt. Yet he says that came from an international sports language and a community into which he taps regularly, often seeking out Brian Goorjian and Jan Stirling (basketball), Wayne Bennett (rugby league), Charlie Walsh (cycling), and confidante Joyce Brown (netball).

He said football teams had followed the lead of soccer, hockey and others, using depth and width to create time and space. Giving up ground to eventually gain advantage was one example of what would not have happened 25 years ago, he said.

Nor, of course, were such huge coaching teams in place back then, although Parkin insists he is still "totally responsible" as he was in 1995, when "empowerment" was the successful theme. Yet there is no doubt the help, and the ability to delegate have enabled him to continue, while also combining a long tertiary education career he continues to cherish.

"I think the milestone reaffirmed where I am with my life," he said, apologising for his at-times "shocking" treatment of the media and admitting a weakness of pessimism.

"I think it's been a long and pretty tough innings. It's been a massive output in my life that I didn't quite understand, and the punishment that you take physically and mentally through the whole thing.

"I started in 1960 or '61 at Hawthorn and I've been fortunate to stay in footy in some form, playing, coaching, developing footy, for the last 40 years. That's a long time to give to any one institution in anybody's life so I'm thankful. I've received far more from the game than the game's received from me."

COACHING'S 500 CLUB	
Jock McHale	714 games (Collingwood)
Allan Jeans	575 games (St Kilda, Hawthorn, Richmond)
Tom Hafey	522 games (Richmond, Collingwood, Geelong, Sydney)
Ron Barassi	515 games (Carlton, North Melbourne, Melbourne, Sydney)
David Parkin	499 games (Hawthorn 94 games, 1977–80; Fitzroy 69 games, 1986–88; Carlton 120 games, 1981–85; 216 games, 1991–present)
PARKIN THE COACH	
Wins	292
Losses	205
Drawn	2
Winning percentage	58.5
Premierships	4 (Hawthorn 1978, Carlton 1981, 1982, 1995)
Runner-up	2 (Carlton 1993, 1999)

PARKIN THE COACH	
Finals appearances	13 (Hawthorn 1977–78, Carlton 1981–85, Fitzroy 1986, Carlton 1993–96, 1999)
Night premierships	2 (Carlton 1983, 1997)
Runner-up	3 (Hawthorn 1979, Carlton 1981, 1996)
PARKIN THE PLAYER	
Games	211 with Hawthorn from 1961–1974, including captaining the club to the 1971 premiership

The Age 21 April 2000

THE MALCOLM BLIGHT SACKING

Rohan Connolly

WHEN YOU'RE A COACH WITH as big a reputation for unpredictability as Malcolm Blight, it's hard to keep surprising people. But it's fair to say Blight's sacking as St Kilda coach yesterday surpasses any of his wild and wacky stunts over the years for pure shock value.

It's only 10 months into the supposed "ride of a lifetime", and a mere 15 games into the new and more professional approach to football that Blight was supposed to be bringing to Moorabbin.

In hindsight, that ride was the "Mad Mouse" going spectacularly off the rails. How did both parties get it so wrong?

St Kilda president Rod Butterss' fairly unconvincing explanation yesterday centred around Blight's seeming lack of commitment to the "core values" laid down by the club's new management team.

At the same time, both he and football director, and now temporary coach, Grant Thomas denied any rift between themselves and Blight. Skipper Robert Harvey said the players had no problem. It doesn't add up.

More and more, possibly the saddest point in St Kilda's recent history seems like a case of two parties completely unprepared for the scale of either's quirks. Or a club that couldn't cope not only with the degree of professionalism expected by its new coach, but all his attendant eccentricities, and a coach who had little idea just how flawed was his new environment.

Blight's coaching record, and surely this will be its conclusion, makes for amazing reading. He's coached four AFL clubs now, and pulled up stumps early at three.

Even in his first ill-fated spell, as North Melbourne's captain-coach in 1981, he lasted 16 rounds before resigning, one more week than he's managed with the Saints. He coached Adelaide for only three seasons, winning two premierships but resigning midway through the very next season.

The sudden departures don't suggest success. A record of two flags, five grand finals and a career winning percentage of 58, as good as or better than all his present rivals bar Denis Pagan, Kevin Sheedy and Terry Wallace, suggests otherwise.

But Blight's success always seemed to go hand-in-hand with his "wackiness". More importantly, it also went hand-in-hand with his supposed dictatorial style, and his penchant for publicly singling out individuals for letting down the team and his coaching philosophies.

At Geelong, Blight threw down the gauntlet from day one, in November 1988, when, in front of the assembled media, he dragged out and dressed down Cat star Bruce Lindner for being a late arrival for a 10-kilometre time trial.

Later on in his tenure, Blight staged perhaps his most public display of his displeasure by sending defender Austin McCrabb away from the three-quarter-time huddle, like an errant schoolboy sent to stand in the corner.

It is the "crazier" Blight stunts, such as the day he made the Geelong players sit around a swimming pool pretending to be Indian chiefs, or lining the same players up as a "guard of honour" for their Adelaide opposition, that have always attracted the most comment.

But those amusing stories have had nothing like the impact of a vintage Blight "bake".

Adelaide hosted two of his more famous, his round-two 1997 labelling of ruckman David Pittman as "pathetic", and the afternoon at Football Park the following season when so annoyed was Blight as the Crows were being overrun by Richmond that he and football manager John Reid packed up shop and went inside the rooms.

Both were huge gambles that could have backfired. Instead, Pittman recovered to play a key role in the Crows' first flag win. The following season, after Blight went AWOL in the last quarter, Adelaide won all but five of its last 18 games to win consecutive premierships.

But the most obvious, and rarely discussed, difference between Blight's time at Geelong and Adelaide, and his short-lived tenure at Moorabbin, was simple—the quality with which he had to work.

The Cats and the Crows had experienced, senior and physically strong lists, both of which had underperformed and needed a good kick in the pants.

St Kilda was a much younger, rawer, lightly framed player group, even with its legion of recruits from other clubs, and not nearly so able.

That's why eyebrows were first raised when Blight declared, as he had with the Crows, that the pre-season before Christmas would be purely fitness-based, the balls not coming out until January.

The eyebrow-raising continued when the Saints stayed out on Colonial Stadium to warm down after their round-10 loss to Melbourne, Blight seizing the chance to address the group out there.

For perhaps the first time since a quinella of flags with Adelaide raised him to god-like proportions as a coach, the more cynical began asking whether there was a bit too much "smoke and mirrors".

Perhaps there was. And perhaps Blight's sacking is evidence that a man surrounded only by excellence most of his sporting life isn't the best-equipped to teach it to a club that sees the same quality only as a lofty, previously unknown ideal.

But given his history—and that of the club he embraced in a moment of what appears to have been foolish lust—it seems that both Blight and St Kilda should have at least known to buckle up when they climbed aboard for the "ride of a lifetime".

VFL PLAYING RECORD	
North Melbourne 1974–82	
Games	178
Goals	444
Honours	1978 Brownlow medallist 1978 North Melbourne best-and-fairest Premiership player 1975 and 1977 Topped VFL goalkicking in 1982 with 103 goals Club leading goalkicker 1978, 1979, 1981, 1982

VFL/AFL COACHING RECORD			
	Wins	Losses	Ladder position
North Melbourne			
1981	6	10	8
Geelong			
1989	18	8	2
1990	8	14	10
1991	17	8	3
1992	18	8	2
1993	12	8	7
1994	16	10	2
Adelaide			
1997	17	9	1
1998	16	10	1
1999	8	14	13
St Kilda (after 15 rounds)			
2001	3	12	14

The Age 20 July 2001

THOMAS, AN OUTSIDER WITHIN

Greg Baum

GRANT THOMAS IS THE STRANGER in town. Everyone knows who he is—but who is he? Down at the AFL Arms, the regulars are staring and whispering among themselves. Some are suspicious, some curious, some openly hostile. But over at the table, he is beginning to win games. What sort of hustle is this?

The way Thomas came in was affronting. As a St Kilda board member, he fired Malcolm Blight and replaced him with himself. But he also had led the deputation to hire Blight in the first instance. If he was driven by personal ambition then, he hid it well.

Perhaps Blight had to go. Jason Cripps spent eight years at St Kilda, and grew to understand the place intimately. "If you ask the playing group, deep down inside, they weren't too disappointed that Blighty did go," he said. "Unfortunately, it just was not what St Kilda footy club needed at the time. He was very aloof. We had a young group coming through the club, at a critical time, and we needed someone like Grant, who would bleed for the place. The club is his No. 1 priority.

"I'm not saying it wasn't for Malcolm, but that's at times how it came across. It just wasn't going to be successful with us."

Cripps, now working for St Kilda and the AFL in Hobart and playing for Tasmania, admitted it was strange initially. "Aaron Hamill was pissed off," he said. "But Grant sat Aaron down and explained the whole story, and there was nothing said after that."

St Kilda president Rod Butterss' voice grew weary when asked about the integrity of the process of replacing Blight, in which a notionally independent panel recommended an insider.

"I knew then, and I know now, that if the sub-committee had come back with a strong recommendation for someone other than Grant, he would not be in that job," Butterss said. "He demonstrated that he understood better than anyone else what had restricted St Kilda from enjoying success historically."

Thomas is seen to have come from nowhere. In fact, it was not nowhere, just somewhere else. He played 72 games for the Saints. He coached Warrnambool to five premierships in the Hampden league, then had a year with Old Xaverians in the amateurs before embarking for the AFL again.

Butterss now believes the Thomas route is the way to go. "I think the current model of assistant coaching is in many ways flawed. You aren't required to make tough decisions. You're sitting one out, one back, and get sucked along in the current.

"I don't believe it is the ideal preparation for senior coaching because it doesn't expose the assistant coach to the realities of confrontation and tough decision-making. You've got to be able to go out into VFL or country football and take the full responsibility for managing a group of people."

He said that even if, say, Terry Wallace or Rodney Eade applied next year when the coach's contract was up, he would stand by his man.

Some find Thomas, if not sleazy, too much like a salesman.

But every coach is a salesman; everyone of them has had, at one time, to sell to a team a line that he did not truly believe himself. Cripps said that with Thomas, it was not spin, but candour.

"He's straight down the line. When I was delisted last year, he was straight to the point with me," he said.

"Honesty is one of his strengths. You look at the Matthew Capuano situation. Once he'd made up his mind that was it, he wasn't going to leave him playing for Springy for the rest of the year and keep feeding him crap about how he's close to getting a game. He's honest and a player appreciates that. We didn't always have that before."

Still, Thomas disturbs the establishment. They dislike his links with Butterss, with his designer stubble, name and lingo. They think Thomas's talk about "empowerment" is pretentious, but no one scoffed when David Parkin first used the same jargon. They suspect he is assimilating power rather than dispersing it, for instance, by inviting chief executive Brian Waldron into the coach's box.

But all the great coaches had their power bases. Besides, Cripps said

Thomas genuinely shared around responsibility. "The leadership group would meet once a week and he'd ask them how the game plan was going, what we needed to do different," he said. "He involved a lot of people."

Andrew McLean played at Old Xavs and later became president, and credits Thomas with building the springboard that took the club from last the previous season to a run of six premierships soon afterwards. "Knowing the sort of person Thommo is, and the way he relates to players, I think you will find there will be a bit of the old Tommy Hafey thing. Players will be playing for him," McLean said.

The orthodox dislike Thomas's dual role as coach and football manager, also responsible for player contracts, like a soccer manager. Butterss admitted that this was a financial necessity forced upon the club, but said it had mothered a working invention.

"Through the adversity, we've had to think laterally and come up with better ways of using the resources available to us."

Some doubt that a coach-manager can make clear-eyed match-day decisions. Again, Cripps said the key was honesty. "If a bloke's got a contract that's heavily incentive-based, Grant is not the sort of person who would drop him because he was coming up for, say, a 20-game bonus. It just wouldn't happen."

The establishment thinks Thomas is paid too much for a novice coach, that he is too outspoken for one yet to pay his dues and that he will squander what in a sense was St Kilda's ill-gotten wealth, the largesse of the draft. Butterss did not dispute that St Kilda was a beneficiary of the system, but did dispute that Thomas had had a champion team fall into his hands.

"I've been in the room when the phone calls came in. We've had some extremely attractive offers for us to trade away our first-round picks," he said.

"We've resisted that. We made a decision three years ago to rebuild the club with youth. We knew we'd have to go through pain. There may be a bit more pain left. We needed somebody with strength and character and vision to implement those difficult decisions. From that perspective, Grant's done a really good job."

Besides, critics agree that even the most sublime list will not add up to the sum of its parts if it is in the wrong hands. The young stars are all playing well, an Essendon reject keeps kicking goals, Robert Harvey is playing his best football since his Brownlow years and Fraser Gehrig has found a new lease. The Saints are young, talented and last week had a stirring win over Brisbane.

The jury, always large at St Kilda, is out still on Thomas tactically. "I suggest you ask Leigh Matthews and Gary Ayres that question!" said Butterss, adding that tactical acumen was important, but not critical, to modern coaching.

"My belief as president is that our football department has adopted a game plan that they believe will be successful in September," he said. "It may not be tricky or sexy. It may be simple, but it works."

Nonetheless, Thomas remains an outsider. When Capuano was sacked, other coaches suddenly had no compunction about minding the Saints' business for them. But what coach does not have some blood on his hands? Mick Malthouse spoke out bitterly, but there were plenty of friends of Shane Watson to say that the Collingwood coach had a selective memory.

So they still stand and stare, doubting Thomas. The man has eight children; that would set him apart in any company. He also has a precocious football team that is beginning to feel its oats.

St Kilda folk look at the draw, see Carlton, the Bulldogs and Geelong in the last three rounds, and dare to think that they will be in this to the end.

If the coach's name was Malthouse, his halo would be ready to be picked up now.

As it stands, Thomas is still being measured up.

The Age 14 June 2003

INTRODUCING MARK WILLIAMS, PREMIERSHIP COACH

Caroline Wilson

MATTHEWS, SHEEDY, MALTHOUSE, BLIGHT, PAGAN—*it's an elite club, those who have coached a premiership in the AFL era. This year, Mark Williams became just the eighth man to achieve the honour. This is his first in-depth interview since Port Adelaide's triumph.*

Success has not changed Mark Williams. If anything, the 2004 premiership coach now seems a more extreme version of the passionate figure that strode from the coach's box in the dying minutes of the grand final and briefly wondered how he should react, before pretending to choke himself with his tie.

Ten weeks have passed since Port Adelaide's historic victory and Williams is the first to admit it has not all been plain sailing since then. The first few weeks that followed the premiership were a little flat, disappointing even, and occasionally lonely.

Denis Pagan said he could not get the famous words of the classic song "Is That All There Is?" out of his head on the morning after North Melbourne's 1996 premiership victory. For Williams, his joy was tempered by almost immediately losing four key members of his football department and one star footballer.

Not to mention the reality of an AFL system that dictates one must move on almost immediately. For Williams that meant that days after the premiership he headed alone to the AFL draft camp in Canberra—those assistant coaches who had not quit the club had taken holidays—where he experienced a couple of interesting confrontations.

One was with Hawthorn pair Alastair Clarkson, Williams' recently departed assistant, and Jason Dunstall. The Hawks' version is that the premiership coach refused to shake Dunstall's hand and stuck out a solitary finger instead. Williams said he could not recall the finger part of the story. When asked whether Clarkson, had he not received the senior job offer, would have been offered the Port assistant position again next season, Williams replied: "I'm not sure."

Williams had just learnt that his gun fitness coach, Andrew Russell, had been poached by Hawthorn, which forced him to immediately scour the country for a replacement in time to set out a pre-season plan. Williams insists he did not take any of the departures personally; along with the shattering loss of vice-captain Josh Carr, the club's recruiting manager Alan Stewart had taken a promotion at the Crows and ruck coach David Pittman quit for family reasons.

But Williams was angry about losing Russell, who has been replaced by Darren Burgess, formerly of the Swans and the Olyroos, among others. To add insult, Clarkson also took on the just-retired Port veteran Damien Hardwick as an assistant, a job Williams had also offered Hardwick.

It was almost two months later at the coaches' conference in Melbourne that, according to the Hawks, Williams approached Clarkson and Dunstall again and apologised for his behaviour at the draft camp. The group all agreed to move on. Williams was in fine form that day also; customarily vocal, challenging but upbeat, he spotted his nemesis from a previous meeting, AFL medical officer Hugh Seward, and commented: "You again!"

Seward and his team were outlining proposed changes to the ruck rules to prevent injury and Williams called out: "Why don't you stick to doctoring and leave the football to us?" Most people in the room laughed. The tinkering of the AFL ruck rules is a long-time bone of contention for Williams, largely due to the effect it has had upon his game plan and that of his captain, Matthew Primus.

Williams did shake Pagan's hand in Canberra, but in the same breath that the Carlton coach offered his congratulations, he half-jokingly suggested that it was time Williams stopped criticising Nick Stevens. Despite all that has happened since Stevens left Alberton to join the Blues, Williams has not forgiven him for his behaviour before departing Port Adelaide and, according to the club, a long list of his former teammates have not either.

There had been a confrontation the previous week off-stage at Channel Nine's grand final edition of *The Footy Show* when Williams spotted Stevens. Despite several claims to the contrary, Williams insists he accepted Stevens' handshake that night.

But there have been plenty of positive interludes for Williams since Port Adelaide's historic first AFL flag, a premiership that has lifted the coach into exalted company and has him now negotiating a fascinating and more generous three-year contract with his club.

(Williams is a laborious list-maker—he makes one every day—and his list of contractual conditions forwarded to the club earlier this week would reportedly make intriguing reading. Both parties hope to have a new deal in place by Christmas.)

After the final name had been called at the 2005 AFL draft last month, Collingwood president Eddie McGuire sought out the former Magpie captain to offer his congratulations on behalf of the club. It was an emotional moment for both men.

The Collingwood connection remains strong for the Port Adelaide coach. On one visit to Melbourne, he noticed he was the only Collingwood skipper not to have his name on a stand at Victoria Park. Williams pointed it out to McGuire, who rectified the issue.

That's how it is with Williams. He is seemingly devoid of guile, can be challenging to the point of pushy and even irritating, but he is always entertaining. His refreshingly honest, if bizarre, response to coaching Port Adelaide to a premiership that seemed the club's and Williams' destiny divided the football industry when he publicly turned on the club's major sponsor—"Allan Scott: You were wrong!"

But those close to the coach say that Scott did far more damage to Williams the previous year by declaring he would never coach Port to a flag. The pressure on the coach and his young family, they say, was intolerable and linked in a sense to the panic attack suffered by his wife Pauline, who briefly passed out in the dying minutes of the 2004 preliminary final against St Kilda.

No one at Port Adelaide will discuss the current Scott situation—his Scott's Transport has a year to run on its deal with the club and the training facility at Alberton is named for him—in any meaningful way. It remains a touchy subject and members of the Port Adelaide board have privately made it clear they wish Williams had not said what he did.

While Port stage-managed a meeting with the old man at his Mount Gambier headquarters, where he handed over a six-figure bonus cheque for winning the flag, Williams and Scott have still not spoken. Williams said the pair might come together in February thanks to the AFL's Mount Gambier scheduling of Port's pre-season community camp.

Still, he has a premiership cup, and despite the post-grand final drama there have been moments of wonderful satisfaction for a mentor who has achieved something Leigh Matthews claimed was harder than winning three flags in a row—finishing No. 1 after the home-and-away rounds three years in succession and finally achieving the ultimate.

"I'm the son of a premiership coach and I know that the primary emotion is relief more than anything," said Williams. "It's less 'thank God' and more 'thank God that's over'.

"The on-going satisfaction was walking down the street and seeing the smiles on people's faces and listening to the people talk about how happy this has made them. And I was proud of the players. They had more input into what happened this year and to have enough gumption to get up again and win it after the previous disappointments was very impressive."

But none of the above has made Williams any more relaxed. The same day in Melbourne that he jovially confronted the AFL medical staff, he also took Andrew Demetriou aside to push the league to look at compensating all clubs losing players due to the "go-home" factor.

"I'm not sure who's ever left Brisbane to go home," said Williams. "We've lost two out-of-contract players in two years in Nick Stevens and Josh Carr."

The ideas never stop spouting out of his eccentric brain. Admiring the living area of his two-storey house just a short walk from the bay at Glenelg, the lack of books around the room is noted. Although he and his sister Jenny recently released a children's book themselves, Williams says he has no time to read books. But he is a voracious reader of newspapers.

He is upset with this columnist for twice singling out Byron Pickett following the Norm Smith medallist's serious driving misdemeanour shortly after the grand final.

Williams first spoke to Pickett about the incident when the footballer called the club at the start of last month on another matter and the coach grabbed the phone. "Byron," he said, "I'm glad no one was hurt." He defended his refusal to publicly take on Pickett and even implied *The Age*'s focusing on the issue bordered on racism.

A friend at the club told Williams that once he finally won a flag for the club he would no longer have to restrain himself. While some at Port Adelaide live in fear of Mark Williams unleashed, others would say it was ever thus.

MARK WILLIAMS ON …

False rumours of Aboriginality

"I hope you write that you asked me this question. I'm not Aboriginal and if you knew anything about it you wouldn't ask if I was part-Aboriginal because Aborigines will tell you there's no such thing. You either are, or you aren't. I was asked once to play in an Aboriginal team in the '80s and I said no because I didn't qualify and [he laughs] one player accused me of not being a brother."

The minor premiership

"I believe there should be a more significant reward for the minor premiership and we should look at going down the Premier League soccer path. I've spoken to the board and we are going to talk to the AFL about it. It's tough to do in this competition (finish No. 1 after 22 rounds) and I can say that now we've won the flag. Who is Dr McClelland? There is no presentation of the trophy, it's almost sent to you as an afterthought. I couldn't even tell you where it is now."

Josh Carr

"He had said he was going to stay and he went and that was disappointing. He was the heart and soul of our club and I would have made him captain. Still, he'll go to sleep at night feeling very comfortable with himself and his role at the Port Adelaide Football Club."

Byron Pickett's car accident

"Write the stories now for next year and put the names in because it will happen again. Alcohol is the No. 1 concern that creates all these problems. His was one of thousands of these things that happen every year. Everyone gets on their high and mighty perch, but I don't see many people controlling their alcohol intake. It's what starts the fights, the smashing of cars and the sexual assaults."

The AFL

"When I thanked the AFL on grand final day I don't think I got my point across. But the institution of the AFL is held so high and I was thanking that institution for providing the magnificent backdrop to what the team achieved. Since I was 10 I went to every grand final, I watched the marathons the night before. All those years watching other people take the flag."

The Sunday Age 5 December 2004

THE ROHAN CONNOLLY INTERVIEW:
RODNEY EADE

Rohan Connolly

RODNEY EADE TURNED 48 EARLIER this week, an age at which most men are slowly coming to terms with their impending mortality, and starting to look back as much as to the future.

But for the coach of the Western Bulldogs, it's 48 years young, not old. Hear his mobile phone ring, and you'll hear not a business-like tone, but the opening strains of contemporary rock band the Foo Fighters' "Best of You".

Attend one of his team talks, and in between electronic slide show presentations of strategy and tactics will appear a comical slide poking fun at this or that Bulldog player. Make an error, and a young Western Bulldog is likely to feel his coach's wrath, followed just as quickly by a smart one-liner to ease the sting.

"The players here keep you young. And I think humour keeps you young," he says. "I like to think I have a reasonable wit and sense of humour, and I like people to enjoy themselves.

"I'd like to think here we have an environment where they want to learn and improve and work, but at the same time, they're actually enjoying it as they go along.

"I'm all about education and teaching and people learning, and I've got a group that's really enthusiastic about improving themselves, so in many ways they've given me a lot of enthusiasm. It's sort of a role-reversal, I suppose."

Surrounded by some of the most precociously talented young players in the country, he knows he has to keep his message, as well as his methods, as up-to-date as possible.

"I try not to talk about myself as a player. Every now and then, I might give an example of people I've played with, but I don't want to talk ancient history. They want to know about contemporaries, people they know. You've got to keep their interest, by talking about what's going to spark them."

And what stimulates the young professional sportsman is something about which Eade knows plenty because sport at the elite level virtually has consumed the four-time Hawthorn premiership player's entire life.

Eade's father Brian represented Tasmania in cricket, football and basketball. He played cricket against the touring West Indies, and one year won both the Tasmanian district cricket batting and bowling averages.

Brian Eade played football with Glenorchy, and was a star of the 1958 interstate carnival held in Melbourne, kicking the winning goal in Tasmania's surprise victory over South Australia.

After a knee injury ended his football career prematurely at only 26, he took up umpiring. Then he coached University in the amateurs. Rodney, the eldest of two sons, followed his father religiously around the sporting traps. And obviously learned plenty along the way.

When the younger Eade played senior football with Glenorchy at 17, incredibly, he'd already been playing district cricket firsts for three years, having been thrown to the wolves at the tender age of 14.

"I was lucky to be in the right place at the right time," he recalls, modestly.

"Dad was captain-coach, and he didn't want me picked. I'd been playing third grade and done pretty well, got elevated to the seconds, and when that got washed out, they put me straight into the ones against a team that was on top and had three of the leading state players. We were playing for a draw, and I ended up coming in at No. 8 and making 30 not out."

Eade never returned to the lower grades. In football, he starred in his one season with Glenorchy's senior team under the coaching of Hawthorn legend Peter Hudson, who urged his old club to snap up the teenage prodigy.

The Hawks obliged. Eade, still attending high school, made his senior debut only six games before the end of the 1976 home-and-away season, held his spot and played on the wing in a premiership side in his ninth game of VFL football.

Thus began a 30-year association with the game's most elite level that has been broken just once, when he quit as Sydney coach midway through the

2002 season, and stayed on the outer until his appointment on a three-year deal with the Western Bulldogs at the end of 2004.

It's a passion that he admits has at times consumed him to the detriment of life's other pursuits and responsibilities.

There's more balance now, he says—the result of that enforced lay-off, and his relationship with his second wife, Wendy, with whom he has an eight-year-old daughter Meggan. Eade has two teenage boys, Jordan and Jackson, from his first marriage.

"I think Wendy has really opened my eyes to a bit more culture in life," he reflects.

"I like the theatre, and I read a lot, I listen to different forms of music. It's about trying to keep a balance between your family and different interests, and not to be totally absorbed. I know you're supposed to be totally absorbed as a coach, but like anything, you've got to get a break away from it."

So has his departure amid some acrimony from Sydney four years ago changed him? Eade concedes he became too immersed in the politics that inevitably surround a football club, and too upset by the various "mistruths" that were spread freely about his intensity, and the breaking down of his relationships with his players.

"I think I fell for the trap of worrying about things that were out of my control," he says.

"Just the small bushfires that were being lit around the place. You get involved in it and it takes your focus away from what your job is, and obviously I was distracted."

He's glad in hindsight that he didn't land the Kangaroos job, which he applied for when Denis Pagan left Arden Street at the end of that same year.

"I thought I was probably ready to go back into it virtually straightaway at the end of that year. I'm glad I didn't. I needed to clean the pipes out, there really was a lot of pent-up frustration and anguish within that. That's all gone."

And what he learned about himself has become a valuable coaching tool, in "just the impact that you can have on people".

"Even things you don't do consciously, not so much in the words you use, but how you say them. It's about getting to know people a bit better, how they'll interpret you, because people can interpret things the wrong way.

"I can deliver the same message to five different people and have five different reactions to it. Some people will say: 'Oh well, he's challenging me.' Some will say: 'He's criticising me.' Some people will ask: 'What's he trying to say?', and then try to read too much into it, and two or three different thoughts going through their head. That can poison them and create doubt, so you've got to make sure the message you want to get across is actually received the right way."

There's little doubt given the steep learning curve the Western Bulldogs have traversed in Eade's year-and-a-half in command, their flying finish to 2005, and the pace and precision of disposal that marked their 115–point demolition of Richmond last week, that the message at Whitten Oval is being heard loud and clear.

"Even last year when we were 6–10, I was still excited internally, and pleased," he says. "I thought we'd made quite good development in the areas we needed to. The results weren't there as such, but I thought we'd made enough ground and thought the future looked reasonably bright.

"There is a buzz [around the club] and I think it's due to the place being down for quite a while, and probably the way we're playing, too, not just the results, but the way we're winning. Whether it's being able to come from behind as we did a bit last year, or playing good, hard aggressive football, or to be able to put away a side like we did last Friday night. They're indicators to everybody that this football team is maturing."

Life for both a traditionally downtrodden club and a coach, who during those darkest final days in Sydney not only lost his "mojo" but a normally cheerful and sunny disposition, is looking pretty good once again.

"I wouldn't use the word satisfying," he demurs. "You tend to use that when something's completed, and in this industry, you just know there's always something lurking around the corner that's going to hit you smack in the face with a cricket bat, but the improvement we're making seems to indicate to me we're building a platform to be ongoing rather than improve for 12 months then fall away.

"You do go through periods where you doubt yourself or your methods, or wonder whether you need to change things, but this has been like a hand in a glove, I think. The way I like to go about the job fitted perfectly with what this group needed. It's like a young, blank canvas I'm working with."

And when you're as young at heart as Eade, even after three decades, painting the resultant picture still can be an awful lot of fun.

VFL PLAYING RECORD	
Hawthorn 1976–87	229 games
Brisbane Bears 1988–90	30 games
VFL/AFL COACHING RECORD	
Sydney 1996–2002	152 games, 81 wins, 69 losses, 2 draws
Western Bulldogs 2005–06	23 games, 12 wins, 11 losses, 0 draws
Totals	175 games, 93 wins, 80 losses, 2 draws
Winning percentage	53%

The Age 8 April 2006

NO MORE MIRACLES, SIMPLY THE DAY THAT HAD TO COME: KEVIN SHEEDY

Greg Baum

AT THE END OF AN ERA—his era—Kevin Sheedy walked into a blitz of camera flash guns. "Japanese making a lot of money," he chortled. When chief executive Peter Jackson spoke of Sheedy's "aplomb and professionalism", Sheedy mouthed the word of "aplomb" again, as if amused by it.

When Jackson asked that the decision to sack Sheedy be judged not now, but in three to five years hence, Sheedy interjected: "I'll be on the board by then."

Jackson, hitherto considered in tone and even in expression, gave up. "I just hope you're not president," he said.

This news conference was as Sheedy's generally are—a pantomime, but bigger. It was as if to say that nothing had changed except that, incidentally, he would not be coaching Essendon next year.

Meantime, he would remain in character to the end—impish, upbeat, calculatedly and infuriatingly oblique, full of wisecracks and asides, revealing little of himself.

But when asked how he felt, Sheedy volunteered nothing brighter than "pretty good". When asked about the wisdom of Essendon's decision, he replied: "It's not necessarily correct or a mistake."

He had been uniquely fortunate to coach the Bombers for 27 years, he said, but also made it clear that he had never entirely given up on the possibility of a 28th. He had miraculously saved himself often enough before.

But this year, it became clear that, rabbits or no rabbits, Essendon wanted back the hat.

Sheedy's sacking was a momentous turning in the tide of Essendon's affairs—and for that matter the AFL's—yet in its moment, the word "sacking" seemed too harsh.

More precisely, it was the day that—sooner or later—had to come. Essendon, knowing the stubborn set of his mind, had been coaching him towards acceptance since January; even Ron Evans, the late AFL chairman, had impressed on him that he and the club had come to the long unimaginable watershed. A finishing date was roughed out.

But the deleterious effect of ever-rising speculation, combined with the falling of coaching vacancies at three other clubs, had forced the Bombers' hand. A meeting on Monday, a little last-minute subterfuge to distract media, and the job was done.

According to Jackson, when the inevitable at last was upon Sheedy on Tuesday morning, he said: "Let's get this over and done with, because we've got to beat Adelaide." Jackson said Sheedy's phlegmatism in such an historic moment was the mark of the man.

But others never would be so dispassionate on his account. Yesterday morning, as word swept town, media and fans descended on Windy Hill, startling pensioners arriving for a social morning. Passers-by on the road were constrained to say their piece, some rejoicing in the Bombers' hurt, one calling choice epithets to the media.

Another, in a white delivery van, yelled: "They ought to be ashamed of themselves: he put you on the map . . ." His voice trailed off in his wake. No more in his leaving of the Bombers than in his long stay would Sheedy leave folk unmoved.

Some players sat in on the news conference in Essendon's theatrette, others watched live on pay television from an adjoining room. It was an age removed from the manner of his arrival in 1981, long before pay television, the internet and—for that matter—the AFL.

The Bombers lost five of their first six games. I recall sitting with him on a bench in the away change rooms at the Western Oval after the fifth defeat. He was wondering what he had let himself in for.

That week, he touted the idea that he might come out of retirement. The Essendon board vetoed it, but rarely bested Sheedy again until this week. The Bombers won their next 15 games in a row, and three years later the premiership, and so a legend was founded.

Coaching exploits aside, Sheedy was—and remains—the single greatest character of his era. Publicly, he was eccentric.

Privately, he was, too: Jackson's several bemused shakes of his head yesterday suggested as much (Sheedy "sacked" Jackson by way of return compliment yesterday, saying that the club was in the throes of the change, with a new president and soon to have a new coach AND chief executive!).

But Sheedy could connect with footballers; his record says so. Periodically, he would fall out with one or another, but rarely for long, or for good.

He was as chirpy as ever yesterday. He would keep all options open, except to stay at Essendon; that would be unfair on his successor. He would remain in football, would continue to enjoy it. Jackson said he had impressed on Sheedy his own advice, that the best might be yet to come.

Sheedy grinned. It was a brave face, or the facsimile of one. On Tuesday night, already half-sacked, he went to a function at the racing museum. Last night, he intended to go to dinner with some old mates from VFA club Prahran, as planned. "I don't think it is a big deal," he said of the day. "It's footy. It's sport."

But at the end of the conference, an odd thing happened. Eighty media folk, including the most hard-bitten, burst into applause. Some surprised themselves. It happens at the Olympics, but not in the dog-eat-dog world of AFL.

It was the first ovation in what will be a long and deserved series. Once the last echo has died, Essendon will never be the same again, and nor will the AFL.

The Age 26 July 2007

BLUE-COLLAR BLUEBLOOD:
BRETT RATTEN

Rohan Connolly

THE HOMECOMING OF CARLTON'S WORKING-CLASS hero holds promises of a return to one of the club's most glorious periods.

The Carlton faithful are overjoyed to have a favourite son in Brett Ratten as their coach for the next two years, but few happier than the "Thursday ladies", who meet in the social club at Princes Park every week.

The ladies adopted Ratten as their own a long time ago. They conduct their own best-and-fairest count every season, which the former Carlton skipper won three times.

When *The Age* arrives to interview the new coach, he's being serenaded by them, sitting around a big round table, sharing a coffee and nursing the bottle of champagne with which they've presented him.

The Blues have been through the toughest five years of their history, starved of wins and money, a shell of the club that set the standard for so long.

But there's a real buzz around the place this Thursday afternoon. And Ratten's comment the previous day that he wanted to revive a little of that famous Carlton swagger has struck a very popular chord.

It's as if Princes Park is rediscovering its soul gradually, and although Carlton hasn't played here for more than two years, it's still very much home.

"I've moved round a few houses, but this place never changes its address. You know where to come, the car's on autopilot," Ratten reflects of the journey he's been making for 22 years since he was a 14-year-old in a scholarship squad.

"I was out there [pointing to the ground] with Craig Bradley one day this year, and I said, 'Do you just look up at the stands and you can still hear them screaming?' He said, 'My oath.'

"You can still feel that Heatley Stand rocking, Carlton kicking 10 goals in the last quarter to that end and the place jumping. I still just look around and think of moments, of games, of people. We might not play games here now, but the memories will last forever."

Carlton is one cornerstone of Ratten's life. The other is family. He grew up in Yarra Glen, and on this evening will head back to give a talk at the local footy club, where he played, younger brother Mark still plays and which has made the finals for the first time in years.

"I still relate to the place because of the freedom I got to grow up and do things," he says.

"I'd go down and watch the seniors, spend all day on the bike, run out and kick the footy, then play on the Sunday.

"I loved growing up there. You and your mates could do anything you wanted to do round town. I had a key to the tennis club when I was 13, blokes had 'paddock bombs', we'd go yabbying. I had ferrets when I was a kid. It was just a great life."

Ratten went to Lilydale Tech, and married Sharyn, the sister of his best friend at school. They live in South Warrandyte, close to where they grew up. Sharyn runs the school canteen at Park Orchards Primary.

He remains proud of the values instilled in him by his parents, Dennis and Adele, who he says "worked themselves silly" in the restaurant trade. It's reflected in the names of his two children, eight-year-old Cooper, and five-year-old Tanner.

"They're strong, working-class names. A cooper was a barrel maker, and a tanner a leather maker. I'm from a working-class family, and Sharyn is as well, and we loved the names and the meaning behind them. Mum and Dad are the hardest-working people I've seen. They've given me a great work ethic, and I'm very proud of that."

It is a work ethic that served Ratten brilliantly as a player over 14 seasons, 255 games and three best and fairests. Those figures belie the obstacles he overcame along the way.

Like the lack of confidence that dogged him over his first four seasons and 60–odd games at senior level, the turning point, he says, Carlton's crushing defeat at the hands of Essendon in the 1993 grand final.

The Blues might as well have played one short that day, says Ratten. "I was like an extra spectator. I wasn't in the moment, I think I had the fear of failure before the game, and everything just went on around me. I think I learned a big lesson from that. From that moment onwards, I vowed that I'd never let another minute go by without being involved in a game. My mind-set changed."

Two years to the day, he'd be standing on the MCG dais, a premiership player and best and fairest winner in one of history's best teams, which had won 23 of its 25 games.

It's a lesson that will come in handy now that he's in charge of an entire, mostly young playing group. "I think it's important that I believe in them, and that's one thing I want to make sure, that we're very positive with the way we go about things," he says.

"But in saying that, they must stick to the rules and structures put in place. As I said to the players early on, if they give me 100 per cent and make a few blues, I can live with it. If they don't give me 100 per cent, I can't live with that."

But confidence wasn't Ratten the player's only handicap. He'd played 189 games and won another best and fairest by the time he got around to tackling the lifelong astigmatism that had left him with shocking eyesight but prevented him from wearing contact lenses.

Ratten had cataract surgery, then laser surgery just after the 1999 grand final, and spent a week lying in a darkened room. His vision improved dramatically, and he requires spectacles now only to read. And there's no more practical jokes at his expense.

"When the club [previously] had said we wouldn't train at night any more, I said, 'Hallelujah,' because I'd be able to see. The lights here are at eye level, and when I was younger, the boys would play havoc with me. I'd say, 'Who's that?' and Justin [Madden] would say it was [rover] Fraser Murphy, but it would be [big man] Peter Sartori," he laughs. "They'd just play games with you."

Not that Ratten hasn't been above playing the odd game himself. He began turning his mind to the idea of becoming a coach when he began to see properly. By the time Wayne Brittain was his coach at Carlton, it was becoming an obsession.

"I drove 'Britts' crazy, to the point where if he wasn't in his room and the team was up, I'd go in and change them, the match-ups and things like that," he laughs. "He'd know it was me, just swing a few changes and walk out of the office." Did Brittain ever go along with it? "I'd get the odd one through and think: 'You beauty!'"

Aspirations became some sort of reality when the freshly retired Blue joined Melbourne as an assistant coach for 2004. The association lasted only a year, and there's been lingering whispers about tension between him and senior coach Neale Daniher.

Not true, Ratten says. And annoying. "There were a few jobs going, and Neale said to me get yourself ready because you never know when the opportunity is going to come up," he says.

"I spoke to Chris Fagan and David Parkin and a few people regarding coaching, and they thought I'd be better off coaching my own team. I thought if I served another year on my contract, then went and coached my own team, I'd be putting myself behind. I was better cutting off now, going back a couple of steps so I could then go forward.

"I thought . . . I knew a bit when I finished playing, but Neale just showed me the way you needed to plan and prepare, and that just helped me when I did coach my own team [a Victorian Country Football League side, then Norwood in the Eastern Football League], then again with Denis [Pagan] here. I really appreciate the lessons Neale taught me. It was invaluable."

Now it's time to put what he's learned into practice. Carlton already has shown some change in Ratten's four games as caretaker coach. The Blues have shot up the rankings for uncontested marks and scoring accuracy, down for inside 50s, indicating not only greater efficiency, but a more possession-based, deliberate style of play.

"I think we may have over-possessed at times, but if we've got the ball in our hands, it's better than the opposition having it," he says. "If you go too quick all the time, you get scored against, and if you go too slow, you can't score enough. It's trying to find that happy medium."

There's some big decisions to be made over the next few weeks. Starting with the futures of Brendan Fevola and captain Lance Whitnall. Fevola looks like keeping his spot. Perhaps "Big Red" may hang on, too.

Fevola has a tendency to get bored, Ratten says. "I think we need to keep him stimulated, on and off the field, so he's got something to look forward to after footy. It doesn't matter what you get [as a trade] for a player of that calibre, it's extremely hard to replace someone who could be in the top 10 in the AFL."

Today's game against the Kangaroos and next week's against Melbourne probably will determine Whitnall's fate. But Ratten wants to at least give him every chance.

If that doesn't happen, one of the coach's first calls might remain one of his toughest. For Whitnall, like Ratten, Carlton is home. The new coach and favourite son is already pondering getting more former Carlton greats back to the club, reflecting more on the special moments in the Blues' history.

And, as we walk back through the social club after our interview, and he glances across, smiling, at the Thursday ladies still chatting away, Ratten doesn't need to add, special people, too.

BRETT RATTEN ON . . .

Growing up

"You and your mates could do anything you wanted to do round town. I had a key to the tennis club when I was 13, blokes had 'paddock bombs', we'd go yabbying. I had ferrets when I was a kid. It was just a great life."

His children, Cooper and Tanner

"They're strong, workingclass names. A cooper was a barrel maker, and a tanner a leather maker. I'm from a working-class family, and Sharyn is, as well, and we loved the names."

The 1993 Grand Final

"I was like an extra spectator. I wasn't in the moment. I think I had the fear of failure before the game and everything just went on around me . . . I vowed that I'd never let another minute go by without being involved in a game."

His eyesight problems

"When I was younger, the boys would play havoc with me. I'd say: 'who's that?' and Justin (Madden) would say it was (rover) Fraser Murphy, but it would be (big man) Peter Sartori."

Coaching ambitions

"I drove 'Britts' crazy, to the point where if he wasn't in his room and the team was up, I'd go in and change them, the match-ups and things like that . . . just swing a few changes and walk out of the office."

Next pre-season

"I think we'll approach the NAB Cup differently . . . it's not the be-all- and-end-all if we don't win it or make the finals, as long as we're progressing."

Coaching philosophy

"I want to have a variety and tactics that are a little bit different so we're not stock-standard all the time."

The Age 25 August 2007

MATTHEWS, A MAN OF HIS TIME, DEPARTS AT A TIME OF HIS CHOOSING

Greg Baum

THERE WAS A TIME WHEN football coaches all wore trench coats and pork pie hats and looked old, or at least much older than the players in their charge, and were little seen and less heard publicly, which gave them the authoritarian air they needed. Some were sacked, of course, some several times over, but by the second or third time, it was scarcely ever a surprise. And some left in what seemed the fullness of their time.

Now coaches wear sponsors' clothing and dye their hair or are fashionably bald, all of which makes them look almost like players. Such authority as they exude seems hierarchical rather than patriarchal.

So it seems constantly to come as a surprise now when a long-serving coach departs, either by sacking or resignation, even when the departure has long been speculated upon, even when it is from his second or third club, even when it is in the fullness of his time. It came as a surprise yesterday when Leigh Matthews stood down as coach of the Lions. But it should not have.

Matthews was, at 56, the oldest coach in the competition. This is a watershed age for coaches, arguably for everyone, an age when a man or woman typically takes stock, contemplates what he or she has done and still has left to do, and, if necessary, makes the change before it is too late.

Ron Barassi, Norm Smith, Allan Jeans, Tom Hafey, John Kennedy and David Parkin were all between 55 and 60 when they packed up their clipboards. Last year, Kevin Sheedy and Denis Pagan both took their (albeit reluctant) bows, both 59 at the time. The exception is Collingwood's Jock

McHale, who was 66 when he finished, but had coached for an improbable 38 years.

Matthews' exit leaves Mick Malthouse as the AFL's oldest coach at 55. Like Matthews, he has a year remaining on his contract. Earlier this year, Robert Walls wrote a column questioning whether the time had come for Malthouse and Matthews. Irritated, Malthouse said it was not about age, but innovation and adaptability.

Of course he had to defend himself; anything else would have looked like equivocation and run through the club like a virus. For the most part, he has adapted. But he is at an age where he can reserve the right to change his mind as Matthews just changed his, without losing dignity.

Next oldest to Malthouse is Adelaide's Neil Craig, at 52, but his circumstances are as exceptional as McHale's in that he did not have a preceding stellar playing career in the AFL and did not coach in his own right until he was 48. The next oldest are Rodney Eade and Mark Williams, both 50, and Terry Wallace, about to turn 50. The youngest are Brett Ratten and Matthew Knights, both 37.

The prevailing wisdom is that coaching has become a young man's game. But the wise sometimes forget that they are also seeing with older eyes. Of the illustrious list above, only Pagan was older than 40 when he began coaching in the AFL. Jeans was an infant at 27. McHale and Barassi were older, but still playing; their likes will not be seen again.

The key to all was that they innovated and adapted, to changing times, to changing demands, even the famously inflexible Hafey. Smith pioneered a new way of playing, Parkin a new way of coaching, by player power. Sheedy endured by force of personality.

Matthews, despite impressions, adapted. Early in his career, he depended on the respect he commanded as one of the game's greatest and most-feared players. He had natural authority. An early premiership at Collingwood, thought impossible, reinforced this moral authority.

But Matthews in Melbourne was remote and formidable and outwardly gruff. Matthews in Brisbane became, as well as an extraordinarily successful coach, a teacher and a sage. Partly, this was what the AFL expected of him and paid him to be, as an evangelist on the game's frontier. Partly, you suspect, it was because he also grew in understanding and contentment.

As a coach, Matthews was not ground-breaking as have been, for instance,

Wallace and Eade. His teams played powerful and irresistible, but orthodox football, hard-working and hard-hitting, some would say in Matthews' own image, although that is too simple. They won premierships, a succession of them. For all their invention, neither Wallace nor Eade has yet won a premiership as a coach. Style is their legacy thus far, results Matthews'.

Walls argued that the game was passing Matthews and Malthouse by. Geelong and Hawthorn were leading the competition for handballs, Brisbane and Collingwood trailing it. They were also both in the bottom four for uncontested possession. Once, handball and uncontested possession marked a team out as remedial. But the game has changed; Geelong has made handball an attacking art form.

There is nothing to say that Matthews could not have adapted again. At the year's start, most thought he had. At the end, Brisbane was about where most predicted. If the whimper had been at the start and the bang at the finish, Matthews might have thought differently.

But he might not. He has nothing left to prove to anyone, not even to himself. And unlike Sheedy and Pagan last year, he goes now on his terms. If we are surprised, it is only because Matthews has out-thought us, again.

MATTHEWS: A LIFE IN FOOTBALL	
1968	Joins the Hawthorn Football Club at age 16
1969	Makes senior debut
1971	Premiership player, Hawthorn best-and-fairest, represents Victoria for the first of 14 times
1972	Hawthorn best-and-fairest
1973	Hawthorn leading goalkicker
1974	Hawthorn best-and-fairest
1975	Hawthorn leading goalkicker
1976	Premiership player, Hawthorn best-and-fairest
1977	Hawthorn best-and-fairest
1978	Premiership player, Hawthorn best-and-fairest
1980	Hawthorn best-and-fairest, captain of Victoria
1981	Appointed Hawthorn captain, Hawthorn leading goalkicker

MATTHEWS: A LIFE IN FOOTBALL

1982	Hawthorn best-and-fairest, Hawthorn leading goalkicker
1983	Hawthorn premiership captain, Hawthorn leading goalkicker
1984	Hawthorn leading goalkicker
1985	Deregistered from the VFL after the Neville Bruns incident, retires from playing football, last match in a losing grand final
1986	Becomes assistant coach for Collingwood replacing Bob Rose as senior coach mid-season
1990	First premiership as coach of Collingwood
1995	Sacked as Collingwood coach
1999	Appointed Brisbane Lions coach
2001	Premiership coach of Brisbane
2002	Premiership coach of Brisbane
2003	Premiership coach of Brisbane
2008	Announces retirement as Brisbane Lions coach

The Age 2 September 2008

FAITH HEALER: ALASTAIR CLARKSON

Rohan Connolly

IT'S FAIR TO SAY THAT Alastair Clarkson's appointment as Hawthorn coach in late 2004 didn't exactly meet with resounding applause, particularly among the Hawk faithful.

The club had overlooked three other candidates, favourite sons no less in Terry Wallace, Rodney Eade and Gary Ayres, not only experienced AFL coaches, but Hawthorn premiership heroes, all integral parts of the club's greatest era.

Instead, it had plumped for a bloke who for all his 130-odd games as a player with North Melbourne and Melbourne, and time spent as a coach or assistant coach at Werribee, St Kilda, Central District and Port Adelaide, was still probably best remembered for an infamous blow to the jaw of Carlton defender Ian Aitken in an end-of-season exhibition match in London all the way back in 1987.

The good folk of Hawthorn were livid at the appointment. They wanted to know why. For most of the Hawthorn players, it was more a question of "who?" Like Sam Mitchell, the man who, all going well, will late this afternoon be standing alongside Clarkson on the MCG dais hoisting a premiership cup.

"I was in South America with Richie Vandenberg and Campbell Brown," Mitchell recalled to *The Age* last year. "We were jumping on the internet to find out about it, and they just talked about how he'd belted someone in London.

"We got back for the best-and-fairest wondering how this person we'd never heard of had got the head coaching job. He only spoke to us for about 10–15 minutes, but we went out of the meeting with our answer."

And four years later, so does everyone else. With the prospect of a first Hawthorn flag for 17 years only four quarters of football away, to the faithful, Clarkson is every bit as brown-and-gold as Wallace, Eade, Ayres, perhaps even Leigh Matthews and Peter Hudson.

If that seems a little fanciful, you only needed to be at Hawthorn's final training session this week on Thursday at Waverley Park to see the proof. More than 10,000 had gathered to watch the Hawks go through their paces.

Just before the players ran out, Clarkson and the rest of his coaching panel made their way down to the ground through the packed terracing. Within a couple of seconds, the entire crowd broke into spontaneous, loud cheering.

The Hawks, inside and outside the club, love Clarkson's meticulous planning and preparation. The tactical smarts that have made midfield zoning and "Clarkson's cluster" the most talked-about football strategy for years. Most of all, though, they seem to love the feistiness and competitive nature that has helped create something of an "us-against-them" mentality. Even those at other clubs who don't necessarily warm to the man readily acknowledge he'd be very handy alongside you in the trenches.

"I just think he's the most driven individual I've ever met, to be perfectly honest. He will do anything and everything to succeed," lauded one of Clarkson's right-hand men, assistant coach Damien Hardwick, before the final training run.

"From my point of view, he's the next long-term coach. I can see him doing this for 15 to 20 years, he's that driven. He's already planning his [study] trip overseas, whether we win or lose, already looking towards the next big thing in football. He leaves no stone unturned in regard to his preparation. He challenges us and makes us better as coaches and better as people."

At the same time Mitchell and those Hawks on holiday in South America were trying to get their heads around Clarkson's appointment four years ago, Ian Robson, being courted for the club's chief executive position, was doing similarly from Edinburgh, having spent the past eight years in the United Kingdom working in sports administration.

It was another Hawthorn great, Jason Dunstall, acting as interim chief executive, who had gone in to bat for Clarkson hard with a reluctant board, and got his man over the line. Now the man who would take on the chief executive's job full-time would find out why.

Robson had worked for Sydney when Clarkson was a player. "My memory of him was as a hard-at-it person on the field," he says.

It's a quality Clarkson has been able to bring to the role of coach with great effect.

"He's demonstrated that in a whole range of different ways off the field as coach, not just at Hawthorn, but in his pathway to getting here," Robson says. "He's someone who just has the most extraordinary family values and ethics. That's obviously a credit to his upbringing in the bush (Clarkson hails from Kaniva) and I don't think he's lost any of that humility and down-to-earth nature.

"But when he wants something, he knows how to go hard at getting it. That's sometimes the thing which has got him into trouble, whether he believes he's been wronged by the media or a journo in particular. But he has enormous resolve.

"That determination is what got him that opportunity at Hawthorn in the first place, and what has taken him through a period of extraordinary criticism when the appointment was made, both inside and outside the club, then again when the club reappointed him. Then we went through some criticism earlier this year when we hadn't reappointed him.

"It's been a funny journey, but here we are within four years playing in a grand final, and he's got a three-year contract in his back pocket now for the future."

Hawthorn football manager Mark Evans, another Clarkson right-hand man, says the coach's single greatest asset is his "ability to be able to assess things strategically". The much-discussed "cluster" defence has its roots in other sports, of which Clarkson is a keen follower.

"He's been to England to learn about soccer, he reads books about soccer, baseball, basketball, gridiron," Mitchell noted last year. "We try so many things from all these sports during the pre-season."

And most likely will be again next pre-season. Because far from having a post-grand final breather, Clarkson, as soon as next week's draft camp then the following player trade week is out of the way, will, with Evans and assistants Chris Fagan and David Rath, head off to the US and Europe on another professional development trip.

Just like the end of last year, when his professional duties took him to the UK. Always searching for that little edge over his coaching peers, and far more importantly, for the Hawks as a team over their opposition.

Relentless. Driven. Intense. Whatever it takes. The words and phrases you hear over and over in relation to perhaps the AFL's next premiership coach. The other one you will hear, at least within the club if not necessarily the rest of the football world, is compassionate.

"He does keep a shield up on some of those things as well," Evans says. "The fund-raising he does a lot people wouldn't know about, but on a weekly or fortnightly basis, he goes into the Monash Medical Centre. It's not a public event, it's just who he is and what he does."

Earlier this year, Clarkson played a key role in helping secure funds for friend Graham Barnell, who had acute leukaemia, to receive specialist treatment and surgery in the US.

Says Robson: "That demonstrated that notwithstanding the importance we obviously place on his role inside the footy club, there were for him things in life that just had paramount focus over and above that."

Barnell's plight, and Clarkson's involvement in attempting to secure the massive amount of money he required, was publicised on Channel Nine's *A Current Affair*. Clarkson would no doubt have been embarrassed at being made a focus, but realised how crucial was his profile in getting the money.

In a life sense, too, for him it was all about the team. As, of course, is today, the biggest of his entire career in football.

Surely, Clarkson's first flag as a coach and Hawthorn's first for close to two decades would allow him just a brief window of self-satisfaction? Not likely, say those who work closest with him.

"I know you guys in the media will hear it a lot this time of year, but we're trying to sustain a team ethic which, yes, is about playing in a grand final, but also about the whole way we operate as a football club," Robson says. "People here aren't just members, they're part of our football club, and I know 'Clarko' takes great delight in driving all that."

Personal glory? No way, says Evans. "It's just not his style. It's impossible to continually push the mantra of team first unless you live it yourself. He'll share every bit of success that comes our way. That's his nature."

One very much in keeping with the "Family Club" image the Hawks pushed to such great effect back in those heady days of the 1980s. And the faithful love that.

They might have been aghast when Clarkson was appointed their club's coach four years ago, but as a 10th premiership beckons, they've been long since convinced that he, too, really is one of them.

His methods might be cutting edge and as contemporary as they come, but in terms purely of profile, Hawthorn's Alastair Clarkson is something of a throwback.

There was a time when much of football's coaching elite seemed to share many similar traits, none the least a playing background that may have produced descriptions such as hard-working and dedicated, but seldom brilliant.

Allan Jeans and Tom Hafey were two obvious examples of players of limited capacity whose clubs were far better served later in life when they turned their hands to coaching, finishing with eight premierships between them.

As a player, Clarkson was no dud, 134 games over 11 seasons with North Melbourne and Melbourne the proof. But he was swamped by the tide of rising young stars who rose through the ranks at Arden Street in the early 1990s, was eventually made captain of the reserves, while in his final two years, the Demons were never more than battlers.

The theory behind the success of men such as Jeans and Hafey as coaches was the fact they'd had to fight tooth and nail to maximise their capacity to play at the elite level. Clarkson fits the mould as well, but it's a mould not so identifiable among recent premiership coaches.

Clarkson's rival in the Geelong box today, Mark Thompson, was a 200-game All-Australian and an Essendon premiership captain. John Worsfold was a dual premiership skipper with West Coast, Paul Roos one of the most feted stars of the 1980s, Mark Williams a Collingwood captain and four-time premiership coach Leigh Matthews arguably also the game's greatest player.

Perhaps it's Clarkson's first league coach, Denis Pagan, who comes closest in terms of playing background, the dual premiership coach with North having played 143 games, like Clarkson, first with the Roos, then for his final two seasons, somewhere else.

They're profiles that seem to indicate two qualities. A determination to keep going, but also the willingness to take the steps required to maximise senior opportunities, which in Pagan and Clarkson's case meant shifting footballing homes.

That's been equally the case for Clarkson the coach, too. Stints as senior coach with Werribee in the VFL, as an assistant at St Kilda, as the head man with Central District in the SANFL, then learning more still about the caper under Mark Williams at Port Adelaide.

If there's always been an innate ability to read and analyse the game, for Clarkson, the coaching path has been equally about picking up knowledge from a host of sources at very close quarters.

Then there's Clarkson's professional profile as a teacher, perfect for the influx of youngsters into Hawthorn that coincided with his arrival at the end of 2004. Hawthorn football manager Mark Evans rates that another significant factor in Clarkson's success.

"He has tremendous belief in people, always sees their development possibilities," Evans says. "Very interested in people, and how to get the best out of them."

And, clearly, himself. Clarkson had a hard time convincing Hawthorn he was the man for the job ahead of three names far bigger and more meaningful to the Hawks than his in Rodney Eade, Terry Wallace and Gary Ayres.

They'd all been genuine playing stars as well. Clarkson could never claim that. But these days, and even more so should Hawthorn pull off a premiership win today, he doesn't need to.

The Age 27 September 2008

NEW RICHMOND COACH DAMIEN HARDWICK EARLY IN HIS TENURE AT TIGERLAND: "WHAT HAVE I GOT MYSELF IN FOR?"

Rohan Connolly

DAMIEN HARDWICK FOUND EARLY ON in his debut season as an AFL senior coach that he was becoming too emotionally involved in games. So he resolved, when it came to his own reactions, to "take the scoreboard out of it a little bit".

Last Sunday, as his exuberant young Richmond team won a crushing victory over West Coast and his spearhead Jack Riewoldt went on an extraordinary goalkicking spree, came the definitive proof the strategy had worked.

Hardwick was coaching the Tigers, as he has nearly all season, from the interchange bench. After just 20 minutes and a rush of Riewoldt goals, he spoke to his assistant, Danny Daly, up in the box.

"I said: 'Jeez, Jack's been good, how many has he kicked?'" Hardwick recalled this week. Told he already had five, Hardwick was startled. And again, midway through the last quarter, when an already vocal home crowd started roaring even louder. "I asked them: 'Why is the crowd going nuts? . . . Oh, right, he's going for 10.'"

Hardwick wasn't so detached from the result he couldn't work out the Tigers were about to record their second win of the season, the immediate future far brighter than it had seemed five or so weeks previously.

But he's got his own ladder, too. The official AFL version has Richmond at two wins and 10 losses. On the Hardwick measure, the Tigers are 2–2, the result of a decision taken immediately his team had done all but win the game against Hawthorn in round eight.

"It was a game our numbers suggested we should have won, but being a young side, we just couldn't get over the line. But the belief the players got out of it was enormous," he explains.

"As we were walking from the field that day, we stood together as a group, players and coaches, and we said: 'Listen, our season starts from round nine onwards. We've set ourselves a standard, now we understand what's required to play at a certain level.' We took a stand there that our season was beginning now."

Hardwick is also into winning behaviours, even if the team isn't winning. "We celebrate every goal as if we're in front, we help our guys get up off the ground, all that sort of stuff," he explains. "It's the chicken or the egg, what comes first? We're saying that we might not be winning on the scoreboard, but we can at least set our winning behaviours up nice and early."

The beautiful irony in all this for the long-suffering Richmond hordes is that in being freed from the potentially deflating pressures of the scoreboard and the win-loss tally, the victories are coming.

The first, two weeks later on a rain-soaked AAMI Stadium against Port Adelaide, preceded one of the most passionate renditions of a theme song ever belted out by a playing group, one which almost moved Hardwick to tears.

"I've been fortunate enough to win premierships, but I still maintain that was the best song I've sung. I nearly teared up. It was just so emotional for the players, they'd put in so much hard work, I was so happy for them and to actually get to sing that song . . . jeez it's a great song, it really does get the passion stirring . . . I'll remember that till the day I finish."

Suddenly the positive signs for Richmond seem everywhere. There's the emerging superstar Riewoldt. One of the most composed and consistent rookies of recent times, Dustin Martin. A surprise packet in Ben Nason. Trent Cotchin hitting his straps. Vast improvements from the likes of Matt White, Shane Edwards and Jake King. And the recent renaissance of even a couple of old-timers in Ben Cousins and Shane Tuck.

Hardwick landed at Punt Road last August with a clear, long-term vision. They've had a few of those over the years at Richmond. But the results are already becoming apparent.

Certainly more so than when the 2010 campaign kicked off with a shattering loss to Hawthorn in the first round of the NAB Cup. Richmond was jumped, never in the contest, and already trailing by more than 100 points come three-quarter-time.

A ruder welcome to the world of AFL senior coaching is hard to imagine, and Hardwick felt it keenly.

"I must admit, after that first loss I felt like the loneliest bloke on the face of the earth," he recalls. "I remember going to bed that night and I actually felt crook, thinking: 'What have I got myself in for?' It was probably the eye-opener for me. The first thing you do is doubt yourself, think have I not done this or that right.

"But the great thing was, though I didn't want to watch the tape, I made myself, and when I watched it, I thought we had some areas that we could improve really, really quickly. And for the rest of the NAB Challenge, we were actually pretty competitive. It's all been a thoroughly enjoyable process, I've learnt a lot about the caper in a short period of time, and some do's and don'ts as well."

There was a "don't" as recently as last Sunday, when Hardwick sent out a message telling Riewoldt not to talk to the Fox TV crew out on the ground immediately after the siren. But when Riewoldt started copping a public whack for following his coach's instructions, the mea culpa was immediate.

"It was my stuff-up," Hardwick says, "and the reason I came out and apologised was that people were into Jack, and it wasn't his choice, it was mine. People are very quick to whack Jack, but he's an outstanding kid."

Hardwick has had far more serious issues to deal with, though. Like the aftermath of the round-three match in Sydney, when youngster Daniel Connors was suspended by the club for eight matches after alcohol-fuelled high jinks in the team hotel, and more senior teammates Cousins, Luke McGuane and Dean Polo were suspended for a game for failing to do enough to stop their teammate's rampage.

"We learnt a lesson about the parameters we had to have in place for such a young group. And we probably didn't have enough in place to knock it on the head," Hardwick admits. A chastened Connors played his first game back in senior company last weekend. So have the lessons sunk in?

"I think so. Dan had a number of issues prior to that, and we just wanted to make sure he understood perfectly where he was at, and that any further instances down that track were going to cost him his career. It's been a massive eye-opener for him about what you have to be prepared to give up in order to have a good time for one night."

Hardwick says he's enjoying developing his relationships with the playing group, and it's certainly not all one-way traffic. "The kids of today are very different to when I came through. They'll always ask why something happens, which, to be honest, I quite enjoy. I actually want them to challenge me, to ask why they're in or out of the side, and I say to them the day I don't respond to that is the day I shouldn't be coaching any more.

"I'm happy to give them some home truths, but I'm also very happy for them to give me some home truths, because as the relationship gets stronger, they know I'm not going to bullshit to them, and it creates that open-door policy that I think good footy clubs are founded on."

That, and balance. Hardwick is big on family.

"To me that's first, and football a long way second, and that's a club mantra as well. If anyone has got family issues, they take care of that first, then worry about the footy." Married to Danielle, Hardwick has three children—Benjamin, or "BJ" as his dad calls him, 13, Isabelle, 10, and Imogen, seven. They've been actively involved wherever he has been. Hardwick recalled how, on the day of his appointment to the Richmond job, his daughters had asked if he could take Cyril Rioli along with him. Now they're converts, too.

"We try to do as much as we can together," he says. "BJ comes to games with me now and scouts, like, 'OK, BJ, who's in the centre bounce now?' The girls watch the footy with me on the couch. They love it, and they'll give me advice, too, like, 'That guy didn't find the body, Dad.' I'll still go and watch them play sport. I was scoring at the basketball the other night."

Which presents its own set of problems, given close friend but now rival coach Alastair Clarkson's daughter is playing for the same team.

"Our daughters play in the same side twice a week," he says with a laugh.

"It was very funny the week we played Hawthorn. On the Tuesday, it was a little bit frosty, then on the night before the game we're both sitting there like this [he strikes a rigid pose, eyes straight ahead, arms crossed defensively]. We're good mates, our families are very close. At the end of the day, footy's a small part of our lives considering we're going to be lifelong friends."

Hardwick has plenty of other football mentors, including Chris Fagan, head of coaching and development at Hawthorn, and former Port Adelaide assistant Geoff Morris. There's his own dad, Noel, who coached him in his junior playing days with Upwey-Tecoma.

But there's a new, even more meaningful relationship being formed with the Richmond Football Club. They're a good fit, Hardwick and the Tigers, a former no-nonsense, hard-as-nails defender, with a club whose origins and character remain distinctly blue collar.

"Just getting back to that workmanlike outfit is something our boys have taken stock of," he says. "I think over the last six weeks, we've started to see some of those traits coming back into it, which will help link us with our past."

And then there's that famous Punt Road passion. "At the weekend, we had 31,000 there for a game between 16th and 14th, staggering, then to hear the passion in the crowd walking on to the ground afterwards," Hardwick says. "Honestly, I just can't wait till we get a crowd of 70,000, and they get to sing that song, to hear that many of our supporters roaring would be amazing."

Indeed it would. And given Hardwick's aversion to taking note of the scoreboard, also some pretty compelling evidence that his young and emerging Tigers had won again.

The Age 19 June 2010

COACH CHANGED THE GAME—AND WON A FEW, TOO: PAUL ROOS

Jake Niall

PAUL ROOS WILL LEAVE THE game on his own terms and as his own man.

Some coaches transform their clubs, others change the way the game is played. Some bring new methods for managing players. Paul Roos did all three and, along the way, he delivered a famous premiership to a frontier market with a team of modest talent.

Roos is the most influential AFL coach of the past decade and when the man Kevin Sheedy dubbed "the Sundance Kid" rides off into the setting sun at season's end, he will become, if he isn't already, the game's most coveted coach.

That he doesn't necessarily want to coach again will only multiply the level of interest and the dollars on offer; persuading "Roosy" out of exile will be like getting, well, Robert Redford, in your movie in 1969. Actually, Marlon Brando, circa 1978, is a better analogy, since it is the reluctance of the star that makes him such a hot commodity.

Prepare for more stories about Roos being the "top priority" for various clubs. Roos has already been the subject of considerable speculation at clubs whose coaches run out of contract next year, such as Carlton. The assumption, always, is that while he says he doesn't want to coach, the Godfather offers will eventually see him saddle up again.

No one can quite believe that a coach as capable as Roos—and low maintenance to the club's administration—will walk away. Coaches, as a rule, don't walk. They get shoved, and most of them are addicted to the caper.

Not Roos. David Parkin, his former coach at Fitzroy and an occasional mentor, never thought his old centre half-back would coach, and judged—wrongly—that he'd be too easygoing to thrive in a job that attracts what Parkin called "aggressive, dominant, autocratic pricks".

The converse, of course, was true: Roos thrived, in part, because he was atypical. His legacy outweighs his contemporary rivals (Mick Malthouse began much earlier) because it is multi-dimensional.

There are five major areas in which Roos has had a marked effect on the game. First of all, he gave the Swans a premiership, their first in Sydney and, for the South Melbourne folk, the only red and white flag since 1933.

In doing so, he used a stoppage-based game style that Andrew Demetriou considered the great Australian football ugliness. The AFL reacted to the ugly Swans by implementing a series of rule changes, with the overall aim of stopping stoppages. The AFL's mantra became "continuous" footy. Every significant rule change since 2005, thus, can be seen as a response to Roos, who crafted his game plan around the good but not supremely gifted players at his disposal. This impact on the rules would be his second major legacy.

The third legacy was a consequence of the second. By becoming a foe of head office and speaking out against rule changes, Roos made Sydney, hitherto seen as an outpost of the AFL administration (much like the incoming teams today), a truly independent operation, albeit one that still required a few props. This transformation was largely about psychology; the Swans saw themselves as in opposition to head office to a greater degree.

Roos had already changed Sydney by the manner in which he'd won the coaching job. The Swans had wanted—and apparently signed—Terry Wallace. The fans rose up and demanded that Roos, the caretaker, get the gig. Sydney had never seen such a display of people power. It was a watershed moment in which the members and supporters asserted their ownership of the club.

The fans were empowered, then Roos began his defining task of empowering his players. He introduced Ray McLean's "Leading Teams" to the club and allowed his players unprecedented control of their own destiny, though one presumes he used gentle prods to get them moving in certain directions. The players branded themselves "The Bloods", adopting the old South Melbourne nickname.

Sydney's success resulted in other clubs following. Others had used empowerment models before, Roos made it fashionable. A dysfunctional Geelong adopted a similar leadership model, with a more attacking and fluent game style using far better players. Geelong, more than any rule change, was the counter to the defensive methods Roos had unleashed.

Parkin considers the empowerment of the players to be Roos' greatest legacy. "He did it from day one."

Coaches don't set out to change the game. They want to win games. By achieving the latter Roos also did the former.

The Age 17 June 2010

THOMPSON EXITS AFTER A DECADE TO REMEMBER AT KARDINIA PARK

Martin Blake

MARK "BOMBER" THOMPSON: GONE. Gary Ablett: gone. Frank Costa: going soon.

Ostensibly, Geelong is reeling after a decade of stability. Realistically, it is slightly different. By 4pm yesterday the Cats had said their goodbyes to the second-longest serving coach in their history, and moved on.

"Mark created history at this club and he'll be remembered for that by a lot of people," said chief executive Brian Cook, at a press conference where Thompson's resignation was announced. "We've all been on a magnificent, a wonderful journey for the past decade, led by Mark. However from today we're on a new journey."

They had a week of warning, of course, for Thompson had told Cook last Tuesday that he was baked. The delay in finalising his departure was merely a precaution; Thompson agreed with Cook's suggestion that he take some time and speak to some confidants, but it changed nothing. Yesterday his assistants and many of the Geelong staff packed into the theatre at Skilled Stadium to see Thompson, dressed in business suit and Geelong tie, pull the pin.

It has been quite some ride. As Costa observed yesterday, Geelong was in strife in 2000 when he, Cook and Thompson arrived at Kardinia Park. The club had no money, its list was poor and its facilities second-rate. As Thompson and Costa depart, the club is sound and strong and successful.

"I'm leaving today but the club is still a fantastic club," said Thompson. "We haven't taken our eye off the ball as far as developing young talent and recruiting the best talent we can. We've got some really exciting players at the

63

club and I'm sure the next coach, and the people here, it's bigger than me, the people here will get it right.

"That's one thing we've been able to do over the years. Every year we finish, we aspire to be better and I think we've done that year after year. The real challenge now is to find a coach who's got that energy, and the skills to take the club forward, and that's not me."

Thompson's 11 years netted two flags from three grand finals, seven finals appearances and 161 wins—more than any other team in that period. Perhaps equally as significantly, his Geelong teams from 2007 to the present played blindingly brilliant football to watch. In a sense, Thompson revitalised the game by encouraging his players to take the game on, surging through the corridor without stopping to think.

Asked to name a highlight, he cited the drought-breaking 2007 premiership triumph, and he talked about the smiles on the faces of old Geelong people like Costa and the late Alex Popescu. "It's something that will never leave me," he said.

Yesterday he revealed that his doubts about continuing had surfaced some time ago, but that he kept them largely to himself. "A long time ago I said I wasn't going to coach forever, and I've known for a little while that this was going to come," he said. "I didn't tell one person or maybe I slipped out occasionally, but I kept it to myself, because if I had done it six weeks ago or four weeks ago the whole momentum of who was going to replace me and the big goodbyes would have been a distraction to the team.

"To be honest, I totally wanted to put every bit of effort into winning the 2010 premiership. It didn't happen, unfortunately, but we got close."

He could not have made the ending of his love affair with coaching any plainer. He is cooked. "I'm just pretty much over the job, the day-to-day relentless work of it. You know, there's a few things in my life I have to fix up and I want to fix up.

"As coach you're totally absorbed by what you do. In the process you miss family functions, you miss certain things, you do a lot of things only half-good, half-done. I've got to get back and look after myself a little bit. I'm looking forward to that."

By choosing to walk away rather than persist against his instinct, Thompson believes he has done the right thing by the club, and Cook agrees. "If we had a coach next year who was half glass full and half an effort, it would be much worse than the position we're in at the moment."

Thompson said he wanted his departure from Geelong to be without acrimony. "Handling it this way is a lot easier on the person. I know I've let the club down by walking away, but we're going to be friends for life because I did it that way. A lot of people do get the sack as coach. They don't end up having a great relationship with that club, and I want it to be a great relationship for a long time."

The Age 5 October 2010

PUMPED AND PROUD: CHRIS SCOTT

Rohan Connolly

CHRIS SCOTT MAY WELL BE the one to breathe life into the ageing Cats' line-up and his enthusiasm shows he is ready for the task.

It's several days after clocking up his first win as coach of Geelong, and Chris Scott is still fielding questions about his somewhat animated response up in the box towards the closing stages of the Cats' nail-biting win over St Kilda.

"I don't see a problem showing some emotion, especially in the last 20 seconds of your first game as coach, when you've won with basically the last kick," he says.

Importantly, nor did the Geelong supporters. Quite the reverse, in fact. As a symbol of the two time Brisbane Lions premiership player's commitment to a new cause, nothing spoke louder than Scott's adrenalin-fuelled pumping of the fist as Darren Milburn ran into an open goal to seal the victory.

Scott had sat as an assistant in the Fremantle coach's box for three years. He'd taken the reins in the Cats' war room for the NAB Cup and a couple of practice matches. But nothing could adequately prepare him for the emotional rollercoaster he rode in his official senior coaching debut.

It was hectic, nerve-wracking, anxious and, ultimately, joyous. But Scott found himself loving even the uncomfortable bits.

"There's so many ups and downs—and I even felt this as a player—a lot of it's not very pleasurable," he reflects. "Like being nervous before a big game. It's not a nice feeling, but at least you feel alive.

"That's what it felt like on Friday night. For five seconds there, where we thought the game was gone, you're the most depressed you can remember being, but then there's the exhilaration of getting over the line. Then, two hours later, I'm in the car thinking about Fremantle [the Cats' opponent in Perth tonight] and what we're going to do about Aaron Sandilands.

"You wake up in the morning feeling like a bit of a goose because you know you're going to see all those replays of yourself carrying on like an idiot, but it's those small moments that really make you feel alive."

Which, in a sense, is pretty much Scott's mission for Geelong. There will be some changes, to style, to personnel and to positions. There's bound to be the odd uncomfortable moment when home truths are told. If last Friday is anything to go by, there'll still be plenty of joy, too. But it's all about the business of making a team—popularly pronounced dead as a premiership contender, and at the end of an era—feel alive once again.

Scott knows he's in relatively uncharted waters. New coaches usually inherit sides closer to the bottom of the ladder and requiring a complete rebuild.

Instead, he's taken over a team which lost a preliminary final after contesting the previous three grand finals.

For Geelong, and its new coach, it's a fascinating fork in the road. The manner of the Cats' defeat at the hands of Collingwood last September suggested time was up. Run your eye over the names on the list, however, even without Gary Ablett, and you see a side that, purely in terms of talent, is still very much in the hunt.

But Scott is perhaps better placed than most to be able to read the situation as it develops through the course of this season.

"I have some sympathy for the players at Geelong last year, because what they had done had been so effective over such a long period of time that they had a lot faith in it," he says.

"Being prepared to change is really hard. I experienced the same thing at Brisbane. When you've got faith in a system [not to mention three straight flags], you tend to back it in at all costs.

"I have an intense desire to make sure I never forget what it's like being a player," says Scott, who retired at the end of 2007 after 215 games. "It's going to be harder to remember in 10 years' time, but I'm determined to have that empathy for players.

"One thing I can guarantee you is that in 10 years' time, playing will be harder than it is today, the same way that five years ago playing was a lot easier than it is now."

Scott has been careful not to throw the baby out with the bathwater, with the list (Ablett and the retired Max Rooke the only losses of note) or the coaching panel, all of whom were there in 2010. But he believes firmly that what might only appear a tweak to the formula here or there could make a significant difference.

"The overwhelming strength here has been midfield depth, and I reckon that's a pretty good template for successful sides," he says. "I'm keen to exploit that to its maximum. The flexibility of our list is a huge strength, and I think we can exploit that a little more.

"In the modern game, what is the difference between a high half-forward, an on-baller or a wingman? They're basically the same thing. So we need a group of 12 to 14 players who can do that. Fortunately, I think we have the personnel to do it.

That doesn't mean that Steve Johnson won't play forward, or that Corey Enright won't play back, it just means, hopefully, they can contribute through the middle of the ground a bit more."

Scott reckons the Cats have at least a dozen players capable of playing in defence. Then there's the kids who are going to get a lot more opportunity.

The likes of Cameron Guthrie, Daniel Menzel and Allen Christensen— all three late inclusions for tonight's tough road trip to Subiaco—along with Taylor Hunt and Mitch Duncan.

Scott's already heard the talk that playing a required number of youngsters is one of the key performance indicators on which he will be judged. Not true, he says. Not that he'll need much prompting to give them their shot, either. But not just for the sake of it.

"If we don't think any have deserved their place, we'll play none," he says. "It's really important to understand the big difference between having a long-term plan with young players and throwing them into the deep end and playing them irrespective of form and health.

"We'll provide opportunities where we think players have put the work in and we think they can do it, but not at the expense of where they'll be in three or four years, and I think we're in a fortunate position where we can do that."

Much of the obsessing over the apparent differences to the Mark Thompson version of Geelong and Scott's 2011 model is, he believes, a little simplistic.

The most superficial indicator to date is the Cats' greater inclination to kick. But that's more a consequence of other changes. And, as Scott points out, Geelong still racked up more handballs than anyone else last week.

"The part people underrate is what the opposition are doing," he says. "I'd be really disappointed if people made the observation of Geelong that they just play a certain style.

"To an extent, we want to play a certain way, but if the opposition dictates that we can't, we've got to be able to adjust, and I think that's what we're seeing within games.

"Take last week, for example. We don't want to be a side that kicks sideways and goes backwards and moves the ball slowly. A lot of those, in our view, from our review, were errors. We might be trying to do something else, we've just made mistakes in the game.

"If there's no opposition out there, we're going to play really fast, direct footy and score quickly. When the opposition make that impossible, we've got to have a plan B. From what I saw in the last seven or eight games last year, compared to what we need to do now, and every side's the same in this respect, when the opposition defends really well, you can't persist in trying to play the same way. You've got to be able to read that situation and make a difficult decision."

And Scott's had pretty good mentoring on the "difficult decision" front, too, having been coached by a man—in Leigh Matthews—not only a certified football legend, but the unsurpassed master of football pragmatism.

"I'd like to think in some way I could emulate his ability to cut through what is a very complicated game and deliver a simple message to the players," he says. "The other thing I always marvelled at was that I assume he had players he liked more than others, but you couldn't tell who they were. I think that's a really important quality in a coach. Naturally, you're going to be drawn to some people, but when the hard decisions had to be made, Leigh's decision-making was unencumbered."

It's that sort of clarity of which Scott will need plenty over the next couple of years, with no fewer than nine Geelong players turning 30 or older this season. But rational thinking doesn't necessarily have to come at the expense of passion. And whatever course Scott takes over the long term, those emotion-fuelled seconds in the coaching box last Friday night are going to stay with Cats fans for a long time.

The Geelong hordes knew at that moment they had a coach who really cares. And, like the new leader soaking up the emotional ride of a senior coaching debut, following a team still feeling very much alive.

The Age 2 April 2011

BUCKLEY AND THE SEARCH
FOR FOOTY UTOPIA

Jake Niall

When you change the government, you change the country.

Paul Keating

THE REAL KIRRIBILLI PACT WAS a secret handshake, witnessed only by four men. Collingwood's version was out in the open. Ultimately, it resembled the furtive Bob Hawke–Paul Keating deal only in the sense that a venerated, silver-haired leader was reluctant to vacate the seat.

Hawke was shoved when his team was battling, while Mick Malthouse spent the final two years—the most successful of his dozen at Collingwood—knowing that he would be replaced by Nathan Buckley at the conclusion of season 2011.

At first hailed as a coup, the arrangement soon became highly contentious because the Magpies won a premiership and were within 30–40 minutes of snaring a second; to tip a coach out, in the middle of such success, was unprecedented. While Malthouse signed on, he never concealed his distaste for the handover.

But a deal is a deal. Buckley is the coach. Malthouse, having spurned an ill-defined "director of coaching" afterlife at Collingwood, has gone to Channel Seven.

The Collingwood switch is a change of leader, not government. Most of the Malthouse front bench—football chief Geoff Walsh, sports science boss David Buttifant and recruiting manager Derek Hine—have stayed on. The playing list is mainly intact, albeit a number are injured and a couple have retired. The coaching change is more akin to Keating following Hawke than Howard following Keating.

Still, Collingwood is already a slightly different team under Buckley. How different? Leigh Matthews, one of the game's clearest thinkers, predicted that "very little" would change in the transition to Buckley. Matthews has met with Buckley to provide some informal mentoring—"a few conversations" was how the phlegmatic Matthews described the interaction. Matthews is one of a number of advisers who've been sought out by an intensely focused Buckley.

Another occasional sounding board and four-time premiership coach, AFL Coaches Association president David Parkin, said Buckley's preparation for coaching was the most rigorous he had seen.

As promised, Buckley has had the footballs out earlier and more often than Malthouse. The workload is said to have increased.

"The altitude camp we did over there was by far the hardest, the hardest session, the hardest training camp we've done over there," said key defender Ben Reid.

The players say the game style has been tinkered with, rather than revolutionised, with a greater emphasis on ball movement. Buckley is renovating, not tearing down the house that Mick built.

His man-management style—seen by sceptics as his major challenge—is still taking shape. Motivating and extracting commitment from players, "getting them up", was Malthouse's great gift. Buckley, to date, has been "very measured" in all his dealings with players. Rodney Eade is providing the experienced hand and one of the jocular foils that Buckley's manager and confidant, Craig Kelly, said his man would need.

The most important difference between Collingwood's 2012 compared with 2011 could prove to be the circumstances that Buckley has encountered, which, due to injury—two of them serious—and Sharrod Wellingham's ill-timed drinking session, have become more problematic over the past month.

In the grander scheme, Buckley has been bequeathed a club with a very strong playing list, huge resources and expectations. On Friday night, however, when Buckley takes command in the box, the Pies will likely be without eight or nine of their best 22 from last year. That's not counting retirees Leon Davis and Leigh Brown.

More ominously, they enter the season with 11 premiership players, including Scott Pendlebury and Travis Cloke, coming out of contract in a market liberalised by free agency and Greater Western Sydney.

Essendon's ex-champion Matthew Lloyd reckons that, as coach of the flag favourite, Buckley will be under more pressure than any rookie coach in AFL history.

Buckley this week dismissed such talk as irrelevant to the task at hand. "Whether I'm under more pressure or not, I beg to differ," he said. "Every coach has an expectation and is trying to achieve an end. The pressure that comes with that is just a side effect."

Matthews called the notion of Buckley feeling pressure a "misnomer", observing: "People like Nathan Buckley, Michael Voss, James Hird, the pressure they put on themselves . . . far surpasses any external forces."

Yet, Buckley has learnt to temper those demands he places on himself. "I think I've learned that that's not necessarily a great way to be. It's not great for the mental state at times, because sometimes you need to be able to smell the roses. But the fact is no matter what anyone says outside of our organisation . . . in the end, you're judged on your performances."

From the outset, Buckley—and by association, Eddie McGuire and the administration that installed him—will be judged harshly if the Pies stumble. Millions are willing him to fail. He did, after all, choose Collingwood for a second time when he might have coached a club that is less offensive to the majority.

The Buckley question—how he will he differ from Malthouse and can he make a difference?—is among the most significant of the season. Typically, coaches begin with teams that have failed and have a mandate for change. Buckley starts with a unit that lost only seven of 51 matches over two seasons. He has a mandate only to win.

THE GAME PLAN

At a briefing in February, Buckley revealed that the Magpies had changed their game style slightly—by "5 to 10 per cent"—for the 2011 grand final. There was "no doubt" they'd been worked out. The problem had been that the Pies hadn't had sufficient time to drill the variations. Buckley believes Collingwood's 2012 game plan will alter somewhat over the course of this season. "I guarantee you by the end of the year, it will shift."

It's clear that Buckley wants the Pies to use the corridor more than they did under Malthouse, who treated the boundary as his team's 19th man. But this should not be overstated. They still play wider than most clubs.

In cricketing terms, the boundary has been Collingwood's stock ball. Buckley has decided it needs another delivery—the corridor, or switches of play—to keep the opposition guessing. It's quite possible that this would have happened even under Malthouse.

The impression of opposition experts from rival clubs is that the Pies won't use the "get-out" kick down the line with the same frequency as they have and will switch play and move in board when held up. Ball movement will remain rapid and, if possible, quickened further as the Pies seek to isolate Travis Cloke, the game's most potent marking forward. As an assistant coach, Buckley liked Cloke and Chris Dawes to play in set positions, rather than swapping constantly.

At Collingwood's sunny community camp in Wangaratta, veteran ruckman Darren Jolly, told *The Saturday Age* that much of the game style was unchanged, but the Pies had placed more emphasis on how the ball was moved. "Still we'll constantly work on our box set-up, defensive side, clearly to stop goals, but more on our, I suppose, attacking ball movement. We're not going to be so predictable to teams because, you know, clearly they figured us out last year.

"Certainly, Geelong in the grand final showed us up with their plus one behind the ball. They really ate us up in that area. We've done a few things over the break to combat that and, hopefully, turn it around." Jolly said Buckley had "certainly freshened up the group, in I suppose aspects of our game that probably we weren't focusing on enough".

THE GEELONG MODEL

Buckley's admiration for the team that wrenched the premiership from the Magpies was evident when he spoke to *The Saturday Age* this week. Geelong was the only team, besides his own, mentioned.

"In recent history, you only have to look at what Geelong were forced and were able to do last year," said Buckley, in response to a question about Collingwood's thinning depth. "They played a lot of their youth, a lot of their young players at an early stage of the year and throughout the season and that gave their established players some rest and recuperation."

He reeled off the names of the Geelong players who'd materialised last year. Buckley, who had been the assistant coach with an opposition brief under Malthouse in 2011, had completed a Masters in Geelong.

If it's natural for all clubs to eye off the premier, Buckley has a particular reason for aspiring to emulate Geelong. The Cats won the premiership, rejigging their game style and freshening up under a new novice coach, after 11 years and enormous success under another man. Crucially, the Cats didn't discard the essence of what Mark Thompson had implemented. Chris Scott sought to retain the strengths—sublime ball movement, hardness, contested supremacy—while upgrading the plan to cope with Collingwood-style forward presses. Geelong toned down its helter-skelter, handball-happy style and kicked it more.

"I think any premiership coach creates a role model for the next year, at the very least," said Buckley. "Some premierships—all premierships—are won on obviously optimum effort and investment by the playing group and the coaches. Some were by tactical advancement or strategic advancement.

"I thought Geelong was a balance of both of those. They were able to maximise their playing list and got great investment from their players, but they also tweaked their existing game plan to the point where they, you know, they were up to date. I don't think there was anything special or spectacular with the way they played the game, other than the fact that it was hard, contested and not easy to beat."

Buckley's challenge is similar to Scott's.

"If you look at premiership sides, or even Collingwood, in recent years, there's been players that—[Jarryd] Blair, Dawes, Reid, [Brent] Macaffer, Brown, probably five that jumped up that wouldn't have been seen as legitimate AFL talent at the beginning of 2010. They've played in premierships that year.

"You've got [Allen] Christensen, [Mitch] Duncan, [Trent] West and potentially [Daniel] Menzel who got injured, stood up and were in their best side, there's three or four that came up in [the] 2011 premiership side. No matter who you are, or what you look like at the beginning of the year, if you've got an established core, then you can develop three or four players that push through . . . and become part of the best 22, then you're in the hunt."

The upshot? Buckley needs to find four or five kids to emerge this year.

DEALING WITH PLAYERS

As a player, Buckley wore a reputation for demanding plenty of teammates. Malthouse, asked in a 2009 television interview about Buckley's potential coaching pitfalls, referred to Nathan's "perfectionist" streak. The inference was clear, that Buckley was a higher performer who might struggle to tolerate less single-minded mortals.

So, the obvious question for the players was whether the perfectionist had been hard on them. "Well, he certainly hasn't been yet," said Jolly, the ruckman adding, with a chuckle, "Who's to know what's going to happen [after] a couple of games with a bit of stress on his back? But, to date, he's been fantastic."

Perhaps because he's so aware of his own intense nature and conscious he's following a popular older coach, Buckley has been measured to the point that sources say he hasn't yet raised his voice in anger. His management style is said to be understated, composed and rational; in dealing with Andrew Krakouer's demons, he erred on the side of the player's welfare and gave him a month's leave.

Malthouse had a bond with his players that had an emotional edge. He showed faith in them, told them he believed in them, that he was proud of them. They responded with effort. He was perhaps most beloved by those who'd been scallywags: Dane Swan, Alan Didak, Heath Shaw, Chris Tarrant, Ben Johnson. They didn't want to disappoint the grey-haired father who'd shown such faith.

Malthouse was loath to suspend players for indiscretions and reluctant to hand power to his leadership group—albeit, he shifted this stance over time. Buckley, as captain, took a harder line and was an advocate for player empowerment. In his book, *All I Can Be*, he explains his disappointment when Tarrant and Johnson were allowed to play in a late-season game after they'd been embroiled in a late-night scuffle. This week, Wellingham was suspended for drinking in what was a standard club response.

If Malthouse was a motivator with an emotional pitch, Buckley takes the view that, in an ideal world, motivation should be the player's responsibility. "I have a great belief in the philosophy that the player is responsible for their performance and for getting themselves up, the motivation comes from within, within the individual and within the team. I believe the player needs to find the necessary arousal level to perform week in, week out and he needs to have a reason to do that and generally the team and the leaders within draw the group together to provide that.

"And the responsibility of the coaches is to provide the right environment and the stimulus for the players to find that level."

Buckley acknowledged that to have self-motivated players was "utopia"—a word the perfectionist used more than once in our conversation. "But to get to that point, players need to understand when they're doing it and when they're not." A strong coaching panel would "give that feedback".

The affable Buttifant is probably closer to the players than anyone at Collingwood, and was even tighter with Malthouse, with whom he recently wrote a book. In the industry, many wondered if Buttifant would leave post-Malthouse, but he stayed.

Buttifant's role under Buckley has been the subject of some conjecture. It was suggested that Buttifant, the high-altitude training pioneer, had less clout under Buckley than Malthouse. Buckley wished to correct this view.

"David's importance with a junior coach, or a young coach, a rookie coach, is probably enhanced, given that I'm leaning on 'Butters' as much as any first-year coach feels like he needs to lean on a person in that role. The fact is, he has a wealth of experience . . . he and I obviously have discussions about philosophically where we need to go to and we set the direction and then we go and roll it out together."

Asked about the workload on players, Buckley said: "I still think there's an ability to develop every player at every opportunity. Our players can be fitter, our players can be more skilful, our players can be faster and stronger and we're not setting a ceiling on our capabilities of that."

Buckley is also managing a host of new coaches, having lost the three men he had earmarked for the main assistant roles, Mark Neeld, Scott Watters and Brenton Sanderson (ex-Geelong) to senior coaching jobs. Eade has taken one slot, in a mentor-like role, with Robert Harvey (midfield) and Ben Hart (defence) joining Matthew Lappin (forwards) as line coaches.

Like Neeld, Buckley also has adopted the West Coast model of having a development coach under each line coach, bringing in old teammate Anthony Rocca, Dale Tapping and ex-Bulldog Mitch Hahn.

The net result is less experience and continuity in the coaching ranks. Buckley took the glass half-full view. "At times, having a fresh perspective is going to be a great opportunity for them. They know what they're capable of . . . and really, you know, the players will get the job done. I'm pretty confident that our coaches have got the experience and the ability and the perspective to be able to create the environment around those players for them to be stimulated and improve."

"Creating an environment" for the players emerges as a Buckley stock phrase. It is also his solution to perhaps the largest storm clouds hanging over the Westpac Centre: those 11 players coming off contract this year.

"Clearly, clubs are not going to be able to match the dollars that are going to be thrown at some of the individuals at the end of the season. So . . . it's important for the players to feel a value and a worth beyond the monetary aspect of it and in the end, there's going to be some circumstances that clubs aren't going to be able to even bridge that gap, because it's a bridge too far. The money will be so extreme that some players will decide that. In the end, you can only deal with what you've got and what we've got at the moment is the ability to create the right environment, build on the relationships and create a football team that players want to be part of.

"We'll go about our business and what will be will be."

FATHER FIGURES

In the corner of the ramshackle rooms at Visy Park eight days ago, after the Collingwood–St Kilda practice match, a tall, bearded man chatted to the coach before Buckley sat down with Eade to dissect the game. This upright figure, Ray Buckley, a former coaching nomad, is the formative influence in his son's football life.

All I Can Be contains searingly candid accounts of how a forceful Ray pushed and moulded Nathan, including a startling letter the father wrote to his teenage boy, in which he accused his son of being soft. "You were a very tough kid from age 3 to 9 and then you slowly eased off the pace, became a thinker and chose the easy way." Ray implored Nathan to harden up, prescribing a series of physical and mental tasks, including runs and lifting weights.

More than a decade ago, I asked a Collingwood insider about Buckley. "Nathan Buckley," he replied, "is Tiger Woods. He's the creation of his father."

As coach, Buckley is seeking out older heads who can help him be all that he can be. Eade fills that role formally. Matthews is lending the occasional ear. Barry Richardson, the ex-Tigers coach and president who Buckley worked for when he arrived at Collingwood, is also on hand to provide counsel. Kelly, the manager and ex-teammate, is another.

For the son, there is some symmetry in the father watching him coach. "We've come full circle. When I was a young player, dad had plenty of advice. At a time when my career went on, he didn't have as much to relate. But he's a big supporter obviously and, you know, I value his opinion and I suppose like any father and son, we speak about it. He's a great confidant and definitely someone I speak a lot to and about what's going on in my life."

It seemed Ray, as a former coach, was more animated about Nathan as coach. "Oh, yes. I don't want to go there," said the son.

Buckley is 39—old enough, as McGuire pointed out, to be father to some players. Matthews was greatly impressed with the person Buckley had matured into, having coached the 21–22-year-old version.

In McGuire's initial concept, the paternal figure in Buckley's coaching life today would be the man he replaced. Buckley said he had seen Malthouse a few times since their parting. "Yeah, we've had a few chats." About? "Just in general and we've run into each other on a couple of occasions and just had a general chat."

Malthouse had not offered advice. "No, he's offered me plenty of advice over the years. I've got 14 years of advice ringing through my ears with every decision that sort of I make . . . as are the words of any of the coaches I've had in the past."

Malthouse and Buckley had mutual respect, rather than deep affection, as the older man recently acknowledged. The old coach knew that his presence at Collingwood was untenable. Hence Buckley has turned to others.

"Unfortunately, it's like me and 'Vossy'," said Matthews of the severance that occurs. "It's the old bull and the young bull."

Malthouse was a father to his players. What would Buckley be? "Yet to be written," said the young bull.

The Age 24 March 2012

MICK MALTHOUSE

Konrad Marshall

As COACH, MICK MALTHOUSE ALWAYS knew that at a certain stage of the summer he would start his pre-season, examine his strategy, attend to his playing list, and generally reinvest all his energy in a group of footballers and their long march toward a common goal. "But all of a sudden that stopped, and it stopped very abruptly. And it was just finished. There were no leftovers. You don't wean yourself off a football club—it was just instant," he tells me, holding eye contact early in his first major interview since vacating the top job at Collingwood. "It's really strange thinking singularly instead of broadly, but I have to. I have to think, what am I going to do now?"

Instead of honing a game plan, he is practising his commentary skills for Channel Seven and 3AW. Instead of consoling injured Magpie Brent Macaffer, he is working with students in a new but somewhat nebulous mentoring and promotions role as a vice-chancellor's fellow at La Trobe University. He's writing a column for *The West Australian*, and talking to another company about a leadership role, all of which is to say he is keeping busy.

"I'm not idle. I've never been idle. I don't think I ever could be," he says. "I really need to be stimulated by something, and there's a real challenge in front of me, which I like." The commentary box, he notes, offers positives the coaching box could not. "Maybe I wake up more clear-minded, not having that ache in the pit of my stomach about who's injured, who's not, who's suspended, how is the team performing." He misses coaching—that much is not in dispute—"but the facts are that you can't change that, and I don't want to look back," he says, pausing. "But I'd be lying if I didn't say I've found things difficult. It's been very difficult. Very strange."

We meet in the lobby of Channel Seven headquarters at the Docklands, where Malthouse recently joined the network's repackaged 2012 AFL commentary team. He offers a handshake with his right hand, and takes you by the arm with his left. His mitts are monstrous, of course, making it hard to ignore the fact that the guy in front of you with the wary smile is the original hard bastard, "Captain Cranky", "Mad Man Mick", he of the so-called "perpetual scowl", "withering glare" and "piercing steel stare"—a guy who "sucks the moisture from his teeth" before spitting venom and contempt. None of that reads true, however. Today he is genial rather than suspicious. Expansive instead of dismissive. Today, the man with perhaps the most taciturn image in football is reflective.

He is happy to discuss his controversial departure from coaching (and the possibility of his return), and before that, willing to take a rare look back—way back—at his childhood, including a few of the trials that perhaps inform the reticent personality he has become.

When Malthouse was 12, for instance, his father was struck down by Guillain-Barre syndrome, a serious and rare autoimmune disorder that causes nerve damage, muscle weakness and paralysis. The episode eventually forced Malthouse, born and raised in Ballarat, to leave school, which he loathed anyway ("I couldn't hate anything in this life as much as I hated school"). He grew up quickly, working part-time in the same plaster factory where his dad laboured, but assumed everyone around him grew up facing similar challenges. "There were a lot of tragic stories to come out of there, and you didn't know any different," he says now. "It's on reflection that you realise the impact of what took place."

If Malthouse has a philosophy in life, beyond the canned quotes from Confucius or Winston Churchill that he used to offer journalists, it boils down to this: "No rear-vision mirror." He doesn't like visiting former homes and makes infrequent appearances at former clubs (blocking out what's behind him "because there's too much of life in front of you"). Ordinarily circumspect, he now casts his mind back: "There's no question in my mind that the past shapes your personality. I'd be the first to admit I was very suspicious of people right through my life, because I just didn't know how to take people."

With his father needing hospital treatment in Melbourne, they had to sell the family car, and his mother was the only person who could afford the train trip to visit his father in the city.

There were times when Malthouse wasn't sure if his father was even alive—if his mother was hoping to protect her son from a harsh reality with a ruse. "You'd spend nights with grandparents, with friends, with your mother," he says. "You tend to get a little—what's the truth here?"

Living in the Housing Commission area of Wendouree West, the born larrikin knows he could easily have drifted to hooliganism in his teens, but he had football. Specifically, he had football clubs—places where, he once said, "you can camouflage yourself among many". As a junior, he remembers walking to the ground, tramping across paddocks with teammates, picking up circular puddles frozen solid and flinging them like Frisbees. Barely half the players had their own footy boots—the rest had to wear school shoes onto the muddy field. When the first gas showers were installed in the change rooms, threepence a hot rinse, Malthouse would try to catch the tail end of a friend's post-match shower.

"You didn't have a towel or anything. You'd wipe yourself off with your dirty jumper, put it back on and walk home. That was your day. That's what took place. No one felt sorry for themselves. We didn't know it was cold." He bangs his plank-like fingers on the table for emphasis. "Under no circumstances should there be any sympathy, because I don't need any and didn't need any at the time. You lived life like Huck Finn—everything was an adventure." It wasn't an exceptional upbringing, he stresses, just a different one. Yes, he had to go rabbiting and fishing to put food on the table, but he enjoyed doing so. (The hardest part was a lazy ferret, or the 20-mile return bike ride to Lake Burrumbeet.)

"That was life," he says. "I really detest the (notion of a) millstone around the neck. Get over it. You can do something if you're prepared to. Yes, there's a lot of bad luck in life, and it follows some people, but you can't let it weigh you down—and, by the same token, you cannot polish yourself up because of it either."

Malthouse has always believed that success—including football riches—flows from the incremental improvement wrought by hard work. That in part explains his frustration with game commentary that focuses on soaring personal narratives—it fails to take into account the minutiae of a group of men improving one metric at a time, making cumulative gains and lifting organisations as they do so.

One of his first public pronouncements when he was recruited in 2000 to coach Collingwood was that he wanted the club he grew up barracking for to improve in all areas—to become the Manchester United of Australian sport. He can still hear people sniggering at that pledge, but feels justifiably vindicated today. "He was the personification of what we wanted Collingwood to be," says club president Eddie McGuire. "Hard-bitten, totally professional, but I also knew him to be a great family man, and community minded."

His impact is unquestionable. To the end there he led the paradigm shifts of modern football—increased interchanges, high-altitude training, and the forward press. One-third of the senior AFL coaches guiding teams into season 2012—six out of a possible 18—have either played under Malthouse or been his assistants, including Mark Neeld (Melbourne), Brad Scott (North Melbourne), Scott Watters (St Kilda), John Worsfold (West Coast), Guy McKenna (Gold Coast) and, of course, Nathan Buckley (Collingwood), the beneficiary of the famous succession plan, the so-called "deal of the century" whereby Buckley would take the reins as coach after two final years with Malthouse at the helm.

Collingwood's version of the Kirribilli agreement was first floated by Eddie McGuire in mid-2009. McGuire says today that at that time he started to believe Malthouse was "closer to the end than he was to the start".

"It didn't matter how much I asked him, begged him, cajoled him to take more time off over the summer, he was still the first back in the office," McGuire says. "With Mick, we didn't want him to be completely shot."

McGuire denies the deal had anything to do with the widely held belief that he was concerned Buckley might go elsewhere to start his career as senior coach, and more because he wanted Malthouse to "pass the baton at full pace". McGuire says he was concerned by Malthouse saying things along the lines of "I don't think I can go on with this."

"No, I've never said that," says Malthouse, flatly rejecting McGuire's version of events. "I'd be the first to get out if I didn't think I had the necessary energy and focus . . . There's going to be times when you're tired and you're disappointed, but that's incorrect. There were pressures, but I've been through a lot worse. If that's his perception, that's fine . . . but I felt very much in control of the situation."

Malthouse's acquiescence did come at a difficult time. His grandson had just had a major operation and his mother was dying. In the end, he accepted the deal to take the pressure off himself and family, but watching the candle burn down on his remaining two years—last pre-season, last Anzac Day, last grand final—was tough. Tougher given how well Collingwood was performing. Tougher still following the grand final loss to Geelong last year, knowing there would be no next year. "That was his family, and all of a sudden he wasn't part of it anymore," says Nanette Malthouse, his wife of 38 years. "It's just like a marriage break-up, I guess. He really did struggle for a while, but I think he's through that now."

Even at this stage, his separation from clubland must be difficult. Malthouse played his first game of footy when he was eight years old. (He is now 58.) By the time he was 15, he had played his first senior game for the North Ballarat Roosters, and by 17 he was plucked to join the Saints. The rest is VFL/AFL history and his own unique place therein.

Early in his professional career he was a mischief-maker, remembered at Tigerland for hiding a dead possum in a committeeman's Rolls-Royce. (Less subtly, he was said to have hurled the odd dead ringtail at teammates while they were showering.) Never one to imbibe beyond a rare glass of white wine, he didn't join the boozers of any club, but neither did he judge their behaviour. (On the way out of the Punt Road Oval car park, he was fond of ramming his Valiant into the rear end of other players' cars.) Those closest to him suggest he has never lost that lightness of heart.

"I think this year people will get to know the real Michael Malthouse," predicts close friend and adviser, Melbourne Heart chairman Peter Sidwell.

His warmth was perhaps obscured by a relentless competitive streak. On the field, he became a backline general, organising meetings and issuing directions. He took to sleeping with pad and pen by his bed, began subscribing to overseas sports magazines and remains an unabashed devotee of soccer luminary Sir Alex Ferguson and legendary American football coach Vince Lombardi.

His potential eluded no one. As a coach, there was an urgency and intensity to his methods. Shane O'Sullivan, a former general manager for the Bulldogs, remembers Malthouse, then 30, dropping Footscray captain Jim Edmond when he was out of form: "Pretty special qualities in a young man, a young coach, to do those sorts of things."

"Every year you're under pressure," Malthouse says, remembering the first moments in charge. "I've never allowed myself to feel safe, right from the start. Year one was the same as year 28 in many respects."

He developed his own inclusive style and a particular set of golden rules such as "Consistency is overrated" (meaning he knew exactly which players would respond to a spray and which ones needed their hands held). He still trumpets the importance of developing not only better players but better people. The causes he supports today, including the YMCA Bridge Project (helping juvenile offenders find work) and GordonCare (helping young people at risk of homelessness find a place to live), speaks to that empathy. "If you're part of the human race, you'd like to think you could help out in some way somewhere," he says. "And these are the ones that sometimes go through life without notice."

West Coast CEO Trevor Nisbett says Malthouse was a "pioneer" in developing his charges into rounded individuals—from boys into men—but that it often went unnoticed because of his "prickly image". "As much as he's been extremely hard on some of his players, I think he's driven them into really good people. They probably don't understand that until they finish playing." Malthouse elaborates: "One of the greatest flaws in any sport is the way the door slams when they're finished. We like to think we look after our own, and we do, when they're playing. But afterwards, a lot of them are left in a precarious position, both financially and emotionally."

Some even say his antagonism toward the media—which at the Eagles included a "bible" for all players with such pointers as "Many private things occur in your club, keep it that way"—was merely an extension of that protective instinct. Basil Zemplas, who tried out (unsuccessfully) with the Eagles and then became a reporter in Perth when Malthouse was at the helm, says he never took attacks personally because, with Malthouse, it never felt personal. "He could be intimidating, no doubt, but I think he used those press conferences to do what he needed to do for the team, or to get a point across to the opposition," says Zemplas, who will work alongside Malthouse this year on Saturday afternoons. "It was almost a game after the game. I'm not sure he ever loved them, but I don't think he disliked them as much as it sometimes appeared."

Yet from his time at the Eagles onwards, Malthouse was routinely called out as "aggressive", "abrupt", "testy", "snarling", "sneering", "combative" and "bullying". Interactions were "skirmishes" and his bile was "customary". If—somehow—a post-game Q & A session was rewarding or chatty, it would be described later as "peculiar" and "almost unnatural". One online columnist side-stepped all euphemism and metaphor about the Malthouse mystique, calling him small-minded, bad-tempered, lacking in discipline and shirking responsibility: "He's quite unpleasant." Malthouse ignores them. "Some people are sheep," he says, smiling and shrugging, "and once something is established they don't know anything else to write, so they continue with their favourite story."

It seems as if there is more than one Mick Malthouse. The truer portrait—recounted by senior sports journalists and reflected in our interview—is of a person more comfortable in small forums and one-on-ones. There, he is inquisitive, affable and charming—completely free of hostility or animus. Put simply, he was not at his personal best under lights, faced with a barrage of questions in the post-game press conference—that was the job. "And to do the job, you've got to be right in or right out," he says. "You cannot be part way."

His players may have felt joy after their premiership victories, but the emotion most felt by their coach was simply relief, particularly after winning "the ultimate".

"I could not explain here in a million years what the relief is like," he says with a sigh. "In my case, you could carry me out of the box in a bucket, because I just feel as if every sinew, every ounce of energy, every bit of myself has been thrown into that effort and there's honestly nothing left. I'm quite happy for the achievement to just sit in a corner and let everyone else celebrate."

On a Thursday afternoon in February, at the celebratory launch of the new-look Channel Seven commentary team, Malthouse is the main man in frame. From playing warrior to warlord coach, the "silver fox" is now one of footy's elder statesmen, with a stature matched only by that of the guy sitting next to him, Leigh Matthews.

The room is filled to the gills with journos looking for a free lunch and ex-footy players in suits emblazoned with the red "7" logo, and the ever-excitable Bruce McAvaney can't resist asking the obvious: "Micky, how many times do you reckon you're going to be asked this year, are you going to coach again?"

"I'm anticipating that it won't die," answers Malthouse, "and I'll regularly give the answer 'Never say never'."

Later he explains: "It's in your blood. From time to time you think, does the future have some football in it? I'm not sure . . . The reality of it is that it's been a difficult couple of years, and do I really want to put my family or myself through that again?"

Nanette believes he would love to be preparing the Magpies for their next match right now, but at the same time, she had had enough and is happy to move on. She doesn't think Malthouse will coach again. "I might be wrong," she adds. "But then I've got to decide if I'm prepared to go through with it, too, because we've always done this as a partnership, so it would be a huge decision for him to come back."

McGuire says he just wants to see Malthouse "relax a bit", but would love to see the "Collingwood icon" back at the club, perhaps at an event in his honour, later this year.

"Mick Malthouse is one of the most impressive people I've ever met in any walk of life. I hope that maybe the upside from all of this is that a year down the track he finds other outlets for his talents that have been largely kept in football," McGuire says. "But he may say, for all the rest of it, 'I actually just love football.' It's a very seductive game. It can totally absorb you. But it's a hard taskmaster, footy."

So what will he get up to?

On his Twitter feed, Malthouse labels himself an "environmentalist, husband, father and grandfather", and indeed, most of his posts revolve around family, with a little green activism: spruiking the pleasures and treasures of the outdoors and lamenting the sorry state of the Yarra River, along which he pushes his bike regularly. He has more freedom, naturally, to sleep a little longer, go out to dinner more often, read all those newspapers he used to ignore.

Those close to the man say he is in a good place, but they will wait until the season proper starts before declaring his transition a success. Their hope is that the commitments on his plate will become routine—that the fullness of a new schedule, career and life will come to him, albeit slowly.

"I know quite a few politicians, and at the time they're involved in politics they think there is only one thing in life and that thing is politics," says Peter Sidwell. "But when they get out of there, they finally see that there is a different dimension to life and that there are some really nice things going on, and I think that will be similar for Michael."

Perhaps then, when this holding pattern becomes an habitual reality, the question Michael Malthouse asks won't be the ponderous "What am I going to do now?" Perhaps he will rub those big hands together with delight, and wonder "What should I do next?"

MALTHOUSE THE PLAYER
Born in Ballarat, August 17, 1953, Malthouse began playing as an 8-year-old in under 14s, his first win coming against a team from the local orphanage. At 15, he played his first senior game for North Ballarat and in 1972 was recruited to St Kilda where he played 53 games. In 1976, he crossed to Richmond and established himself as a backline leader, playing a further 121 games including the Tigers' 1980 premiership.

MALTHOUSE THE COACH
Over 28 years, Mick Malthouse coached three clubs (Footscray, West Coast and Collingwood) through a combined 664 games, second on the all-time list to Jock McHale. In Malthouse's time in the coach's box, he guided his teams to 19 finals campaigns including eight grand finals and three premierships. Among many honours, he was twice named All-Australian Coach.

MICK MALTHOUSE ON. . .
Gambling in football
"Heath Shaw pulled $10 out of his pocket and got eight weeks. Silly boy, we all know that. But there's one hand saying 'don't do this', and the other hand taking money from advertising gambling. That doesn't make sense. It looks great in the coffers, but the AFL hardly needs that money. We've seen enough families who've been affected by gambling—let's not promote it."

The match review panel
"It was formed to get rid of the inconsistencies and I think it's created inconsistencies."

The sub rule
"My view is it was a knee-jerk reaction, without enough evidence. What we saw at Collingwood was the interchanges went up, and the soft tissue injuries went down. But once the AFL make up their mind, that's it."

The fixture

"The draw is 18 sides with 22 games. Without doubt, you cannot answer in any other way than to say it is compromised. But when people say it's not fair, I say get over it. I'll tell you what's not fair: an 18-month-old kid with cancer, a two-year-old that loses an eye, a five-year-old gets run over by a car. That's not fair. Don't worry about the draw."

Free agency

"I hate free agency. I detest it. Mark this down right now—mark my words— there will be a two-tiered system. The big clubs will have the money and the profile and the pull, and little clubs will be fighting for survival, and we'll have the very thing we tried to get rid of by introducing the draft and the salary cap in the first place."

Nathan Buckley

"You might have good ideas, but to be a good coach you've got to have a good side. In principle, he's got a very, very, very good football club, so he has a wonderful chance to be a good coach."

The Melbourne Magazine, The Age 30 March 2012

THAT ONE DAY

THIS IS THE DAY ANY football-loving child dreams of—playing in a grand final. Actually, it's what any football supporter dreams of, no matter what their age. This is that one day in September or, on the rare occasion, October, that can make or break a player or club. For the Brisbane Lions, 2001–03 would ensure they would be remembered as one of the greatest teams of all time. The Bombers had started the decade as the team to beat, but they would fade into obscurity. Another expansion side, Port Adelaide, would have its moment in the sun, sparking a memorable celebration by coach Mark Williams.

The Hawks would secure an unexpected flag in 2008, with coach Alastair Clarkson embracing a story penned by Jake Niall on the morning of the game as an analogy to his players about how they could stop the Cats. Niall drew on a line used by Woody Allen in the film *Annie Hall*, the Cats and their relentless running game were compared to a shark in that they had to move forward or they died. With an image of a great white shark projected on to the whiteboard behind him and Clarkson tracing the outline with a marker pen, the coach urged his men to stop the offensive-minded Cats from running in straight lines and to kill the "shark" as quickly as they could. To the surprise of many, they would do this.

A year later there would be heartache for St Kilda. "In the end, the ghosts of 1971 and 1997 came back to haunt St Kilda," Martin Blake wrote. More pain would follow against Collingwood in 2010—first in the drawn grand final and culminating in defeat in the replay a week later. "Win, lose or draw, Collingwood does grand finals hard. It might as well be written into the club's motto beneath "*Floreat Pica*". "The premiership wasn't, isn't and seemingly never will be, a cakewalk," columnist Greg Baum observed.

While the Magpies would celebrate in 2010, it was the Cats who enjoyed a remarkable dynasty, claiming three flags in five years, the third, in 2011, under rookie coach Chris Scott and without brilliant playmaker Gary Ablett, who had defected to new club, the Gold Coast Suns.

A DYNASTY? HISTORY SAYS THE DEVIL'S IN THE DETAIL

2000 GRAND FINAL, ESSENDON v MELBOURNE

Greg Baum

THE PREMIERSHIP WAS WON. The sun was starting to set. The great bowl of the MCG was aglow. The cup was standing in the centre circle, the Essendon players surrounding it in a tight circle, lustily singing the song they had not dared to sing for the previous month. The world was black and red and rosy.

This dusk was the dawn of a seeming era. Somewhere in the night, coach Kevin Sheedy spoke of the "marvellous times" ahead for the Bombers, and was only slightly less hyperbolic on television yesterday morning. "If we get it right at Essendon, there's a good year or two coming," he said. Forty thousand members would bear witness.

And why not? Sheedy had gone to bed not long before what must have looked to Essendon folk a beautiful sunrise. The Bombers had come closest of any team in history to the true meaning of champion, losing just one of 25 games, not to mention an undefeated run through the Ansett Cup as a precede.

They are young, with an average age of just 25, a figure which will drop with the retirements of any or all of Wallis, Bewick and Long; Wallis, a heroic figure at last, has already announced his intentions.

They are skilled and poised; it is difficult to remember a spilled mark, or an indiscriminate kick or handpass by an Essendon player in the grand final. With nine players aged 23 or less, they are still developing. With Barnard on the bench, they are even. With Rioli and Jacobs not even on the bench, they are deep. Depth is the spur within.

They were as indomitable this season as the Essendon premiership team of

93

1985, and as youthfully irrepressible as the triumphant Essendon team of 1993. Both were expected to burgeon into dynasties. Neither did, and as the sausages sizzled and the champagne fizzed at Windy Hill yesterday, it needed only a glance into the club's archives to know that when it comes to eras, Saturday's win not only looked easy, it was in truth the easy part.

In 1986, Essendon won its first four games, by which time it was widely and deliriously expected that it would go through the season undefeated. But in rapid succession, Paul Van Der Haar and Daisy Williams broke their legs and Tim Watson did his knee.

Further, the Bombers had packed off popular clubmen Stephen Carey to Geelong and Peter Bradbury to Collingwood to make way for disgruntled and highly paid Collingwood pair Geoff Raines and Mike Richardson, promoting rumblings of unrest at the club.

Defeated in round five by Carlton, the Bombers did not regain their momentum, and after finishing fifth lost a famous elimination final to Fitzroy by a point. Raines and Richardson moved on to Brisbane. In the next two seasons, Essendon did not make the finals.

Again in 1993, the world seemed at Essendon's feet after a new generation of baby Bombers romped to a much celebrated premiership. But injury and complacency again intervened, and the next year they finished 10th. A series of finals disasters, board division, murky financial dealings and turbulence surrounding Sheedy's coaching followed, and only on Saturday did the club have its catharsis.

Now, for the third time since Sheedy became coach, the Bombers are on the threshold of an era. Injuries or their lack will be telling. Essendon had a charmed run this year, but knows that even with the most scientific management, and notwithstanding that fitness guru John Quinn was arguably recruit of the season, it cannot last.

Carlton went through the 1995 season without significant injury, scarcely changed its team from beginning to end and lost only two games. This year, the Blues were on a mighty run when injuries cut down Koutoufides, Bradley and, at the end, Silvagni, and they could not patch themselves up. On Saturday, Wallis was tough enough to reset his own dislocated finger, but the rest can at best cross theirs.

History teaches that never does the same 22 repeat a premiership. The Bombers, like all clubs, will have to cut their list by at least two, to 38. Tony

Shaw speculated yesterday that they will have to trade at least one of their top six players to make room in the salary cap for all the pay rises now merited; retirements alone will not be enough.

This pruning process will have to be delicately handled, for in the rarefied atmosphere of a professional sporting club, ill-contentment can become a debilitating plague. "This is the greatest bunch of guys you could ever play footy with," said James Hird on Saturday, but that bunch inevitably will be changed next year, and so will its dynamics.

In Essendon's favour, it knows the lead it has over the competition will not easily be reined in by the other clubs in this time of massive regulation. In 1986, Hawthorn could buy in Gary Buckenara and John Platten, and Carlton could add Kernahan, Bradley, Motley and Dorotich to its books at the stroke of a pen, and so play off in that year's grand final and the next. Now, Carlton, Brisbane and Melbourne will have to work with what they have.

But the Bombers' greatest guarantee that this premiership is a beginning, not an end, lies in their past two defeats. The hurt of last year's preliminary final sustained the club all through this season, and ought for years to come; it became perhaps the first club to do the complacency thing before the premiership.

These Bombers are young, but not so young not to have learned cruel lessons already. No one at Essendon will surely imagine, as Paul Salmon yesterday admitted to imagining in 1985 and others certainly did in 1993, that more premierships will follow as if by birthright. The memory of last year's vanishing pennant is still too vivid.

There was about Hird's every action and word on Saturday a sense that a man can only turn the other cheek to the vicissitudes of fate for so long. His voice was croaky, his edge hard. "There's a devil in there somewhere," remarked Sheedy.

This year's lone defeat at the hands of the Bulldogs will remain a sore point, but also a counterpoint. More than any of the string of victories, it legitimised Essendon's achievements this year; it showed that nothing is gained in this competition that is not hard-earned, nor liable in one lax moment to be lost. It created a legacy.

"This is the greatest football club ever," exclaimed the half-hoarse Hird on Saturday night. It's not. Not yet.

The Age 4 September 2000

LIONS DEVOUR THE MEEK PIES

2003 GRAND FINAL, BRISBANE v COLLINGWOOD

Caroline Wilson

CHAMPIONS FIND BRILLIANT AND BEAUTIFUL and different ways of walking into history, but Brisbane yesterday built a football dynasty on its wounded but fearsome pride. Michael Voss did it with a cyst the size of a golf ball on the side of his damaged knee. Nigel Lappin did it with a broken rib and Jason Akermanis with silly words and handstands but five devastating goals.

And Leigh Matthews did it with a humility that belied his achievement. The greatest player of them all yesterday coached his football team, which is after all only seven years old, to a third straight flag, destroying Collingwood by 50 points in front of close to 80,000 fans at the MCG.

Matthews has never lost a grand final as coach and the Lions' victory lifted him into territory inhabited by the likes of Barassi, Sheedy and Parkin. But he took little credit for the achievement, saying he was as surprised as the rest of us.

"I'm amazed myself at what we did today," said Matthews with that dapper little smile that has come to define Melbourne in September.

Simon Black, the Norm Smith Medallist, was humble too, despite his remarkable 39 touches. In the words of his coach, he had his own ball yesterday afternoon out on the ground. In his own words, the Brownlow medallist of 2002 knew he had to play a special one because Voss and Lappin were so hurt.

Collingwood and its Magpie army had joined forces like never before during grand final week to become the star of the show. But in the end the Lions reduced Mick Malthouse's side to a bit player in a much bigger story. In the opening seconds its star, Scott Burns, ran into the centre square and felled Brisbane's fearless Jonathan Brown, but his impact on the incident symbolised that of his side in the end.

Brown talked the talk earlier in the week. "I know that we've got more blokes that'll keep their head over the ball for longer than they will," he said bravely. But he walked the walk in his third straight premiership victory.

It is close to half a century since the competition's last hat-trick. But when Melbourne achieved its string of victories the competition was Victorian and it boasted no draft or salary cap. Still Matthews and Voss dismissed any talk of Brisbane being the greatest ever. Voss, in fact, described himself as a passenger, in this the Lions' third premiership season. "I've enjoyed the ride," he said.

"I kind of had this foreboding that we were limping in a bit today," said Matthews, who kept saying his side had found new ways this September to surprise him. Not only have the Lions won three in a row but they have done so by never once finishing atop the AFL ladder after 22 rounds.

Eight weeks ago, revealed Michael Voss, Matthews called a meeting of all his players and their partners and asked them to give that little bit extra. The club was up against it and struggling even to finish in the top four.

Brisbane has been on the ropes so many times since then it seemed that Matthews' sense of foreboding was well founded. When Collingwood over-came the Lions three weeks ago the feeling among some senior members of the champions' camp was that the journey that lay ahead was no longer achievable.

Twelve months ago today Collingwood was shattered but proud, a young team that had almost achieved a long-shot victory. Matthews appeared more relieved than overjoyed for several hours after the final siren and Malthouse famously cried. This year the script appeared to have been written for the Magpies.

"Play Brave Play Tough Play Like Bobby Rose", read the Collingwood banner. The club was young and fit and knitted together by hunger. Only the loss of Anthony Rocca loomed as the shadow over the occasion. Elsie Rose, Bob's widow, had been chosen to present the premiership cup but in the end all she could offer the devastated Buckley was a sad hug.

"We got close last year and that was painful," Buckley said, "but to know today that we didn't really perform to the level that we have throughout the season was even more disappointing and I'm sure the pain will last longer and hurt more . . . simply because we didn't put our best foot forward."

The mood in the rooms after the game was angry. Eddie McGuire has rebuilt his football club over five years from a basket case into a powerhouse but yesterday, admitted the coach: "We have embarrassed ourselves. We have paid a high penalty with new players coming into the side playing their first grand final who, unfortunately—we had too many that didn't fire a shot. We were gobbled up by a highly professional organisation that has been here, done that, and knows how to win."

Malthouse could have been describing the three minutes that probably defined and decided the 2003 premiership. Nineteen minutes into the second quarter young Richard Cole lifted his head and fumbled the ball on the Lions forward line, allowing Voss to send it down to Alastair Lynch who put his side five goals up.

Three minutes later, it was Rhyce Shaw, whose father knows all about days like yesterday, who slipped and lost the ball only to watch Lynch stretch around him—half gazelle–half rover—to kick his third.

This has been one of football's great years. It was the year the fans came back and cheered for Australian Rules around the country even though they tore down the Ponsford Stand. It was the year that Paul Roos reignited Sydney and Jason McCartney staged one of the greatest, briefest comebacks of all time.

It was the year Port Adelaide choked—again—and Fremantle turned from the team that made up the numbers into a threatening purple haze from the west. It was the year Wayne Carey became human on the field as well as off and the power changed hands at the AFL's head office. It was the year Carlton shattered and not even Denis Pagan or Ian Collins could put it together again. It was the year of the non-Victorian teams and the greatest Brownlow count. When Nathan Buckley finally won a Brownlow but failed to fulfil his destiny.

In the end, 2003 finished as it began. With Brisbane. The heavyweight champion, or some of its parts, lingered a little too as the shadows stretched over the MCG. Alastair Lynch, 35, and Justin Leppitsch, 29 next week, were among the last to leave, with the injured and unavailable Chris Scott along-side them. It was as if they couldn't bear to walk away from the paddock they have made their own. Those fans who stayed and stretched over the fence to congratulate can say they witnessed football history.

The line from the song sounds stranger every year: "We will always fight for victory, Like Fitzroy and the Bears of old . . ." Because there is only the Brisbane Lions now. And there has never been a team like this one.

The Sunday Age 28 September 2003

WHEEL TURNS FOR HUNGRY PORT

2004 GRAND FINAL, PORT ADELAIDE v BRISBANE

Rohan Connolly

IN THE END, THE BRISBANE LIONS handed over the baton of AFL power in much the same fashion as had their predecessor four seasons ago.

In 2001, on grand final day, the Lions had been the fresher, hungrier challenger, hunting down and then running over the top of a tiring Essendon, completely spent after three years of being forever the hunted. That set the scene for what, in the modern era at least, has been an unprecedented run of dominance.

Yesterday, the wheel turned full circle. It was Brisbane, sore, tired, carrying too many injuries, not to mention the psychological burden of equalling a record that had stood for 74 years, that hung on gamely, still leading by a goal into time-on of the third quarter until, once again, the wall of resistance broke and the challenger came bursting through the gap.

In 2001, it was a younger and more sprightly Michael Voss, Simon Black and Jason Akermanis who crashed through. Three years on, they could only watch on as the likes of Byron Pickett, Peter Burgoyne, Kane Cornes and Gavin Wanganeen sped eagerly through the chasm their side's earlier efforts had punched through Brisbane's defences.

Port Adelaide had the fresher bodies and minds yesterday. It certainly had the quicker legs. But it also had the driving force of an unsated appetite, the cravings only heightened by the fact it had outperformed Brisbane in the home-and-away season three years in a row, the Lions' efforts over the last few weeks of each of those seasons the stuff of legend, the Power instead infamously branded chokers.

You only had to watch victorious coach Mark Williams make that gesture with his tie on his triumphant march from the coach's box to the boundary line to realise just how heavily that tag had weighed not only upon him, but an entire club.

An enormous burden has been lifted, and Port Adelaide has the premiership its efforts over the past three years well and truly deserved.

Williams took his medicine last summer and emerged with a slicker, harder line-up that played a better brand of football more conducive to September success. He gambled and won big time with the drafting of journeyman Josh Mahoney, held his faith in previous bit players such as Toby Thurstans, Domenic Cassisi and the flighty Shaun Burgoyne, and oversaw the most inspired positional move of 2004, the shift of Chad Cornes from key forward to key defender.

The upshot is that never has the AFL seemed a more truly national competition than right at this moment. Eight of the past 13 premiers have hailed from beyond the boundaries of the game's supposed heartland. That's just over a dozen flags spread around four different states.

Yesterday's was the first grand final played without a Victorian representative. You can expect to see plenty more. But that will sit a lot easier with locals than many fear if they continue to be blessed by games as good as yesterday's—a classic tough and skilful contest to which the final margin of 40 points did little justice.

The Power has won a flag in its eighth season of AFL competition. That's a year longer than it took bitter local rival the Crows, and two years longer than West Coast had to wait to become the league's first non-Victorian premier in 1992. But unlike Adelaide, whose two flags were perhaps the most unexpected of the AFL era, the Crows having finished fourth and fifth after 22 rounds and having lost nine games each time, this was far more than a case of being in the right place at the right time.

A proud and brash club whose success began to outstrip the confines of its local competition, Port's quest for success at the highest level began as long ago as 1990, when it stole a march on a reluctant SANFL and launched its own bid for inclusion in the AFL.

That ultimately unsuccessful attempt was in no small way responsible for the birth of the Power's now fiercest rival the following season.

It would take Port until 1997 to get its chance. But the Power has been unrelenting in its determination to reach the top, making the finals five years out of eight, and over the past three, winning 53 of 66 home-and-away games, half-a-dozen more victories than that achieved even by yesterday's opponent, roundly acclaimed as the greatest team of all time.

Now, having finally seized the mantle that might have been its as long as three years ago, the question is just how long can Port Adelaide carry it. It's not being churlish—more realistic—to suggest that a run of Brisbane proportions is at very long odds.

Port had the second-oldest list in the AFL this season behind Adelaide, its average age even fractionally higher than was Brisbane's. While the retirement of Damien Hardwick might reduce that a fraction, Gavin Wanganeen, a star yesterday with four second-half goals, and Brett Montgomery are 31, Josh Francou and Darryl Wakelin 30, while injured skipper Matthew Primus and Jarrad Schofield will be 30 by the time next season starts.

It's going to take extraordinary durability, in the end yesterday beyond even Brisbane, for the Power to keep this level up for another couple of years. Perhaps the Lions' demise signals the end of the genuine "superpower". But whatever happens to Port Adelaide from here, the Power will always have the satisfaction of having achieved the ultimate, and having beaten the ultimate team to do so.

MAIDEN FLAG		
Premiership breakthroughs		
Season	Club	Year
1st	Essendon	1897
2nd	Fitzroy	1898
4th	Melbourne	1900
5th	Brisbane Lions	2001
6th	Collingwood	1902
6th	West Coast	1992
7th	Adelaide	1997
8th	Port Adelaide	2004
10th	Carlton	1906

MAIDEN FLAG		
Premiership breakthroughs		
Season	Club	Year
13th	South Melbourne/Sydney	1909
13th	Richmond	1920
28th	Geelong	1925
30th	Footscray/Western Bulldogs	1954
37th	Hawthorn	1961
51st	North Melbourne/Kangaroos	1975
68th	St Kilda	1966
Nil	Fremantle, Brisbane Bears, University	
Geelong (1916) and St Kilda (1916–17) did not compete due to World War I.		

The Sunday Age 26 September 2004

NOW, AS ZEN, SYDNEY REMINDED OF ITS UNSHAKEABLE, UNBREAKABLE BELIEF IN EACH OTHER

2005 GRAND FINAL, SYDNEY v WEST COAST

Jake Niall

No one individual act could define the spirit the Swans rode to a premiership. It happened when they exhumed an all but buried season against the Cats and it was the entree to their final-quarter consumption of the Saints.

The strike-rate was 100 per cent in finals, and so, for the third consecutive week, Brett Kirk, Sydney's spiritual leader and resident Buddhist, again intervened at the three-quarter-time huddle with the game in the balance.

Kirk had given the eccentric Nick Davis a rocket before the forward's four-goal explosion against Geelong, and he'd gathered the Swans together in a calm before they stormed over St Kilda.

These triumphs formed the basis of the Zen warrior's message, which was nothing profound, just a reminder that they'd prevailed in similar circumstances. The Swans are nothing if not accustomed to tight games.

"I pulled the boys in and had a bit of a chat and just said we'd been there before, and we just knew we had that belief in each other that we could do this," Kirk said.

Much as it would be tempting to attribute this moment as the catalyst, the Sydney premiership was a mosaic of 1000 little moments, one percenters, long-term and split-second decisions—on and off the field—with dozens in the final term alone.

The grand final story has been based largely on the two Barrys, Leo and

Hall, the bookends that fittingly provided a beginning and end to Sydney's grand final week.

And it's true, as Swans officials acknowledged, that they wouldn't have won if Hall hadn't beaten the tribunal rap, and they still might have lost, with seconds left, had leaping Leo not leapt.

Ricky Quade, the former player, coach and current club director, was one of the inner sanctum who deliberately averted his eyes when Dean Cox sent his bomb to the top of the goal square.

From the boundary, Sydney's football operations manager, Andrew Ireland, was able to see only Barry becoming airborne. "I couldn't see what happened." Ireland pleaded: "Please be one of our blokes who's grabbed it."

It became THE MARK only because of what had preceded it: Amon Buchanan's goal, Jude Bolton's smother before Buchanan's goal, Hall's gun-barrel-straight shot from outside 50, the runs of Tadhg Kennelly and the ruckwork of Jason Ball in the final moments of his career.

Indeed, Bolton might not even have been on the ground for the moments when his influence was most decisive. He was heading for the interchange bench when he smothered Chad Fletcher's kick.

"I was coming off the ground," said Bolton. "They told me to come off and then I managed to get involved in the play and then they just said, 'Stay on.'"

Bolton, by then, was wearing the same helmet an equally bloodied Kirk had donned in the third quarter of the preliminary final. Blood brothers, indeed.

The Bloods, as they call themselves in honour of their club's past lakeside life, won the premiership through equal parts passion and professionalism, heart and brains.

If they made the right turns amid the mayhem, it was because they have been trained to play a defence-based brand that, whatever its aesthetic faults, tends to flourish in September.

Paul Williams, a premiership player in his 294th game (a record), said of coach Paul Roos: "He said that from day dot, he's preparing something that will get you success in September."

To contain the midfield might of Chris Judd, Ben Cousins and co, the Swans had a plain equation. "Both coaches were playing to their own game plan," said Sydney's opposition scout, George Stone. "We were trying to close it down. They were trying to open it up."

Stone felt that the Eagles had assisted them on occasion when they had extra talls in attack. "I thought when they went really tall, they just lost a bit of run."

Of all the pieces that joined to produce the premiership jigsaw, the central one was surely the decision, forced by the irrational Sydney masses, to hire Roos as senior coach instead of the more proven Terry Wallace. At the after-match function, television icon and Swans stalwart Mike Willesee called Roos "the democratically elected" coach.

Club chairman Richard Colless has been generous, too, in his praise of Ireland, who left the Brisbane Lions after their first premiership and now has presided over the other frontier flag. Mindful of the Lions' success, one of Ireland's first acts at Sydney was to ensure it had the best possible medical, fitness and conditioning team.

While St Kilda's quest sank on the reef of soft-tissue injuries, Ireland observed that the Swans had been settled for weeks and, remarkably, had entered the match without a single player requiring a fitness test. Lucky, yes, but the medicos did their one percenters, too. The recruiting department, meanwhile, placed great store in psychological profiles, what it called the "no dickheads" policy.

The Swans were banged up, to be sure—Bolton had carried a grade-three AC joint, Hall, too, bore a sore shoulder, Williams a quadricep injury and Kirk, doubtless, had more dents than a '72 Monaro. None, however, was inca-pacitated. They were all standing and, on the day, enough of them stood up.

True to his understated ways, Roos yesterday reduced the premiership to its essence: "It's just the ability of all the players to do the right things at the right time.

"Whether it's Kirky throwing his head over the ball, Jude getting a quick clearance or Hally taking a mark or whatever. Everyone did their role today and that's why we're the 2005 premiers."

The Age 26 September 2005

NEW RIVALS SHOW WHY THEY'RE HARD TO SPLIT

2006 GRAND FINAL, SYDNEY v WEST COAST

Rohan Connolly

SO INSEPARABLE HAD BECOME WEST COAST and Sydney over the past year, and so inevitably tight their every epic contest, that, for all the pre-grand final speculation about yet another nail-biter, you couldn't help but wonder whether perhaps yesterday might be the day the bubble burst.

And, for a little over a half, that's exactly what appeared to have happened. The Eagles began the grand final like a side intent on rewriting what had become a very familiar script and, with a little more efficiency, might have had their third AFL premiership close to sealed considerably earlier.

Well, that's how it looked. But we should have known better by now. Of course, Sydney came back. Of course, the finale was suitably dramatic. And of course, like 12 months ago, we'll be talking about this premiership play-off for the rest of our lives.

This one might not have finished with a Leo Barry-type mark for the ages, nor a first flag for 70-odd years. But as a game, it was a cracker. More open than the 2005 version, perhaps with a few more blunders, but moments of brilliance and heroism no less marked. And a one-point margin for the first time since perhaps the most famous grand final of them all, in 1966.

West Coast ended up needing all the breathing space it created for itself with its early superiority. But the Eagles had earned it fairly and squarely, from the moment Ashley Hansen took his third mark and booted the game's opening goal six minutes in.

If anyone personified the determination to turn the tables of fate, it was the young key forward, who'd had an ordinary grand final last year opposed to Lewis Roberts-Thomson, but beat his man comprehensively when it mattered yesterday. He was quick on the lead, sure of hand and foot. Just like, as you'd expect, champion teammates Chris Judd and Ben Cousins, who posted the second and third goals of the match before Sydney had managed a reply.

But significantly, both came after the sort of slips you wouldn't expect of their opponent, Judd's goal off the ground the result of a fumble by the Swans' Amon Buchanan, Cousins' clever snap following another fumbly moment from ruckman Darren Jolly.

Barry Hall missed from 20 metres, Michael O'Loughlin failed to make the distance with one attempt before finally putting his team on the board, Jude Bolton missed two more very gettable goals. Then Hansen nailed his second right on quarter-time.

It was a 16-point gap that continued to grow, thanks to West Coast's centre-square superiority. Dean Cox turned in the sort of game he does so often, not only dominating the hit-outs, but winning the sorts of possession numbers more typical of those at his feet, and the clearances to boot.

Jarrad McVeigh made a fair fist of keeping Cousins under wraps, but Judd was having the better of his battle of the superstars with Adam Goodes. And then there was Embley, running himself into the ground with nine possessions and a goal in the second term alone, 15 by the long break, as the Eagles continued to belt the ball forward, two quick goals to Quinten Lynch and another to Cousins after an unfortunate slip by Tadhg Kennelly blowing the gap between the sides to within a whisker of 30 points.

Sydney might have thought then that the good fight had been lost. But this is the Swans we're talking about. And you sensed change was on the cards from the moment Adam Schneider chased and dragged down Michael Braun in the first minute of the second half, the resultant turnover ending with a goal to O'Loughlin. Embley replied soon enough, but Nick Davis bobbed up with another. Lynch gave the Eagles room to move with a superb set shot from the boundary, but then the unlikely form of Roberts-Thomson, thrown forward, wobbled one through on the run. He wasn't the only unlikely Swan to stir his team, Ted Richards bobbing up everywhere.

More significantly still, Brett Kirk rose another gear and Goodes began to impose himself. Kirk hit the post. Hall missed what he should have kicked in his sleep. And, when Davis booted his second of the quarter, the margin had narrowed to under two goals.

Thus began yet another incredible finale.

From the first centre break, Hall handballed to Goodes, who banged it through with just 14 seconds of last-quarter action elapsed. Five points now.

Hansen missed for the Eagles, and Kennelly rushed a behind, before, with just 7½ minutes left, Schneider's snap crept just inside the goal post. One point the difference, the Swans with the momentum, but both sides now looking all but spent.

A withering run from Daniel Kerr and clever snap from Steven Armstrong gave West Coast a seven-point buffer, cut back to the barest of margins again immediately when the hard-working Ryan O'Keefe slipped a tackle, and a long, speculative left boot bounced over desperate Eagle clutches.

What happened next was perhaps the Leo Barry moment of the 2006 grand final. Deep in attack, Eagle Daniel Chick brilliantly smothered the attempted clearing kick of O'Keefe, recovered to take possession and handball to Adam Hunter, who ran in to boot West Coast's final goal of the game, and make it seven points once more.

Still Sydney would not die, Nick Malceski's snap curling back to bring the Swans within one point again with about 2½ minutes to play. And the final moments of the season said it all: desperate bodies from either side throwing themselves headlong at ball and man, the consequence of every possession, every lunge, every step never greater.

Like last year, it was a denouement of almost unbearable tension. Like last year, the game ended with the ball deep in the scoring territory of the trailing team, one that had fought back from deep trouble to almost pinch victory. Only the roles had been reversed.

Five clashes for an aggregate margin of 12 points. Two flags decided by a total of five points. And now, one premiership each. These two great teams could go on like this forever. And after a grand final like yesterday's, who could complain about that prospect?

	WEST COAST	SYDNEY
Score	4.2 8.7 10.10 12.13 (85)	1.4 4.6 8.11 12.12 (84)
Goals	Lynch 3, Hansen 2, Cousins 2, Embley 2, Judd, Armstrong, Hunter	O'Loughlin 3, Davis 3, Mathews, Roberts-Thomson, Goodes, Schneider, O'Keefe, Malceski
Best players	Embley, Cox, Kerr, Judd, Hansen, Waters, Cousins, Glass	Kirk, Kennelly, Richards, McVeigh, Fosdike, Buchanan
Injuries		Ablett (hamstring)
Coaches comments	John Worsfold: "We put the work in and had faith in what we did even though we were questioned on a lot of issues. I have no doubt we put the work in to win a premiership."	Paul Roos: "We deserved to win two premierships but they also have deserved to win two premierships and we both deserved to win one. So I am happy to be at one all and sometimes in life you have to be happy with what you are given."
Umpires	Allen, Goldspink, Vozzo	
Crowd	97,431 at MCG	

The Sunday Age 1 October 2006

A VICTORY FOR THE AGES

2007 GRAND FINAL, GEELONG v PORT ADELAIDE

Greg Baum

IT WAS MIDWAY THROUGH THE third quarter of yesterday's grand final and the conclusion was already long foregone. High in the Great Southern Stand, a middle-aged Geelong fan danced along a precipitous concourse brandishing cardboard cut-outs of two premiership cups. One was marked 2007, one 2008.

His extravagance was understandable, but misplaced. The other cup should have read 1967, or 1989, or 1992, '94 and '95, or indeed almost any year in the last 44. If ever ever a premiership was won as redress and redemption, rather than simply to consummate a moment, this was it.

Rarely in any sphere of endeavour can ghosts have been exorcised so wholly and ruthlessly.

It showed everywhere, and in every way. Milling in the players' race as the formality that was the last quarter was played out was a conclave of lost generations.

Most were crying, even—or especially—Billy Brownless. Grand final tears are nothing new at Geelong, but these were different, not bitter and salty, but cleansing. These were tears to dissolve years.

Mark Blake hid his behind sunglasses.

He was the exception; he alone was living the experience of missing out in the big one, an old Geelong fate. He alone would have had a mind for 2008.

Somewhere in that madding midst, Gary Ablett snr reappeared. Romanticists might have seen this as a kind of second coming, affirming salvation at last for all. Truthfully, it was as the proud father of two premiership players.

When the final siren sounded, there was an inordinate delay before the Geelong theme song began to play on the PA. It was as if someone did not dare to believe, not quite, not yet. But when at last it did ring out, it was as if on a continous loop, never to stop.

This also was right, for it had to echo in a lot of places, and the here and now was only one of them.

All those underachieving years.

All those unfulfilled players. All those broken hearts, now mended at last.

Geelong is one of only two clubs in the competition that still represents a particular place (Port is the other). It also represents a particular way of playing the game; Geelong's finest teams always have had flair and flourish, too. It is why the club has always attracted a disproportionate number of creative minds to its cause.

The saviours of 2007 were true to that tradition: not just the best team, but the best to watch, too.

But premierships are not won by weight of sentimental favour. Geelong showed from the start of this season that it would not be compromised in any part of its campaign when it suspended Steve Johnson because of an off-season misdemeanour.

This single-minded resolve was apparent in all its work again yesterday.

At half-time, the game was as good as won, but still the Geelong players left the field with their heads down and eyes narrow, still in the attitude of combat. At three-quarter-time, when they might have been forgiven a backslap or two, they formed a huddle.

Only in the last quarter did they relax. Back-line stalwarts Tom Harley and Matthew Scarlett have been po-faced all season, but now Scarlett began to conduct the Geelong cheer squad in its chanting, and Harley, while retrieving the ball from the gutter for a kick-in, shared high-fives with fans. The party had begun.

When the reckoning was done, the Cats had won by more than any previous premiership team, and Johnson, the selfsame ne'er-do-well of the summer, was the Norm Smith medallist.

Deliverance was at every turn.

Really, it could never have been otherwise. Geelong yesterday was making up for lost years. Port was a year ahead of itself, perhaps more.

When Geelong won the minor premiership with four rounds remaining,

Port was not even guaranteed to play in the finals. Its time is still to come, but for Geelong, now was not soon enough.

It meant that this was for the Cats a great season, a great occasion, a great performance and a great moment, but not a great grand final. The AFL had a patchy day. The pre-match tribute to retiring players was touching, but the delivery of the premiership cup to commission chairman Mike Fitzpatrick by a nymph suspended from a balloon was twee. Damn Nicky Webster. Fitzpatrick found himself reaching out for the cup in vain, a position Port came to know well.

The amenity of spectators was spoiled again by the never-ending verbiage of the ground announcer. It was painfully loud, mostly superfluous and sometimes infantile, and in its entirety a gross insult to football fans, implying that they are not capable either of hyping up a grand final by themselves, nor of making their own understandings and appreciations.

Still, nothing would or could ruin Geelong's day. Gary Ablett was flattened early, twice, but that was the last time the match had the guise of a contest. The rhythms of the season quickly asserted themselves, each Geelong player drawing confidence from the next, until it suffused the whole team. It was a complete display, awesome in every way, and frequently exhilarating.

Harley, the understated captain, spent the last few minutes of the match holding the ball, as if to make sure that it was his at the final siren. When at last it rang, it came as a kind of anticlimax.

Geelong remembered itself at the presentation ceremony, coach and captain thanking all the right people and patting each of the children who presented the premiership medals on the head. It was as if they were determined not to be West Coast. Geelong's 1963 premiership captain Fred Wooller presented the cup to Harley, so at last closing the loop.

True to the spirit of the season, the Cats were more animated on their lap of honour than during the formalities.

Some gave away boots, others socks. The footballers have waited all their careers for this, but the fans have waited lifetimes. This, the players appeared now to recognise. The lap was like the season, a sustained performance.

In the prelude to the grand final, a perverse dichotomy was in play.

The fans, knowing too much, were apprehensive. The players, knowing themselves, were calm. Pre-match, Gary Ablett was seen sharing a joke with a teammate, whereupon supporters gnawed off more fingernails.

Now, though, player and fan were as one.

When at last the Cats were done, and dusk was falling on the MCG, they formed a circle on the arena, amid the detritus of the celebrations, and sang the theme song as lustily as it ever can have been sung. So were the ghosts and demons of 44 years driven out at last. Not one for Churchillian speeches, Harley chose just the three words that he knew would resonate with a club, a city, and a following liberated at last: "We are Geelong."

The Sunday Age 30 September 2007

FAIRYTALE FINISH FOR SKILFUL JOHNSON

2007 GRAND FINAL, GEELONG v PORT ADELAIDE

Martin Blake

THIS WAS A SEASON OF FAIRYTALES and within Geelong's romantic story, there were dozens of sub-plots. Steve Johnson's was the most uplifting of them.

Johnson serves as the most potent symbol of Geelong's rise to the premiership in 2007. He won the Norm Smith Medal yesterday by dint of a sometimes brilliant, sometimes clinically efficient game, kicking four goals and handing off a few others. This, 12 months after the Cats offered him up at trade talks and little more than six months after the club's leadership group told him to go and find somewhere else to carry on his business after he was locked up for drunkenness.

Nobody in Geelong colours had come from further out of the picture. Yet such is the range of his footballing talent, no one was especially surprised. "Someone asked me before the game, 'Who's your favourite player?'" said Gareth Andrews, the former Cat and now vice-president. "I said, 'Stevey Johnson.' He's a country kid who just acts like a country kid sometimes. Somehow I think he realised that he had real talent. The way we handled it, and the way he handled it was fantastic. It's not easy when you're like him to turn around, face the truth."

The 24-year-old Johnson was "on" from the start at the MCG yesterday, hit up by Cameron Mooney on the lead for his first goal at the 11-minute mark. In this, the pivotal period of the game when Geelong established its ownership, he was everywhere, gathering a second goal late in the quarter and another on the run early in the second term. Only once, in the first quarter, did he deviate from the Geelong ethos of team-first.

Caught out on the flank, he tried a banana-kick at goal that missed, leaving a disenchanted Mooney wide open and in a better position. Instructively, Johnson squared the ball all day after that. "I knew when I kicked that I should have given it to Cam Mooney. You just have to make decisions when they confront you. At half-time, a couple of blokes said, 'Take the easy options.' After that, it's what I tried to do."

A big grab at full-forward in the final quarter and a fourth goal rounded out his day. He and fellow half-forward Paul Chapman, along with full-back Matthew Scarlett, jousted for the medal long after the game had expired as a contest, although Johnson said it scarcely mattered. Holding up his premiership medal, he said: "I was just worried about getting the big one. That's all that matters. At the start of the day we said it's not about individuals, it's about playing as a team."

The story of Johnson's ousting from the club by his teammates has been told ad nauseum, but upon reflection, coach Mark Thompson said the first part of the equation was easy enough. "It's easy for the leadership group to hand out a punishment," said Thompson. "The hardest part was what Steve had to do. Steve explained how hard it was. It would have been enormously difficult, lonely and hard to get through."

Johnson, who went and trained alone and with local teams, was not even allowed to socialise with other Geelong players during his exile. He spent most of his spare time playing pool, stopped drinking, and lost weight. "I didn't have any choice, really. It was either change and be a more professional person around the club and a more professional footballer, or 'you're out the door' . . . I really wanted to succeed in footy and that's what drove me."

Not for a moment did he consider quitting. "I couldn't think about giving up footy. I've wanted to experience these sorts of feelings since I was a young kid. I've always come down and watched AFL games, I've never had a footy out of my hands. So this was always my dream. I suppose it was a good kick up the butt."

Up near the dais after the grand final, they called out Johnson's name on the public address. Water bottles rained upon him as he walked up, slightly embarrassed but not surprised, since he had been told by an official moments before that he had the vote.

"He's basically become responsible for his own life," said Brian Cook, Geelong's chief executive. "He makes decisions, he's made some hard ones and he's hung in there. He's stayed with it. He's a symbol for the club the way he's turned it around."

Said teammate Joel Corey: "It's a great story. We told Stevey how it was. The character of the bloke to go away and train by himself, come back, and now he's an all-Australian, he's a premiership player and a Norm Smith medallist. I don't know if you'd ever get a better story than that."

Johnson was headed off for a couple of drinks, and well-earned ones. "I suppose you don't really think you're going to get to this stage. I knew if I worked my butt off I could get back, I could get the respect of the players. I always knew this group was good enough to be a premiership side with the personnel we've got. But you never dream of playing in a grand final and winning a premiership when you're at where I was at. I was pretty much out the door. Things have turned around and I wasn't thinking this far ahead. It's just a fairytale."

NORM SMITH MEDAL VOTES	
Danny Frawley (Triple M)	**Jake Niall (*The Age*)**
3 S. Johnson (Geelong)	3 P. Chapman
2 M. Scarlett (Geelong)	2 S. Johnson
1 P. Chapman (Geelong)	1 M. Scarlett
Daryl Timms (*Herald Sun*)	**Josh Francou (5AA)**
3 S. Johnson	3 P. Chapman
2 M. Scarlett	2 S. Johnson
1 P. Chapman	1 M. Scarlett
Steve Butler (*The West Australian*)	**TOTALS**
3 S. Johnson	Johnson 13
2 P. Chapman	Chapman 10
1 M. Scarlett	Scarlett 7

The Sunday Age 30 September 2007

HOW THE CATS SAVED FOOTBALL

2008 GRAND FINAL, GEELONG v HAWTHORN

Jake Niall

JOHN KENNEDY, HAWTHORN'S MOST revered figure, could not resist a dig at the Cats this week. "The Geelong theme song says, 'We are Geelong and so on'," said "Kanga", the triple premiership coach who forged the hard-nosed Hawthorn culture. "But they also say, 'We play the game the way it should be played.' How precious can you get?" It might be precious, Kanga, self-righteous even. But the club song is in tune with the current Geelong team, which truly does play the game the way it should be played: fast, skilful, free-flowing, yet flint-hard and fair.

Whether it completes a near-flawless season with the second leg of a premiership double today, Mark Thompson's Cats have already changed football, shifting its centre of gravity from defence, flooding and static "tempo" football to run, risk and attack. Rodney Eade, the Western Bulldogs coach and the AFL's most feted tactician, called the 2008 Cats "a fantastic advertisement for our game".

AFL chief executive Andrew Demetriou, too, praised the Cats for their game style, which has coincided with record crowds in 2007 and 2008, increased scoring and the more "continuous"—i.e. flowing—game that a concerned Demetriou and his commission craved.

Remember the hysterical debates about what was happening on the field? There was serious discussion, at one point, of lines being drawn across the field to prevent the game from drowning in the flood. Commissioners were worried, leading figures complained about the great Australian football ugliness.

Sydney's highly successful trench warfare methods were winning games, but not friends (Demetriou the foremost critic). Adelaide's zone defence, devised by its scientific coach, was stifling the life out of oppositions and prompted Richmond to spend an entire game chipping staccato kicks to unmarked players—an unsightly "cure" tantamount to the introduction of cane toads.

By purloining less attractive elements of rugby, soccer and basketball, footy appeared to be losing some of its unique, anarchic qualities.

Then along came Geelong.

The Geelong game style—plan is too prosaic a word for an intuitive, jazzy system—is about constant motion.

The Cats don't kick backwards, they play on without hesitation.

They're willing to risk turnovers, or tackles, to keep the ball moving forward quickly. As Collingwood coach Michael Malthouse observed of their high-wire act—which involves high numbers of handball and possessions—they give you a chance.

Flooding is rendered impotent against a team with Geelong's motion and skill. As one of football's most influential figures put it this week: "Geelong f—ed the flood."

The best analogy for the method is a shark, which has to be constantly moving forward to stay alive. The awful Geelong of 2006 was, to borrow from Woody Allen (describing his doomed relationship in *Annie Hall*), "a dead shark". Ball movement was stunted and the Cats, despite their talent, lacked running capacity.

Thompson and his assistants devised the new game style at the end of their annus horribilis. "Bomber", then seen as having one foot in his coaching grave, decided upon a bolder way. Thompson accepted that mistakes would be made, and would not chastise players who sought to attack and use the corridor.

Geelong also developed a loose zone defence. Its players have responsibility for an opponent, but as rival clubs have noted, the defenders often stand several metres from their man, patrolling an area and anticipating where the ball might land. Outnumbering the opposition at the contest is another trademark.

A moment in the preliminary final exemplified how Geelong is willing to chance its arm, on the grounds that the greatest risk of all is to take none.

Gary Ablett had the ball on the edge of the forward 50-metre arc. He spotted Tom Lonergan in the goal square, and in his haste to kick the ball over the head of Lonergan's opponent, ran into trouble.

Ablett improvised and before he was nailed by the tackler, kicked the ball across his body. It just reached Lonergan, who marked and goaled.

Ablett's manoeuvre required rare ability—he had to stand up in the tackle, keep balanced and execute a difficult kick. But what was most striking was he didn't even consider retreating backwards.

He dared, and won.

Eade said the important change Geelong had ushered in wasn't "so much the style or the intricacies of their game, but the premise . . . of trying to win by playing attacking footy, rather than trying not to lose by playing defensive footy. And the way they've done it has set a real benchmark that other teams are obviously trying to copy."

"Rocket" said the Cats aren't simply the best users of the ball; they're nonpareil in the other two phases of the game—when the ball is in dispute or in the opposition's hands. "The way they play is terrific. It's a chance of scores, it's a chance of good play, but it's very much a contested brand as well. They're hard at it."

Seeing the new order, the Crows, Swans and the rest have loosened up.

"The defensive pressure is improving," Eade said. "Therefore if you want to be slow, or too slow, you can really get hurt today. You won't score.

"The mind-set of teams has changed."

Demetriou noted that the AFL's football operations and rules committee had resisted the "temptation" to draw lines and establish zones. "They let the game evolve. They tinkered with a couple of interpretations, and really did a lot of research into how they could make the game more continuous and have less stoppages. And what that translated into was clubs . . . working it out.

"And Geelong were probably the first to work it out, and play a style of football that was attacking and entertaining, and there's been lots of other clubs follow suit."

In truth, it was Eade's Bulldogs who first cottoned on to the lightning, play-on-at-all-costs method for beating the flood—in 2006, when the Dogs finished finished sixth. Eade, who had invented flooding with the Swans in '96, had shown everyone the antidote. The Doggies, however, didn't have the Cats' hard bodies or a power forward.

So it would be Geelong, by dint of its supreme talent, that oversaw the new order. While Bomber's game style was about winning games, not attracting fans, in a happy coincidence it fitted the club's historic liking for fluent, attacking football.

If Kanga Kennedy was responsible for a spartan Hawk hardness that bordered on brutality ("injuries above the neck don't count"), then Bobby Davis, coach of the scintillating 1963 Geelong team that defeated Kennedy's "Commandos" in the grand final, is the torch-bearer for the Geelong tradition of skill and verve.

Davis had been a star, "the Geelong Flyer", in Reg Hickey's 1951–52 premiership teams, which were renowned entertainers. Bob believed footy was entertainment—he gave up coaching and eventually became the third banana to Lou Richards and Jack Dyer on football's funniest program, *League Teams*.

Davis is proud of Geelong's tradition of skill and aesthetically pleasing footy. "We've always encouraged people to show their skills."

He is delighted that Bomber's boys have been true to his legacy. Geelong, he added, was ensuring the game's appeal to future players, as much as fans.

Davis pinpointed an important aspect of the 2007–08 Cats: that while individually brilliant, they have an innate sense of what a teammate will do. "They all know where the other one's going," he said. On song, the Cats are like a team of 22 (Krakouer?) brothers.

Bobby didn't like Kanga's jibe about the "precious" song. He said Kennedy had been "a roughneck player" in the '50s who had coached accordingly. "He wasn't a great skilful player himself."

Kennedy and Davis represent different strains of Australian football. Kennedy was a hard man who insisted on rigid discipline and sacrifice. Davis, a carefree coach, emphasised individual flair, risk-taking and enjoyment.

While Geelong is tough and Hawthorn is highly skilled, there's also a sense that each of today's teams has reverted to type: the mighty fighting "unsociable" Hawks and the team that plays the game the way it should be played.

The Age 27 September 2008

FACES TELL OF A MISSED OPPORTUNITY

2009 GRAND FINAL, ST KILDA v GEELONG

Martin Blake

IN THE END, THE GHOSTS of 1971 and 1997 came back to haunt St Kilda. The Saints blew it, and you could see it in the contorted faces of the players in those desolate dressing rooms last night. A third straight grand final defeat goes on the report card of the AFL's cursed club.

Lenny Hayes, so brave all day in close, was in the arms of his mum, his lip quivering as he came out of the players' area to greet family and friends. Farren Ray was crying too, consoled by his partner. Jason Gram sat in a solitary corner for 20 minutes, seemingly unable to move from his position, and crying as well.

Leigh Montagna, another of the midfielders who fought so hard against Geelong's great on-ball brigade, bravely faced the media but his lip was moving as well. "It's hard to describe, actually. It's just disappointment. We let an opportunity slip. The boys are gutted. Gutted is probably a good word."

Here was the nub of it: the Saints could have lost by 10 goals but did not. They could have played badly but they did not. Either of those prospects would have felt better, almost certainly. But a handful of missed opportunities in the second quarter cost St Kilda the grand final. It was not through lack of effort; more, failure of skill under pressure when it was in a mood to blow Geelong away.

"At the end of the day we did everything we wanted to do and everything that was asked of us and sometimes that's the way footy goes," said Montagna. "A lot of people say it, but you've got to take your chances early and apply some scoreboard pressure. We missed a few goals we'd normally kick. That made it difficult. If we'd kicked a few goals early maybe it would have been different."

122

Witness Stephen Milne racing towards goal at the city end in that second quarter, taking a bounce, sizing up his options, and then butchering an attempt to dribble it through from 40 metres. Witness Milne feeding Andrew McQualter a minute later, the latter running to the top of the goal square and then slicing the shot across the face. Milne missing again at the 10-minute mark, and conceding a 50-metre penalty for refusing to return the football. Zac Dawson taking a courageous mark deep in defence, then playing on and having his hurried kick smothered by Tom Hawkins for a gifted goal to Geelong.

At the start of this stretch of play, St Kilda was nine points up and Geelong figuratively on its knees. At the end of it, Geelong had regained the lead. "We left the door ajar, and they took the opportunities," said coach Ross Lyon. "It's pretty simple."

St Kilda ended up having more scoring shots and took the ball inside its 50-metre zone 16 more times than Geelong (58 to 42). But such numbers don't count for anything—only the scoreboard tells the tale. In the desperate final quarter of a classic grand final, Geelong booted three goals to none. With Nick Riewoldt and Justin Koschitzke well covered up forward, St Kilda could not find another score to turn the blowtorch back on the Cats. The two pillars of St Kilda's forward line, neutralised by strong opponents and by the wet weather, managed just a goal each.

It was so close. The final margin of 12 points is unfair to St Kilda, for Max Rooke's goal after the siren with the mark not even attended was irrelevant. The pivotal play was at 23 minutes in the final quarter, with scores level. Dawson's desperate spoil of Gary Ablett in the centre of the ground could have won the game for the Saints. Instead, it flew straight to Matthew Scarlett, whose deft kick went three metres and into the hands of Ablett. Geelong surged forward for Norm Smith medallist Paul Chapman to snap the winner.

Ross Lyon praised his team's effort and he was right. There were heroic efforts, like little Steven Baker shutting down Steve Johnson all day, keeping him without a touch for the entire first half, and then, late in the final quarter, sprinting back to get a hand on the shot at goal from Rooke that could have buried St Kilda then and there. There was Hayes (18 contested possessions, 10 clearances) and Luke Ball and Brendon Goddard smashing in at the stoppages, the latter having his face rearranged by the knees of his own teammate, Baker, but coming back strapped up to finish it off.

There was Gram, who had been a poor player in the preliminary final, winning the football on the flanks regularly, playing one of the games of his life.

"I think we all saw their effort," said Lyon. "We did a lot right. I thought we had opportunities we didn't take. I can understand how the Bulldogs felt, a little bit. To Geelong's credit, they're a great side. When they had to stand up, they stood up."

Hayes said he felt for the St Kilda fans. "It's absolutely gut-wrenching. No doubt they're feeling it as well. It's very disappointing but they've stuck with us for so long I'm sure they'll be with us again next year. We want to get back and get that cup."

"We feel we have got a game plan that stands up, anywhere in any conditions at any time. We can make it better, we'll work hard, we need to move with the trends.

"We'll continue to add draft talent, trade for talent, improve our football, improve our training . . . we'll leave no stone unturned to get better. If anyone is not up for the challenge, they can walk in and tell me and I'll move them on."

The Sunday Age 27 September 2009

IT'S STILL NECK AND NECK AFTER 44 YEARS

2010 GRAND FINAL, COLLINGWOOD v ST KILDA

Caroline Wilson

IT WAS A CLASSIC GRAND FINAL that had everything except a result. It was a contest that saw the underdogs apparently beaten at half-time and yet somehow manage to unbottle the devastation from a year ago that Nick Riewoldt had instructed his side to absorb. It was yet another grand final in which Collingwood turned failure to win into something like art.

It was a game which saw Brendon Goddard, the bandaged warrior from 2009, take a Jesaulenko-like grab with 10 minutes remaining, outmarking his near-mark of the home-and-away season. And yet he has to do it all again next week. For the second time in three years, more than 100,000 crammed into the MCG. They witnessed the third draw in AFL grand final history. St Kilda kicked one extra goal and yet levelled Collingwood on 68 points.

Separated by a solitary behind for 44 years in the one contest of the year that truly counts, the Magpies and the Saints seemed destined for a stunning role reversal this time around when Travis Cloke kicked his second goal of the game during time-on of the final term, atoning for some costly earlier misses. And then Lenny Hayes, the game's Norm Smith medallist, wobbled through a behind eerily reminiscent in style of Barry Breen with 90 seconds remaining.

What followed was a gut-wrenching minute-and-a-half of exhausted desperation. St Kilda had several chances to will through another point and should have. Collingwood should have had the game won an hour earlier but couldn't. No team was robbed. Both teams were mighty.

"It was bobbing around the forward line," observed Nick Riewoldt. "I was just waiting to see if Barry Breen was on the ground, but he wasn't." In fact Riewoldt had provided a game-saving heroic with a superb pack mark on the half-back flank two minutes before the finish.

Thirty-three years ago when the siren sounded to mark the second draw in VFL–AFL history North Melbourne ruckman Peter (Crackers) Keenan and Collingwood's Rene Kink began a punch-on near the southern wing of an MCG unrecognisable from the stadium as it is today.

This time around the atmosphere was one of equal part devastation and exhaustion but the aftermath was shrouded also in civilisation. AFL bosses quickly made their way onto the ground. There is an infrastructure surrounding the game now that did not exist in the 1970s and some quick thinking by all concerned was required. And some private celebration. Chief executive Andrew Demetriou, who has stated at every appearance this week when asked for a tip that he was hoping for a draw, congratulated both captains immediately after the stunning result with the Saints skipper responding: "I bet you're happy."

Collingwood president Eddie McGuire, who oversaw something of a Magpie carnivale in the week leading up to yesterday's encounter, provided the usual theatre and then some for the broadcast cameras during St Kilda's second-half comeback. He appeared almost elated after the game in the Magpies' inner sanctum and quite intoxicated by the historic significance. "I'm a bit of a fatalist in all of this but this is history in the making and it's exciting," said McGuire. "I don't know if it's the showbiz in me."

His coach Mick Malthouse, who appeared certain at half-time to be heading towards his third premiership as a coach and his first after 11 years at the Magpies, refused to pour scorn on any of his troops. But debate will rage about Leon Davis's potential place in the side next week despite his 30-metre running snap early in the final term that was his side's first goal since Harry O'Brien had put the Pies 22 points at time on in the second term. Only for that moment did Davis have any impact on the game, not the first time he has struggled to influence a final for Collingwood.

It will rage, too, about Travis Cloke's nerve in front of goal. Cloke put Collingwood a point in front with the last goal of the game at 26 minutes after missing from a long direct shot but his two crucial misses before half-time had kept the Saints within reach. The half-time statistics showed that Collingwood had moved inside 50 metres 21 times to St Kilda's four during that quarter and yet led by only 24 points. For the third year running, crucial misses in front of goal cost a team a premiership. At least for the six days.

Ross Lyon too managed to seem upbeat after the game. He described his feeling as: "Just a sense of numbness, a whole range of emotions, frustration, anger. Relief, every ounce of our well-being will go into preparation and recovery, and we'll come to rumble next week."

The two captains actually chatted briefly during the awkward moments after the shock of the final siren, before Riewoldt was the first to gather his players together and Maxwell lured to the dais. "Thanks for coming along," said the Magpies captain whose match-saving mark on the wing was matched only by his oppositie number at Collingwood's half-forward flank.

"It's a pretty unique situation," Riewoldt told the bewildered fans, "and I'd encourage everyone to come back next week." A diehard Collingwood supporter noted that back in 1977 the Magpies had significantly more players prone and shattered on the MCG turf. In 2010 the numbers were more even. Both coaches immediately strode onto the ground to briefly address their players, but neither hung around for long and both appeared buoyant and confident in their makeshift dressing rooms afterwards.

(In the spirit of what was one of those truly epic but strange days in sport, both teams were forced to evacuate to the Southern Stand dressing rooms due to a plumbing disaster in the bowels of the northern side of the ground.) It was in the rooms and briefly back on the sidelines where the Saints' one true ruckman, Michael Gardiner, spent the second half of the game, injured and unable to take part.

Justin Koschitzke did a capable job as his replacement but yesterday's frustration is probably good news for the discarded Ben McEvoy. At half-time, with Darren Jolly dominant, Lyon's one ruck decision seemed folly. By the game's completion it seemed irrelevant. Football fans from both clubs desperate to see a grand final live are winners, too. Close to 15,000 extra tickets for Collingwood and St Kilda members will now become available.

Lenny Hayes, strangley rejected earlier this month by the all-Australian selectors, sparked the St Kilda second-half comeback and simply refused to accept defeat. He was the runaway winner of the Norm Smith Medal, but could barely speak when he accepted it, the first of two to be awarded in 2010.

Lyon, in the less buoyant St Kilda rooms, said he would have liked a result yesterday.

AFL chairman Mike Fitzpatrick conceded he expected the AFL's grand final replay policy to come in for some savage criticism but told *The Sunday Age*: "I don't have a burning desire to change it. Everybody knows about this rule and it's been around for a long time. It was a sensational match, wasn't it?"

The AFL rejected a bid by the happiest group at the corporate function— David Leckie and his team of Channel Seven executives—to schedule next week's rematch under lights at twilight saying that in the end the game had to be played in similar conditions. But the ramifications surrounding the draw and the October grand final continued to unfold.

The 2010 premier is now unlikely to be known before Gary Ablett quits Geelong for the Gold Coast or James Hird follows his heart back to Essendon. Trade week will be upon us, the draft camp will have begun and the World Cycling Championships and the VRC's launch of the spring racing season will be badly hurt by the draw. Last night overseas trips were being cancelled, holidays postponed and the television schedule rewritten. Jeff Browne, the Channel Nine boss, was spotted outside the MCG's Olympic room attempting to book the Rod Laver Arena for a reprise of last week's *The Footy Show*.

But the TAB was rejoicing last night to the tune of $7 million despite the most heavily backed draw in AFL history. The players will be spared a palaver of another grand final parade and Collingwood's elaborate imagination when it comes to grand finals and ways of not winning them has created another historic chapter. And the AFL has promised a result come 5.30 next Saturday. Or 10 minutes later if it comes to extra time. This is the AFL grand final. Not the federal election.

The Sunday Age 26 September 2010

STOIC PIES WIN THE GAME, LOSE IT, WIN IT BACK, BUT STILL NO SPOILS

2010 GRAND FINAL, COLLINGWOOD v ST KILDA

Greg Baum

WIN, LOSE OR DRAW, COLLINGWOOD does grand finals hard. It might as well be written into the club's motto beneath "Floreat Pica". The premiership wasn't, isn't and seemingly never will be, a cakewalk.

This Collingwood grand final channelled so many others. There was 1966, against the same opponent, when Barry Breen's wobbly behind beat them. Yesterday, Lenny Hayes' wobbly point denied them. There was 1970 when they led Carlton by six goals at half-time and didn't win. Yesterday, they led the Saints by four goals at half-time, but they did not win.

There was 1977, playing North Melbourne, when they won it, lost it, but in the end neither won nor lost it. The Magpies won this one, lost it, won it back, but came away with no spoils. In 1977, Twiggy Dunne's pack mark saved them. Yesterday, Nick Maxwell's pack mark saved them. You might even draw a parallel with 2002, Collingwood's last grand final, when it led Brisbane midway through the last quarter of the finals, but lost. Yesterday, ditto. The Magpies have now played in 13 grand finals since 1958, and won one.

At the sounding of the fateful final siren, unable to laugh or cry, most players showed no emotion at all. Many sprawled on their backs, limbs splayed like beached starfish. At length, they did not so much gather themselves up, as congeal. In the rooms—which weren't their rooms—their faces were blank, their hearts empty, their legs heavy. All those organs and limbs and adjectives are interchangeable.

Dane Swan said he felt "nothing", "weird". Leigh Brown said the feeling was "surreal". Dale Thomas said he was disappointed, but was the first to glimpse a silver lining: at least the Magpies had qualified for another grand final, he said. An hour after the siren, most were still in their guernseys, as if they were already kitting themselves mentally for next week. But Swan admitted that the reloading would be hard.

Collingwood looked to have put the grand final together the way it put the season together, piece by piece, until its position was impregnable. Its football was like the pre-match ceremonies, eschewing flourish, pared back to fundamentals. Swan won the first clearance of the match, leading to the first goal 20 seconds later. Ben Reid was flattened but got up. Thomas kicked a 55-metre goal from the boundary line with a torpedo. The Magpies had bolted.

In the second quarter, Collingwood was dominant. Nine shots to one fairly reflected the balance and flow of play. Nick Riewoldt was not a factor because the ball rarely came near him. Nearing half-time, Travis Cloke twice missed straightforward shots. It seemed no more than irritation then.

But the tally of behinds continued to grow. Nearing three-quarter time, Thomas and Jarryd Blair missed. Kicking at goal has been the Magpies' Achilles heel all year, and now they were limping on it. All the momentum was with Saints.

In a breathless, deathless last quarter, Collingwood first fortified its lead, then surrendered it, then reclaimed it when Chris Dawes, sitting on his backside in the goal square, searched out Cloke with a handball. Then Hayes' hither-and-thither snapshot looked momentarily as if it might fall propitiously into the arms of Stephen Milne. Instead, it dribbled through for a behind.

The siren was a pin to a balloon. No one knew what to do or where to look. It was the same in the stands; all were rooted to their spots. Considering the dead weight of history brought to this encounter by both sides, all were prepared for some sort of wrench at the end, but not this stalemate.

The speeches were short and perfunctory. Few players exchanged handshakes; there was nothing to shake on yet. The two gatherings on the field were like two encampments, done with the battle, but not with the war.

McKenna, an American band, was scheduled to play a song called "Last Man Standing", but could not, because two were still standing—just. This had been a titanic contest, but that was beside the point, or technically, beside the behind. The Magpies hadn't lost, but they hadn't won. Again.

Collingwood's unofficial mantra these last 50 years has been that there was always next year. But first there is next week. When the sun comes up this morning, and Magpie heads are clear, they might dare look forward to both thresholds. This team is young—seven of yesterday's 22 have played 50 games or fewer—and it will still be young next week and next year. By next week, Blair, for instance, will have played 12 games for two grand finals, Reid 28 games for two grand finals. That is experience not even Collingwood's money can buy.

Youth is indomitable. Youth recovers quickly. Youth cannot wait for next week to come. Youth was Sharrod Wellingham, trudging purposely across the MCG an hour after the final siren, guernsey still on, making for the Westpac Centre, a recovery session and the start of another grand final week. Shortly afterwards, a shower of rain washed over the MCG as if to cleanse it. A fresh start.

The grand final is over; let the grand final begin.

Fast Fact : The Saints hit the front for the first time after a Brendon Goddard mark and goal with six minutes 47 seconds left in the match.

The Sunday Age 26 September 2010

IN GLORIOUS LIVING COLOUR,
A BLACK AND WHITE FAIRYTALE
FINALLY COMES TRUE

2010 GRAND FINAL, COLLINGWOOD v ST KILDA

Greg Baum

FOR COLLINGWOOD, THERE WAS DELIVERANCE, for St Kilda only desolation. These are the emotional alpha and omega of grand finals, made more acute this day by the premium of the rematch. It is a football axiom that premierships are hard to win, but few have been harder won than this.

Collingwood's change room was overrun by family and friends soaking up a euphoric cacophony, and a fine mist of beer, but also a sense of shock among the Magpies about what they had just achieved. It was the shock of the new. For president Eddie McGuire, this was the culmination of his remaking of the club, and he cried with joy.

The milling crowd in the Magpie room, with not a body's width of room for anyone, was a motif for the way they won this premiership.

On the field, they were a formidable and overbearing physical presence, giving St Kilda not a scintilla of breathing space.

Over the two games, they laid 176 bone-crushing tackles, cumulatively and finally breaking St Kilda's famous resolve. Now the tackles had become hugs, the bear variety for men, tender for wives, girlfriends and especially mothers.

In the St Kilda huddle, there was a different sense of shock: that it had happened again. Collingwood coach Mick Malthouse and captain Nick Maxwell acknowledged the Saints, but on the faces of their counterparts Ross Lyon and Nick Riewoldt, not a twitch was discernible. Somehow, they had played three grand finals in two years without winning a premiership. For St Kilda, premierships are like fairytales, once upon a time.

For Collingwood, premierships are many upon a time, but nearly all a long time ago. The highlight of the pre-match ceremonies, necessarily simplified by short notice, was a parade of Collingwood and St Kilda players from the epic grand final of 1966. Not all made it, and for the rest, it was as well they were in cars. The median age of Australia's population is 37, which means that for at least half of yesterday's crowd, Collingwood's last flag was half a lifetime ago. Their support has been a matter of blind faith.

And that is only the half of it. In the heart of the crush in the Collingwood rooms was former captain Ray Shaw. Between him and sons Heath and Rhyce, they have played in nine grand finals, and this was their first win. Ray was proudly wearing Heath's medal, which for now they will have to share. But they will believe after yesterday that it is never too late for a collection.

The day, like the week, did not reach last week's heights. The crowd was smaller, though not the sound effects. Pre-match, the cup sat in splendid isolation on a plinth in the middle of the ground. The ball was delivered by helicopter; these touches constituted a return to traditional values.

For a half, the match had the same shape and temper as last week's, and the contest was, if anything, even more ferocious. But the auguries were different. Two moments stood out, both smothers. The first was Heath Shaw's desperate lunge to deny Riewoldt as he galloped into an open goal in the first quarter. No one could have known then that Riewoldt would finish the grand final goalless.

The second was Alan Didak's smother of Jason Blake as he searched for a way out of defence in the third quarter, which he followed by gathering the loose ball and screwing a right-foot goal. The Magpies then led by 46 points, and not even the malign weight of their ill-fated history could subvert their mission from there.

St Kilda was still good for its place in the contest until a few seconds after half-time, when Adam Schneider's running shot hit the post. For the second year in a row, the Saints kicked themselves out of contention. But that is an over-simplification. For most of this match, the play ran towards Collingwood's goals as if the MCG were tilted that way. The crowd's noise acted as a fan.

On the night of Collingwood's last premiership, in 1990, Lou Richards declared that the monkey was off the Magpies' back, and that a run of 10 or even 12 premierships would ensue. Victorious captain Tony Shaw, brother of Ray and uncle to Heath, implored the Magpies to make it a beginning, not an end. As it transpired, not one of that Magpie team played in another winning final. Hubris told.

This time, you sense it will be different. This team is still far from fully evolved. Its personnel are young and fresh. Nine have played 55 games or less, and nearly all were prominent yesterday. The least sung of these were key defenders Ben Reid and Nathan Brown, both 21 and now enshrined in Collingwood legend. Last night, Brown guarded the premiership cup as he had guarded Riewoldt, zealously.

In the rooms, Nathan Buckley, Anthony Rocca and Gavin Brown rejoiced. The Magpies cherish their own like few other clubs. In the past they have sometimes suffocated them, but now it looks to be their fortification. Buckley is the coach in waiting; one day, very soon, all this will be his. He can hardly wait.

As per tradition, two hours after their triumph, the Magpies returned to the middle of the MCG last night, still in their guernseys, for one last song, one last hurrah. This was a hard and truly won premiership, 20 years and two weeks in the making, but in the end, it had at last become a cakewalk.

Fast fact : In the first half, St Kilda was able to score a goal from just one of its 19 entries into the forward 50 ; Magpie Darren Jolly recorded 35 hitouts—the second-most of any ruckman in a grand final this decade .

The Sunday Age 3 October 2010

HEROES AND LEGENDS: CATS GRAB A PLACE IN HISTORY

2011 GRAND FINAL, GEELONG v COLLINGWOOD

Caroline Wilson

ALL GRAND FINALS CREATE HEROES. The game demands it. Great grand finals create legends and stories that become the stuff of it. Yesterday's stunning victory by Geelong over Collingwood was one of those.

The Cats upstaged Mick Malthouse's grand finale by 38 points on a chilly October afternoon in front of a crowd that fell agonisingly short of 100,000 people. But the scoreboard doesn't show that it took Geelong three-and-a-half quarters to break Collingwood and make history for its rookie coach Chris Scott, claiming the club's ninth premiership and its third in five years.

After the game Malthouse declared he would walk away from Collingwood almost immediately, putting paid once and for all to the prospect of a handover which would see him mentoring Nathan Buckley. "Mick is finished," declared president Eddie McGuire after the game. "He's hit the wall mentally, emotionally. He gave everything—there's no more."

More of that later. The breathtaking emotion after the game was won and lost came from the man coaching just his 25th game.

"It's such a humbling experience to be here tonight," said Scott. "We are extremely fortunate to be a part of this football club and we should never forget it."

It was close to time-on, with captain Cameron Ling having just put the Cats 37 points up, that Scott bounded to the interchange bench and began embracing his troops.

Ling won a massive hug from the coach after nullifying Brownlow medallist Dane Swan, as did the injured James Podsiadly, who sat on the boundary line for most of the second half nursing his dislocated shoulder. Ling and Podsiadly are two of six 30-somethings in a team that can now rightfully claim to be the greatest of the modern era.

Norm Smith medallist Jimmy Bartel summed up Geelong's year as simply "incredible". Scott called the experience "an amazing day".

The numbers for the Cats are a beautiful set. Yesterday's win was its 105th in 125 games. Since losing the 2010 preliminary final to Collingwood, Geelong has won nine from nine games at the MCG.

Tom Hawkins and Steve Johnson stood out in the story of Geelong's premiership. The latter was stretchered from the ground one week earlier and his knee the talking point of grand final week. Yesterday, he had spectacular cameos in each quarter, finishing with four goals. Darren Jolly and Ben Reid, the two Magpies under injury clouds, were less successful.

Johnson is a proven grand final performer. Hawkins went into the game with a point to prove, a point that became sharper when Podsiadly became wounded. Hawkins was bailed up in the rooms at half-time by retiring team-mate Cameron Mooney that perhaps helped turn him finally from a schoolboy hero to a man mountain.

Hawkins rewrote his own story with a performance in which he finished third in Norm Smith Medal voting, behind Bartel and the Cats' future captain Joel Selwood. But he would have been a worthy winner—beginning the game with a question mark beside his name and finishing with an exclamation mark. Seven of his nine marks were contested, he shepherded, presented and kicked three goals in the second half, missing two more following Carey-like marks in the opening minutes of the final term.

When Hawkins marked a third time, he offloaded to Johnson who obliged. "It's just the ultimate," said the 23-year-old. "I've had a pretty down year and they stuck with me."

The tears that flowed after the siren did not come from Malthouse, not publicly anyway. In the sombre Magpies dressing rooms, the coach confirmed what has been suspected for months: he would not be at the club in any form next year. "I think those [at the club] need a bit of space to go in the direction that they feel is going to take the club forward," said Malthouse. "I could be selfish and stay on . . . but I just don't see any point." McGuire embraced

Malthouse on the MCG after the game having tried, according to the coach, to convince him to stay.

McGuire said: "I'm pretty happy to be able to see the club coached by Nathan Buckley in season 2012 . . . The plan we put in place bore fruit. It gave us an opportunity to really give Mick two more years to do what he did and he finished off as a premiership coach at Collingwood."

The emotion came from some of his players as Malthouse shook their hands.

Leigh Brown, also retiring, shed tears, and his younger teammate Chris Dawes seemed inconsolable. It will be a topic of debate over the coming days as to whether Malthouse's struggle with the handover to Buckley created an unnecessary distraction at the club. Captain Nick Maxwell admitted to "a sense of guilt that we let Mick down".

And yet the loss was only Collingwood's third of the season, with all three against Geelong. Standing atop the premiership dais, Ling described the Magpies as "probably the best side of the last two years".

The Pies were aiming to equal Carlton and Essendon's shared record of 16 flags. But back-to-back flags continue to elude Australia's most famous football club, as they have for 75 years. In fact, yesterday brings Collingwood's losing grand final tally to 26. Malthouse has now overseen three of those defeats.

All week, all season, Malthouse and his football future—or lack of it—has punctuated the competition's narrative, but Scott continued to lurk beneath the headlines. At 35, he is the first coach since Alan Joyce took Hawthorn to a flag in 1988 to win a premiership in his first season. But Joyce handed back the reins the following season. Scott, rejected by Port Adelaide for the senior coaching job last year, is going nowhere.

In the dying minutes of the third quarter, as the hottest ball of the season was fought over in Geelong's forward line, Malthouse stood on the boundary line staring at the contest clad in rain jacket and shrouded in emotion as he awaited his final address. Prophetically, Buckley stood to his right. Literally the coach in waiting held a magnetic board. Figuratively, he held the club's future.

The teams were split by three points at half-time after close to 70 minutes of a classic contest punctuated by moments of brilliance. Andrew Krakouer continued his football redemption and created a postscript to his official mark-of-the-year midway through the second quarter.

Travis Cloke kicked three thumping goals—two from almost 60 metres out. Cloke's third, early in the second term, was followed by a Ben Johnson goal from a free and Collingwood led by 18 points. Then the chant began to drown all else around the arena. Minutes later Podsiadly was stretchered off in agony. But the Cats almost drew level shortly before half-time when Bartel threaded the goals. But Cloke was subdued for most of the second half after Scott moved Harry Taylor from him to Chris Dawes and Tom Lonergan onto the Magpie centre half-forward. Lonergan was thought lucky to be alive after losing a kidney and lucky to have remained at the Cats after struggling as a forward. Now he is a premiership player—one of five yesterday to win a first medal.

Ten Geelong players have claimed a hat-trick of medals. Two more who did not quite get there, the retiring Mooney and Darren Milburn, seemed overcome by emotion after the final siren as their coach demanded the micro-phone a second time having forgotten to mention them and determined they feel a part.

Yet another, Gary Ablett, watched the game reportedly from a bar in Las Vegas. The suggestion was by one former teammate that Ablett would be happy for the boys. This time last year the Cats lost their champion just days after losing its dual premiership coach. Mark Thompson had had a gutful of coach-ing and was reinvigorated by the prospect of mentoring James Hird. Ablett was offered too much money to refuse. Twelve months later, Ablett is one of the wealthiest players the game has seen and the All-Australian captain. Who knows whether he would hand it all back to have been back there yesterday at football's happiest place.

The Sunday Age 2 October 2011

DEEPER GAME

WHILE FOOTBALLERS AND COACHES can often seem bland when they hide behind a wall of sporting clichés, scratch below the surface and that can quickly change. It's then that we can learn what really is going on in their lives and the challenges they have faced to reach the big time—and to stay there. Former St Kilda coach Ross Lyon tells of his family heartache through 2010 when he lost two family members within four months. "I'm really just starting to deal with it now, it's still a bit raw," he told Rohan Connolly in late 2010. "It's been a tough period for my family, we're dropping like flies." Lyon would use the black humour as part of a coping mechanism.

Swans co-captain Jarrad McVeigh also opens up about what he and his family went through when their baby daughter, Luella, fought for her life in 2011. Speaking for the first time about the family's loss in an interview with Michael Cowley, McVeigh admitted his emotions span the spectrum when he looks at pictures of his daughter's month-long life. "Sometimes I just find myself looking at them and maybe cry, or I'm happy," he says of the photos. "I think after every game I played at the end of the year, I'd go and sit in the toilet and just look at my phone."

Western Bulldogs champion Scott West detailed the personal pressures he faced while former Melbourne star David Schwarz would also open up about his background. Former Hawthorn champion Shane Crawford was the toast of the football world in 1999. A year later he would wish he hadn't been. Andrew McLeod is one of the greats of the Adelaide Crows, but there was a time when his passion for the game diminished. "You can get away from why you actually do things," he told Martin Flanagan in

2008. In 2005, Emma Quayle helped explain why Mark Ricciuto, another Crows great, was such a fine leader.

In an age when statistics are often used to tell the tale, it's this chapter that explains the real story.

SCOTT WEST CLIMBS THE SHRINE TO FORGET, NOT TO REMEMBER

Caroline Wilson

ON MANY NIGHTS THIS YEAR, usually around midnight, one of the AFL's most talented footballers has visited the Shrine of Remembrance.

Once there Scott West climbs the steps of his favourite building and sits at the top in a small alcove staring over the city of Melbourne. His city. The four-time Western Bulldogs club champion says the peace and the view can be quite beautiful.

Not so the thoughts that have clouded his head for the best part of a year. Nor the persistent question that will not leave him alone. "I sit there and I think, 'Is it all worth it?'" he says. West is not talking about football.

The truth for this troubled 26-year-old, who touched the football more times this year than any other player in the AFL bar one, is far more frightening than the rumours that have plagued him in recent months.

The truth is that West has been in the grip of a depression that on some occasions has seen him shut alone in his bedroom crying for hours before escaping into sleep.

"I think there are people in the footy world who would be shocked to hear that it's got to the stage this season where I've just spent hours and hours crying myself to sleep," he said.

Scott West has chosen to speak publicly about his condition in the hope of some salvation. His estranged wife, Lechelle, who still loves West and believes in their marriage despite his erratic and unreliable behaviour these past 13 months, has given her tacit approval for this interview.

As he spoke over coffee in Richmond this week Stephen Silvagni wandered past and greeted West. They chatted, West wished him luck for the finals and Silvagni wandered off. "I'd love to be able to really talk to blokes like that and ask them how they deal with life and footy year after year. It might help put things in perspective," West says.

Perspective is a word Scott West uses a lot. Perhaps there are other young men who will read this and realise that they are not alone in their despair if a good-looking and wealthy champion footballer is living in the same darkness.

He cannot quite pinpoint how it came to this, how the downward spiral began for this Essendon Grammar boy from a good and stable family who just over a year ago was playing in the finals as the all-Australian wingman.

Back then he was less than two years into his marriage with Lechelle and the adoring father of his baby son Riley.

Those close to West date it back to the dying seconds of the 2000 Brownlow Medal count. West received one vote in round 22 to place him level with Melbourne's Shane Woewodin. The feedback from the nearby West Coast table (the Eagles had played Melbourne in the final round) was that Woewodin would not get a vote and that West had tied for the Brownlow.

West admits that having got to that stage he desperately wanted it. And then Woewodin received two votes.

"I was shattered," said West, "and why wouldn't you be? It was a shattering experience."

When West woke the next morning all that remained from those few euphoric moments was a hangover. He turned on his telephone and saw 15 messages. The telephone did not stop ringing.

He grabbed his wallet and his telephone and jumped on his bike, riding 90 kilometres from Moonee Ponds to the family holiday house at McRae where he stayed for two days. West denies this was the catalyst for the despair that followed but certainly this was when things began to go bad.

West has searched for answers. Finding little solace from the Bulldogs' psychologist, he has lunched once or twice a week all year with former clubman and close friend Steve Wallis. Somehow though they never quite get to the heart of the matter. Still, says West, he finds solace in Wallis's company.

Being alone with his thoughts is what West fears most. Then he can sense, he says, that he is "inches away" from getting himself into trouble. One night he drove from his Moonee Ponds home to Kangaroo Ground and turned up unannounced and late at coach Terry Wallace's house. Wallace has been terrific, said West, telling him the door is always open, asking how he is. "But we talk about things more generally than specifically. It was only fair that he knew."

Three times earlier this year, West tried to talk to friends about his emotional problems. All three offered the same answer. "They all said they were sorry but there was really nothing they could do," he said. "After that I decided there was no point talking about it."

West has not lived at home for much of this year but is sharing a house nearby with a mate. His son has been a constant lifeline, one he does not wish to play a big part in this story except to say: "That's probably the one thing that there is to hold on to. He has the best mother in the world but I would not want him to be left without my support."

It has been said this season of West, the Bulldogs' vice-captain, that he fell out with teammate Simon Cox because he was having an affair with Cox's girlfriend.

When West finally fronted Cox about the story, he referred to Cox's girlfriend as Carolyn. "Simon told me her name was Clare," said West. "The stupid thing was I didn't even know her name. Someone just sat down and told the biggest lie and it went crazy. My friends tried to correct the e-mails by answering them but in the end I went to the club and told them they had to do something."

Still the stories persisted. That a pre-game punch-up with Cox—or teammate Nathan Brown, depending on the version you heard—before the Brisbane game on August 5 kept him benched for the entire match with a headache.

The club flirted with the truth over the Brisbane incident, correctly stating that West had suffered a migraine but incorrectly saying a 23rd player was available.

"There was no other player there and I still don't know why," said West. "I'll probably get my arse kicked for this but they knew I wasn't right. By 7.30 the night before I knew I was getting a migraine. I was up all night vomiting, I rang the doc at 3am and he gave me a shot and the next morning I could still barely see.

"They put me on a drip for two hours … I still felt like shit, I couldn't do the warm-up and I knew I wasn't right. Sitting there I still couldn't focus but it made me look selfish, as if I'd taken another player's spot."

There have been other issues with the club. Like the humiliating night on Channel Nine's *The Footy Show* when Bulldogs chairman David Smorgon, in a desperate bid for members, paraded a group of star players in opposition jumpers. West, who came close to being bought by Collingwood last year, was asked to wear a Collingwood jumper. How did he feel? "Prostituted," he said.

Then, late last month, West learnt via this newspaper of Smorgon's plea for money to the AFL, saying without an immediate six-figure injection the club would not operate beyond 2001.

"For that to come out publicly without the players having been told disappointed me no end," West says. "If there hadn't been that five-hour meeting and the AFL hadn't stepped in, then where would we have been? A few of the players felt disappointed. We tried to joke about who we'd be playing for this year."

Even Terry Wallace's well-intentioned public statements regarding West caused problems because Wallace referred to his player's marriage problems and that devastated Lechelle, who had been trying to keep the separation quiet even from some of her friends.

Worse has been the persistent whisper that captain Chris Grant and deputy vice-captain Brad Johnson have refused to re-sign unless West left. West has been told many times this is patently untrue but these things can make you paranoid.

"When the rumours are being spoken about you, you realise these are people's lives you're playing with. The only gratifying thing for me is that no one gave it to me on the ground about it. Only one player (Hawthorn's Tony Woods) mentioned it, saying: 'What's going on with you?'"

In the two days at McCrae after the Brownlow count West took calls from his parents and pretty much no one else. They have always been close, he says, but he has struggled to share this. "It's probably hard," he said, "because they've been so successful in their marriage it makes you feel worse, more of a failure."

So West has sought peace at the Shrine where he and the regular on-duty security guard are now on a first-name basis. His most recent visit there was last week.

"It's a beautiful piece of architecture and not many people go there," West says, "especially at midnight. The hours seem to go quickly and it brings the life I lead into perspective and when I think about what it's there for and what it means, it puts my own problems back in their place."

Where to now for Scott West? On Wednesday he visited Terry Wallace and was relatively buoyed by the coach's words. "I know I haven't had as good a year as last year but I still finished second in the overall stats and Terry said he was pretty happy.

"This is not meant to sound vain but I'm proud ... that I've managed to do OK playing with everything else that's been going on."

West has also launched a landscape gardening business in the past six weeks and plans to lay pretty low over September, his first season out of the finals in five years. Perhaps he will watch the Bombers train. He cannot answer whether his marriage will survive. "This is hard for me to explain to people," he says. "But while football is everything, being an AFL footballer isn't. I am three-dimensional. I'm a loving father, I've got a job and there is more to me than playing footy."

As for the answer to the terrible question that won't go away, West remains unsure. "Is it all worth it? I still don't know," he says.

The Age 8 September 2001

AFL COACH REVEALS 11-YEAR SECRET: MY BATTLE WITH BRAIN TUMOUR

Emma Quayle

MARK HARVEY WAS 34, RETIRED and in his first full-time season as an assistant coach at Essendon. It was 1999. At work, around his friends and in the newspapers, people kept asking him the same questions: do you want to be a senior coach one day? Why aren't you applying for jobs? What are you waiting for?

Each time, Harvey tried to deflect the attention, to avoid answering, to buy himself some time. He wanted to coach his own AFL team, absolutely, but he was in no condition to. What he didn't know then was that a small tumour had grown on the pituitary gland in his brain, flooding his body with human growth hormone, making his organs swell and messing with his mind.

How could he contemplate his next career move when he thought he was going mad?

Harvey isn't sure when he started to get sick. But for more than a year after he retired in 1997, things weren't quite right.

First, he'd get bad stomach pains. Then he'd have pins and needles running down one arm. He'd feel murmurs in his temple and suffer horrible headaches. He had an irritable bowel, and he was taken to hospital in agony with a kidney stone. Then his wife Donna, who used to sell shoes and bring new pairs home for him, noticed that his feet had grown. "No, they haven't," Harvey insisted.

He had no idea what was going on. Were these random symptoms somehow connected? Was there something badly wrong with him? Or was he losing his mind?

"It was one thing after another. It kept moving. It lasted over such a long time and it was playing on my mind all the time," Harvey told *The Sunday Age*. "I'd think, is this really happening or am I making it up? It was doing my head in. I was sure that I was losing it."

Each time a new problem arose Harvey would be on the phone to Essendon doctor Bruce Reid, the man who had helped him through three broken legs, several knee, ankle and calf surgeries, countless bouts of concussion and even a four-year battle with the eating disorder bulimia. "Reidy, tell me what's going on," he'd implore him.

Dr Reid knew something was up, not only because of the hard-to-connect physical symptoms but because the normally unflappable Harvey—so tough, so resilient, so able to handle stress—was anxious, all the time. "He was an intense bugger, but he was never a stress-head," said the doctor. "With this, he was getting so anxious he couldn't sleep. Something was affecting his body, something was affecting his psyche, and we couldn't put it all together."

Eventually, Dr Reid sent Harvey to see Ross Elliott, a gastroenterologist. Harvey walked into his office, sat down and placed both hands on the desk in front of him. As soon as he did, the specialist knew what was up.

"Have your hands gotten bigger?" Dr Elliott asked and, looking at them, Harvey could see that they had. His nose and jaw were thicker, too, as were his cheekbones. His whole body was wider than it had been; it was weird. He was sent for full blood tests, plus a brain scan and the tumour was discovered, sitting right at the front of his brain.

Harvey was told he had acromegalia, a condition caused by the excessive amount of hormones in his body. A normal person's level is between three and five, and his was more than eight times that. Had the AFL conducted blood testing for drug use in his final year, and had he been tested, Harvey would have been wrongly sprung as a drug cheat. When a person is born with the condition, or develops a tumour as a child, they can grow to seven feet tall, but because he was an adult, Harvey was instead growing outwards, placing extra stress on his internal organs and the excessive hormones messing with his head.

Two weeks later he was at Royal Melbourne Hospital being prepared for major brain surgery, placing his faith in neurosurgeon Andrew Kaye, who had told him the tumour needed to be removed before it gained a greater hold of him. He knew there was a chance he might not survive the operation.

Watching her husband being prepped, and hearing Professor Kaye explain to his team of a dozen doctors and students what he was going to do, Donna Harvey understood how serious the situation was.

"They took him in, it was an eight or 10-hour operation and I sat there waiting, trying to read a book," she said. "I was thinking, we've got two young kids, and they're in there, inside his brain," she said. "I tried not to show him it was scary, because you don't want to scare the fleas off them before you send them in. But it was, it was incredibly scary. I didn't know if he would come back out."

Before and after the operation, Harvey experienced a raft of emotions, too. Looking up at Professor Kaye, as he prepared to go into surgery, everything hit home, yet he knew he needed to trust him.

"That was the moment when I thought, this is really serious," he said, "but I didn't have a choice. I couldn't go on, feeling like I was feeling."

After the operation, during his stay in hospital, he relied on Dr Reid. "He never let me get into a rut. He has a way of making you feel like things will be all right."

Harvey looked forward to the surgeon's visits, to finding out his thoughts on the surgery.

Although Harvey had known Professor Kaye only briefly before his surgery, the surgeon later returned to play a second part in his life. In 2003, when former Essendon wingman Adam Ramanauskas was diagnosed at 22 with a soft tissue cancer in his neck, Harvey called Professor Kaye and asked if he would see his young coaching charge.

Professor Kaye went on to twice save the player's life and Ramanauskas, after undergoing radiotherapy and chemotherapy, made three inspiring AFL comebacks. After each of his operations, Harvey was one of the first people to see him.

In Harvey, Ramanauskas found someone who understood what it was like to be told your life was under threat, what it was like to be wheeled into an operation you might not come out of, what it was like to wait for the results of tests and scans.

"It helped that, with him, I didn't have to explain anything," said Ramanauskas. "He just knew."

All Harvey wanted, though, was to help. "It was a difficult time for everyone when Adam got sick, but Adam was the one who had to deal with the fact that his life might be cut short and he was so strong-minded," Harvey says. "Not at any stage did he show any sign of wanting sympathy. He made up his mind that he was going to beat it, and that was that."

Both men also understood the highly personal relationship they developed with Professor Kaye after placing their lives in his hands. "In those first few days you find yourself waiting for him, waiting for him to come and see you, to tell you how the operation went, to tell you how your body is coping, what you need to do next," Harvey said. "You hang on to those moments. You spend all day waiting for him to come into your room. And you're always trying to read him before he starts speaking, to know whether he's going to say something positive or negative."

At home, he did more thinking. He did it mostly on his own, having decided to tell only a few people of what he had gone through. His family knew and, at Essendon, so did Dr Reid, coach Kevin Sheedy and recruiting manager Adrian Dodoro, a close friend. Others have found out since as he became more relaxed about it, but at the time he wanted to keep it from everyone else at the club.

Harvey didn't know if he was back to normal or if he ever would be. He didn't want people to wonder if he was mentally all there, doubting his capacity to do what he'd done, and what he aspired to do: coach. And he had always been a person who dealt with adversity on his own.

"Men don't cry. That's his motto," said Donna. "We had really close friends we didn't tell; that's how quiet we kept it. We were pretending nothing had happened, that everything was just like it always had been."

For Harvey, who went back to work after two weeks with his nose plastered, telling everyone he'd had a sinus operation, seeking sympathy wasn't an option.

"It's funny. When you think you've got something that perhaps is life threatening, I think that's the biggest debate you have with yourself. Do you want sympathy or do you want to handle everything on your own?" he said. "I never wanted any sympathy. That was how I looked at it and I was probably never a guy who liked to show any sign of weakness.

"I was told to have six weeks off after the operation because if I overdid things it was going to affect my nervous system, and things like that. I had maybe 10 days off and then I couldn't help myself; I went back to work and there were a couple of times where I didn't collapse but I half fainted because I was putting myself under too much pressure.

"In the end, Reidy said, 'That's it, you're going home for two more weeks,' and that's when I knew I actually had to toe the line and rest up, that everything wouldn't go back to normal straightaway.

"A lot of things cross your mind in that time. The obvious thing I suppose you ask yourself, straight afterwards, is how long have I got to live? What will the results say? And then after that, it's, OK, is it ever going to come back? Will I get my faculties back? I wondered if I'd be the person I was, if I'd be able to go back to coaching, if I'd be able to think clearly. That's what I spent my time thinking."

It took a while. For the first couple of years after his operation, Harvey needed to have his hormone levels checked every six months, and after each blood test he tended to think very negatively. "Those three or four days where you're waiting on the results, it's mind boggling," he said. "You'd look for signs, pick up on things that maybe weren't there, worry if it might be coming back. I had a few months in those first few years I'd just find myself slumped in a chair, not able to do anything for an hour, not really able to move. Then I'd get up and get on with things again."

Slowly, he started to feel like himself again. After those first two years Harvey felt fine, ready to pursue the next phase in his career, determined to become the senior AFL coach that, at Fremantle, he now is. He still has his blood tested once a year, just to be sure, but he feels well and truly better and he no longer feels paranoid or stressed while waiting for the next all-clear.

"It could come back. There's obviously a possibility there that it could still happen, but I don't think it will," he says.

"It's more than 10 years now. They say once you're through those first few years you should be fine. It took me those two years and once that had passed by, I started to feel like it wouldn't come back and I felt like the person I was before it happened. I was able to move on. That's when I felt ready to coach."

The Sunday Age 13 June 2010

GRIEVING LYON TELLS OF A YEAR MARRED BY LOSS

Rohan Connolly

THERE ARE DISAPPOINTMENTS AND THEN there are tragedies. Sometimes tears cloud eyes, blurring the boundaries. But on this point, St Kilda coach Ross Lyon has a cruel clarity. He knows the heartbreaking difference.

Losing an AFL premiership is a disappointment. Losing two beloved family members within four months is a true tragedy.

"Footy's really, really important to me, but, you know, well, we're still alive, and we get another opportunity," he says.

As Lyon knows better than any of his shattered players, some people don't.

Unbeknown to all but close friends, the 44-year-old has been coaching the Saints against a backdrop of family tragedy since his older sister, Julie, died in July.

Julie, who had been battling breast cancer for 18 months, succumbed quite suddenly to an undetectable cancer that had spread to her blood vessels.

Then, just three weeks ago, Lyon's nephew, Kane, the 24-year-old son of his sister, Michele, was killed in a motorcycle accident while on holiday in far north Queensland.

"I'm really just starting to deal with it now, it's still a bit raw," he tells *The Sunday Age*, speaking publicly for the first time about the tragedies. "It's been a tough period for my family, we're dropping like flies."

The black humour is just one coping mechanism. Lyon became so practised at handling his grief during the final critical months of the AFL season that he managed to hide his personal turmoil from almost the entire club as it locked on to the task of winning that elusive flag.

Lyon explains it thus. "There's a real responsibility leading an AFL team, that you've got to dig in. It's easy to talk about it, but sometimes it's your turn as a coach, or as a father or whatever, to practise what you preach a little bit and not crumble."

The St Kilda coach certainly didn't. Julie passed away late on the Tuesday evening before the Saints' important round-16 clash with Collingwood. Her brother kept a corporate speaking appointment the following day. He continued to work through the week and he addressed his players before they ran out that Saturday afternoon, the Saints oblivious to his loss.

"I knew it was a big game, and I didn't want to distract the players," he says. A flat-looking St Kilda was well beaten that afternoon. A score of Saints had been ill during the week. But in the post-match analysis, Lyon refused to use excuses for his players, and certainly not for himself. No one could have blamed him had he done so.

Julie was talented at sport like him, having represented the state at junior level in squash. Although she had fought a lengthy battle with breast cancer, enduring a mastectomy, her death still came relatively suddenly. Lyon did not have the chance to say goodbye.

"I got a bit crook myself, and run down, and missed a family birthday," he recalls. "All my sisters had been into the hospital to see her, but as much as we knew she was in massive trouble, we thought she had some time left.

"I rang her on my way home from work and left a message saying, 'Sorry I haven't seen you, hope you're going well, give us a call.' I'd been working hard and it was a pretty important game, so I said to [wife] Kirsten I was going into the spare room because I needed a good night's sleep.

"I went to bed about 11, then at about 12, Kirsten came in in tears. I asked what was wrong and she said, 'It's Julie, she's passed away.' I sort of erupted because it came as a real shock. So we drove into the hospital pretty late. We saw her, I gave her a hug. Then I went and picked up her nine-year-old daughter Sarah and brought her in. It was really horrible."

That task was made even more poignant by the fact that Kirsten had lost her own mother to breast cancer when she was only 12.

Julie's funeral was a private affair, save for the presence of assistant coach and Lyon's close friend Stephen Silvagni. "I said I didn't want anyone from the club at the funeral," he reflects. "At some point, you just want to be the brother. I didn't want to be the AFL coach, I just wanted to be Julie's brother."

Lyon says he doesn't want his stoicism to be "seen as some sort of badge of honour", nor have anyone think his situation is different from anyone else's.

"People talk about the pressure AFL coaches are under, but mate, everyone's got pressures. The printer, the plumber, they all go home to a mortgage and kids . . . It happened, and I'm dealing with it, but so are a lot of other people. Cancer is everywhere."

But further tragedy was awaiting Lyon and his three surviving sisters. Choked with emotion, he tries to detail the recent motorcycle death of his nephew, Kane, in Cooktown.

"He'd gone up there with his girl to visit her old man. He came off the bike on a dirt road, his helmet came off, and . . ." Lyon's voice trails off.

"I think you find out a fair bit about yourself in these sorts of times," he says later. "Whether you're going to give up or keep working. And I think AFL football prepares you over a long period of time to keep putting one foot in front of the other.

"I think they [the deaths of his relatives] are stark reminders about embracing life and people . . . At Kane's funeral, there was a quote from Tennessee Williams: 'Death is one moment, and life is so many of them.' That resonated with me a lot."

Lyon, who lost his mother, Louise, in 2004, has lately seen a lot of more of his father, Maurice, now 80. "There's an acute awareness of what you value. I think it highlights that, that's what it's done for me."

It's also a reminder that "there's always someone worse off than you", he says, talking about young St Kilda supporter Madison Bartlett, who lost her entire family in the St Andrews' bushfires two summers ago.

Closer to home, there's the now widowed husband trying to comfort his motherless nine-year-old daughter, and the grieving mother who has lost a son in the prime of his life.

These are real tragedies—something Lyon knows a St Kilda grand final defeat, however upsetting, will never be.

The Sunday Age 5 December 2010

ALL ABOUT MY FATHER

Jake Niall

THE MOST PAINFUL RECONSTRUCTION OF David Schwarz's life wasn't the first, second or even the third time he snapped the anterior cruciate ligament in his left knee. It was his decision to finally confront what that eight-year-old boy saw in a Mt Beauty motel room, at 5.30am, a tick over 26 years ago.

Schwarz's recall of that terrible day has grown more vivid since he began belated psychotherapy last year. He remembers the "massive" sound of the .22 rifle, from a few feet away, which woke him. He remembers that the killer wore black, and looked "like an army guy". He remembers the blood "everywhere", and the recognition that his dad, Heinz Schwarz, 31, must be ead.

He can still see the woman, whom his father had been seeing, wrestling with the gunman, her estranged husband. "She was fighting with him, grappling with the gun . . . I didn't know what to think. I just thought, 'Dad's in strife. I've got to get out and try and get some help.'

"So, [the room] had those breakfast chutes—you know, you open up and put the tray in. Because they were fighting near the door, I couldn't get through, so I didn't want them to see me, so I just kind of snuck out through the breakfast chute.

"And I ran around the back, because I knew where the manager was, and knocked on the door and said, 'You've got to help. Someone's broken into our room and shot dad.'"

Eight-year-old David stayed in the manager's room, as police arrived. Soon, he would learn that his father had died from the rifle shot to his head, and that the shooter, 51-year-old Richard Martin, had subsequently turned a gun on himself.

The coroner's report, dated May 1981, noted that Martin and his wife had been separated for some time, a court having ordered him to "keep the peace" with her.

Albury's *Border Morning Mail* ran the story of the shooting on its front page, with a photo of the cordoned off motel crime scene.

The boy Schwarz went back to Beechworth, where he lived with his mother, Mary, and sister, Rebecca, and spent lots of time with his mum's sister, Margaret. Mary would subsequently move the family to Sunbury. David's parents had been separated, his dad living in Mt Beauty, working as a chef at the pub across the road from the fateful motel.

David was visiting his father for a few days during school holidays. They had planned to go fishing on the day of his murder. "Because mum and dad were separated, it was one of those times you used to always look forward to, school holidays. It was my turn to go to dad's by myself—normally me and my sister went together.

"I always think, and I think mum thinks that a lot, too, how lucky I was.

"I was lucky to get out. If I couldn't get out of that servery, I probably wouldn't have got out. That's probably being melodramatic. I don't know. But it was the only door."

In February of last year, at his partner Karen's instigation, Schwarz decided to see a psychotherapist in an attempt to quit smoking. He had beaten "the punt", the gambling habit that had cost him a sum he estimated at "seven figures". The smokes were his next opponent. Karen, with whom he has a two-year-old son, Cooper, and baby daughter, Indiana, was mindful of what the therapy might uncover.

Inevitably, the topic of his father's murder, and what he had seen, was raised during therapy, initially attended by Karen. Soon, it became the focus of numerous solo sessions with his therapist, Jan Beams, a niece of cricketing colossus Keith Miller and daughter-in-law of the distinguished (Melbourne) footballer-cricketer and noted sportswriter, the late Percy Beams. "It was all dad. It was 25 years of having something build up inside you."

Schwarz had never addressed the issue of his father's death, its impact upon him, and how it shaped him. He said he discussed it "briefly" in the media only once, on *The Footy Show*, when he was a panelist, several years ago. The topic was seldom broached by teammates, though the Ox's burden was known to some, such as close mates David Neitz and Guy Rigoni, and Jim Stynes once wrote a short column in *The Age* about it.

The Melbourne Football Club had numerous psychologists available for his use throughout his storied 173-game, 27-operation career, but he had never seen fit to sit down with one and talk about this central, defining trauma.

Why not? "I'm six foot four, I'm tough, I'm known as the Ox. The last thing I want to see is a bloody psychiatrist, or a psychologist—imagine if word got out? And that's the thought process that went through me as a football meat-head. But after being through it, you realise that like a physio, like a doctor, they're there to help. They're there to get you on the track and get you right."

Schwarz now believes he ought to have had therapy when he was recovering from his knee reconstructions in 1995–96, the injuries that denied him prolonged superstardom. "Probably at that stage, my head was the thing that needed fixing. I had a lot of down time, I was on the punt."

He is certain that, in today's environment—in which players undergo psychological profiling before they are even drafted, and the AFL Players' Association has vast welfare programs—such a horrific trauma would be treated via the AFL system.

"I'm sure that it would be dealt with. I think by the club. I think the clubs are that in tune now with all the help."

Fittingly Schwarz, who retired from league football in 2002 and has become a highly visible Channel Seven and SEN commentator (who will do special comments tonight for Seven), was persuaded to enter his mind's no-fly zone when therapist Beams asked him to imagine how Cooper would cope with witnessing his dad's violent death.

"So we get in there and we're talking about, you know, footy and everything I've been through—the gambling and the whole lot," he said. "Then we spoke about dad, and this dad thing. And I thought, 'Oh, we'll clear that up in an hour.' And she [Beams] goes, 'Do you reckon that affects you?' And I said, 'No, it was pretty hard at the time, but, no, I think I'm over it.' She goes, 'Really?' She said, 'You ever cry about him?' I said, 'No, not really.' And she said, 'So you don't think it's affected you?' And I said, 'No, I don't, I don't think it has.' And she said, 'Well, just put yourself in your son's shoes for a moment and you're sitting in bed and the same happens to you and he sees you. Do you think he would be affected?' And with that I thought, 'Christ, yeah, it must have.'"

By exhuming memories of his father's death, reading the coroner's and police reports, bringing his sister along to some sessions and shedding some tears, Schwarz has learnt much about himself. He believes that there is a connection between what happened to his dad, and his gambling and smoking. He recalls that his father, too, was a punter and wonders if he was subconsciously attempting to emulate him.

"I just buried it," he said of his dad's death. "Just put it away. And I think I used sport and anger and . . . anything I could cling on to to cover it over."

The punt was a refuge. "It takes you out of reality. I reckon that was a real escape for me."

Schwarz has always needed company—another trait he attributes to losing his father. "I hated being by myself. Always had to have people around me." He had played basketball "seven days a week" as a kid.

Schwarz temporarily halted his therapy a few months ago, in part because he's working seven days a week during the footy season (including Friday nights and Sundays with Seven), but also since he had dealt with what Beams called "the core" issue. He said he will return at season's end.

"We're at a level now where it's just maintenance. All the hard work's done . . . I've given up the smokes, I've given up gambling, I've spoken about my dad. Karen and I have never been better . . . I'm just more level."

He says he has "an air of calmness" now. His hitherto unrealistic optimism has been tempered. He recalled how the Demons once tested the senior list for optimism–pessimism, scoring each player between plus and minus seven on a scale.

Neale Daniher was in the zero, like right on the middle, rock solid.

"I was plus seven and the bloke said, 'This is most optimistic, this is the biggest number we've ever had on an optimistic test ever.' It'd be raining outside, and I'd be wearing my speedos thinking it's a sunny day.

"I reckon that's another defence mechanism to this thing of dad . . . I think once I went through all this, with my psychologist, my optimism and pessimism is a lot more together now. Realistic."

Schwarz said he had tended to recall "the good stuff" about his dad, and block out the bad. Heinz Schwarz, who migrated from Germany as a young child, was a capable sportsman, a handy footballer for the Beechworth Bombers and excellent barefoot skier. "I remember he had a temper. I remember he gambled. I remember we used to go rabbiting all the time—he was good at rabbiting, really good at ferreting and trapping . . . really good cook. He was a chef."

Heinz barracked for Hawthorn. So attached was David to dad's old team, for which he retains "a soft spot", he remained a member of the Hawks' cheer squad even when playing under 19s and reserves at Melbourne."

"I loved the Hawks. I was always at the footy. I always had idols and my idols were Dermott Brereton, Terry Wallace, these type of people."

Memories of his father are clearly precious. And while Schwarz has a clearer vision of the shooting and its awful aftermath, post-therapy, it is the final hours he spent with his dad that have been fully restored.

"It's more the lead-up stuff I remember now—getting up to Mt Beauty, and playing pool over in the club."

An eight-year-old boy and his dad, hanging together in school holidays. That part of the reconstruction lives happily in David Schwarz's mind.

The Age 25 May 2007

SHANE'S PAIN

Caroline Wilson

THE 1999 BROWNLOW MEDAL, LIKE its owner, has been locked away in darkness for most of this season. The darkness of Shane Crawford's briefcase. "Out of sight, out of mind," he said without much conviction. The way he has so dearly tried to be for most of this year.

Except that when you're the good-looking star of the only game in town, there is nowhere to hide. Even letting your hair grow dark and covering it with hats and buying a mobile telephone your club doesn't know about has proved pretty useless.

Crawford's fall from the graceful heights he scaled last season has been one of the perplexing issues of the season. Several times, he said, he has run out on to the ground and, terrifyingly for him, not wanted to be there.

"I didn't want to play," he said. "I'd think to myself: 'I don't want to be here. I want this game to be over.' I knew this wasn't how it used to be, not enjoying the idea of footy any more."

At Hawthorn, Crawford's struggles with post-Brownlow pressure and subsequent poor form have been the subject of a series of meetings, some hastily convened by a desperate Crawford in which not only the coach was summoned but also his staff and club chief executive Michael Brown and football manager John Hook.

But the football club was no longer a refuge for him. "The best escape was to go home," said Crawford. "I'd turn on the TV and take the phone off the hook and think: 'This is heaven.' I insisted that Thursday was a complete day off and I made sure I wasn't sitting there with a whole bunch of stuff to sign."

To say the Brownlow Medal became a millstone around Crawford's neck would be an understatement. He admits now that he was obsessed for a long time about winning the thing and didn't take his mother Dianne to the count for fear he would lose.

And yet there have been times this season he has contemplated selling it.

"I thought I might just sell it and my name will still be on the board, but I don't have to think of it as mine," he said. "Look, I'm obviously not going to sell it, but those things go through your head when you get desperate.

"Everyone handled it a bit poorly. The club's a bit to blame. It's not totally responsible but even Schwabbie admits it was handled wrong. He [new Hawthorn coach Peter Schwab] has been excellent, but during the pre-season I'd be halfway through a weights session with a partner and I'd be pulled away to sign something or do a photo.

"I went from loving training and footy to hating it. I was just hating it. I thought if this is what it's like, they can have it [the Brownlow] back.

"I was going nuts. I wanted to tell everyone: 'Just let me be,' but with you guys talking about it all the time it didn't help."

Of his attempts to disguise himself, Crawford admitted: "I've tried that. It doesn't help no matter what hats or dark glasses you try."

That's what happens when you go from being a 30 to 40-possession man down to 15. Crawford agreed to talk to *The Age* partly because he can now see some signs of light, and friends have noticed he has been less flat in the past few weeks. He was reasonably happy with his performance against Fremantle two rounds ago.

But the situation remains fragile, with Crawford yesterday deciding against being photographed. For him, some turning points have proved deceptive.

After struggling for the football during pre-season games, Crawford found himself looking at Schwab during the half-time break of the Hawks' round-two game against Carlton and seeing the pressure on his face.

"I just felt so bad for him that he was trying so hard and I was letting him down," Crawford said. "I promised myself I was going to lift and I had a better second half. I keep telling myself to lift and I know I'm not far from it."

But still the theorising continues. Where have you gone, Shane Crawford? Our football club turns its lonely eyes to you and it has seen all sorts of crazy things. Crawford has chronic fatigue syndrome, Crawford is suffering from depression or all manner of sinister illnesses. None of the theories are correct.

But he does admit to being depressed. For the first time at Hawthorn he has started talking to club psychologist Simon Lloyd, big brother of Essendon's Matthew. "It really helps to just open up to someone and know he's not going to talk to someone else about it," Crawford said.

Apart from that, Crawford's main solace has been to vanish, whether it be to his house and TV set, to his girlfriend's family holiday house at Lorne, where he has been working on a film script on and off for two years, or to Cranbourne racecourse, where he has several horses in training.

The film script is proving a welcome escape. It tells the story, he said, of "three guys going nowhere with their lives and then one breaks away". The focus for the script is the Hawaiian triathlon, an event for which Crawford harbours passionate ambitions.

"I don't see myself as someone who'll drag out my playing career and be forced to leave," he said. "There are other things I want to do."

Back to the less golden present, Crawford's first quarter against Sydney on Sunday was encouraging, but while he finished the match with some 20 possessions after an occasionally torrid tussle with Wayne Schwass, he has still to perform anywhere near his peak and would have struggled to win a vote from the umpires to date.

"Crawf," said Schwab early in the season, after being drawn for the first time on the subject of his captain's struggle for form, "I'm sick of talking about you. I had to say something to get them off my back."

Crawford has always tended towards the loner, but he admits this season he has been remote from his teammates, which he feels bad about. "It's affected me as a leader as well," he confessed. "I'd always liked being the sort of person who'd say to the young guys, 'Let's go and do a few laps,' or organise going to a movie. I haven't done that this year. I was remote from everyone."

Recently, filming a TV commercial for multiple sclerosis with James Hird, Crawford hesitated but eventually sought advice from the Essendon captain. Hird was sympathetic, telling him: "I totally understand what's happening, you're everywhere," referring to the Brownlow victory. The trick, said Hird, was to try not to be everywhere.

"Rob Harvey is a good example," said Crawford, almost admiringly, of the dual Brownlow medallist. "He just says, 'No, no, no' to everything."

Crawford admitted he found it hard to say no. The club has told him this, and the 25-year-old admitted that after-effects of all the "yesses" had made him paranoid.

"I told them [the club] I didn't want people to hate me," he said. "I didn't want to be in people's faces all the time. I didn't want to drive around a corner and see my face on a billboard."

Off-field it has been a strange, occasionally devastating, 12 months for Crawford. Last July, his girlfriend Olivia's father, John Anderson—the chairman of corporate finance at KPMG—disappeared while holidaying in Mykonos and was later found to have died accidentally after a fall and a suspected heart attack.

Crawford was not seeing Olivia at the time but the two became reunited after the tragedy and remain together. "I've probably driven her mad," he said.

Then, earlier this month, his maternal grandfather was hurt in a car accident on the first day of a holiday in London. Crawford's brother Justin, now working in a restaurant and playing amateur football in Perth, was dispatched overseas to bring his grandfather home.

"I should have sent Justin with him in the first place," said Crawford, who clearly takes these things on board. He suspects his mother and Olivia have spoken about him this season several times, but added that he saw no reason to burden Dianne Crawford with his troubles.

"I look back now and wonder how she did it when we were growing up," he said. "Dad died of cancer but he wasn't really around before that and she'd be up every day doing her tomatoes from 6am to twelve.

"Then she'd come home and have a shower and something to eat and then she'd go to work at the RSL club from three until midnight and managed to put three of us through boarding school."

Big brother Andrew left home for an apprenticeship in Melbourne, and the legacy from Shane's childhood is that he remains a cleanliness fanatic—"I'm constantly wiping up"—who hates cooking. "I'd be left to cook for Justin, and when he wouldn't eat I'd bash him up.

"I guess the work ethic comes from mum. It can't have been easy for Justin at the club with me there and people always asking, 'Why can't you work as hard as your brother?'"

No one really knows what's wrong with Crawford. Was the Brownlow such a holy grail for him that the follow-up year was never going to present the challenge required? Has the combination of all the pressures really proved such a horrendous burden, even now that Crawford is doing less than he was at the same time last year?

His obvious affection for Schwab belies the theory that the coaching change has hurt him, although the catchcry from Hawks fans is to put him back into defence where he began his 1999 season with such promise. Confidence can be such an elusive quality.

Gavin Wanganeen, the 1993 Brownlow medallist, believes the issue could be more than emotional. "Maybe with Shane Crawford, he's had a few niggling injuries," he said, "and you can't be expected to perform at your best when you have injuries. People have been a bit hard on him. We're not robots."

Crawford, who said he has confided in Nick Holland and who counts Ben Dixon among his close friends at the club, along with the Hawks' fitness coach, Bohdan Babijczuk, said he had also received moral support from Wayne Campbell at Richmond and, indirectly, Anthony Koutoufides, who sent the struggling skipper a message through a mutual friend.

"Tell Crawf I know what he's going through," Kouta said. "Give 'em nothing. They're all trying to crawl back to me now that I'm going all right but I'll be giving 'em nothing."

The Age 6 June 2000

DAMAGE CONTROL

Samantha Lane

IN THE THROES OF HIS worst bout of concussion, Daniel Bell could not remember his girlfriend's name. He held his mobile phone but stared at it blankly. He knew who he wanted to call but he had no idea what buttons to press.

Sitting in unfamiliar dressing rooms, with familiar out-of-body sensations intensifying and his vision so blurred that he could not see his hands was nothing new for the 25-year-old. But an April day in Ballarat, when he received his last big physical hit, was nothing compared to the jolt that would come six months later.

That day—it was October 4 last year—a neuropsychologist Bell was referred to by the Melbourne Football Club, his AFL home for eight years, diagnosed him with brain damage. The expert view was that this damage had come about because of the string of concussions that had littered Bell's career and would end up seriously altering the course of his life.

The neuropsychologist's most dramatic short-term recommendation, which came after hours of testing, was made in the strongest possible terms—Bell should never play football again unless he wanted to risk further brain trauma.

But the initial sadness and financial strain that reality was to inflict on the brown-eyed sportsman, who seemed prone to hitting his head from the time he could walk, did not compare to the frightening prospect of the early onset of Alzheimer's disease or dementia.

By the time of that last big, bad hit in Ballarat—Bell was crunched playing in the VFL but doesn't know much more about the incident—he knew his days as a Melbourne player were numbered if he couldn't shake the assortment of injuries that had dogged him since he became a semi-regular senior player. In retrospect, having the conversation that all footballers dread—when Melbourne coach Dean Bailey told him of his delistment last September—was the easy part.

Bell's history of concussion pre-dated his 66-game senior career. The South Australian defender was regularly praised by his coaches, teammates and fans for on-field acts of blind courage. A link on the Demons' website still points to a story from 2007 in which Bell discusses a "warrior club" that only select Melbourne players became members of when they were judged by their peers to have committed six "warrior acts" on field.

Bell detailed how he had earned a "warrior point" from his teammates following his brief return to the field in a recent match after he'd been concussed in a clash with Chris Tarrant. "I probably should've got a stupid point because I shouldn't have gone back out there. It was a bit silly," Bell joked then.

Now, he understands that his initial insistence to Melbourne medical staff that day that he was perfectly capable of resuming play was dangerous.

But as Bell details his history of concussions—he spoke to *The Age* in his Bentleigh home this week in the hope that his story might influence other footballers to be less reckless than he was—he stresses that he is the only person guilty of mismanagement. "The only mismanagement was from my own will to play," he said. "The doctors did everything they could, and they've done everything they can to help me after footy as well."

In fact, since last September when Bell first lodged concerns with Melbourne's long-serving club doctor, Andrew Daff, that he was experiencing worrying memory loss, the Demons have wanted to support him. It was Dr Daff who directed Bell to the Elite Minds brain-training program the club has offered as a resource to players for some time with which Bell—after committing himself to the online exercises for 15 minutes every second day—has already enjoyed success.

Daff also referred Bell to the neuropsychologist who concluded the former Demon's alarmingly poor cognitive function was linked to the concussions he had sustained playing football. That report now forms the basis of the compensation claim Bell has lodged with the AFL Players' Association.

Bell estimates he was concussed 15 times before he was drafted and as many as 10 times during his time at Melbourne. His first memory of experiencing blurred vision came when he was a child, after he flung himself off a swing and crash-landed. He was concussed playing soccer and tennis, after falling off a motorbike, attempting high jump and in junior footy games all before he was recruited to Melbourne as a 17-year-old, No. 14 draft selection.

His parents, from country South Australia, had insisted on him wearing a helmet in football games. But the hot, restrictive and decidedly uncool head-gear had been dispensed with by the time the kid who grew up wanting to be a football or cricket star turned 14.

As a member of the Australian Institute of Sport AFL academy, on account of his outstanding performances at junior level, Bell had rigorous physical examinations before joining the big league. His concussion history, even as a youngster, led to his first appointment with a neurologist who told Bell he appeared to be susceptible to concussion migraines. "No one ever sat down to say this could actually be serious," he recalls. "But I'm not sure if that would have stopped me anyway, I wanted to play AFL."

Equipped with Bell's medical history, the Demons were aware of the raw facts, but until his delistment last year they had no idea of the related problems the defender was experiencing off the field.

Bell's girlfriend, Jayde, who is clearly still deeply concerned about the recent past and the future, recalls the day last year that Bell forgot they had a trailer to move a piece of furniture. This was particularly disturbing because Bell had only recently used the trailer to help a teammate move house.

"That was the time I said, 'You've got to tell a doctor about this,'" said Jayde, his girlfriend of four years.

Increasingly, concentration lapses and memory loss have become bigger issues.

"In the last couple of years I found it really hard to concentrate in games. Especially last year. Last year I was all over the shop," Bell said. "It would actually make me feel sick after a game because I'd know about the mistakes I'd made, because my opponent had got too many possessions or whatever. I'd think about it the whole week, dreading the meetings because I knew it was going to come up. I'd be asked about my poor positioning at stoppages and I just couldn't give an answer because I didn't know why I hadn't done something.

"I'd feel physically ill for most of the week and that was pretty much most of the last two years. It's actually a pretty big relief not to be on a list now because I don't have that big weight over me that I'm always doing something wrong with my decisions."

Bell would feel more comfortable if his compensation claim could be settled in the same discreet fashion in which it was prepared and adds that it would have felt considerably easier to pursue if it was the AFL, and not his former club, that stood to foot the bill.

But Bell has chosen to detail his experience because he believes it can have a positive ending.

Upon learning the full detail of Bell's condition, Melbourne put him in touch with Duncan Ferguson, a Demons supporter and co-founder of cognitive assessment and training enterprise Elite Minds.

Bell has been using the company's computerised brain-training and rehabilitation programs for the past five months and last week, when he visited the same neuropsychologist that gave him a bleak early appraisal, his test scores—particularly related to memory, concentration and task-switching skills—were markedly improved.

But given the battering his brain took over so many years and the specialised medical diagnosis he now has to measure the damage that has been done, Bell wouldn't be so naive as to think a miracle like a quick fix exists.

The Age 31 March 2011

HEATH WAVE

Michael Gleeson

HEATH SHAW HAS THE BLOODLINE to be a good footballer—and to be stupendously loud. He runs true to his pedigree; even among the Shaws, he is regarded as loud, which is no small feat.

He is the quintessential kid at the back of the classroom. Easily bored and more easily distracted, he talks, fidgets and cracks jokes. He is boisterous and confident, but fortunately also funny and charming.

He has the irrepressible enthusiasm of someone with attention deficit disorder. That is unsurprising because that is what he has.

Diagnosed with ADD as a teenager, he took tablets to control the condition but stopped the medication when he joined the AFL as it remains on the competition's list of banned substances. He could seek an exemption, but the medication robs him of his appetite and he loses weight. He thus chooses steady body over steady mind.

"When I was taking it at school, I was down to about 64 kilos in year 11," Shaw says. "I would take two apples and two roll-ups to school and that was all I would eat for the day, so it makes it really hard.

"If I feel it coming on, I just sort of muck around and act out. Some days, I will be hypo and all over the place and then some days, I will be tired and relaxed. It's ups and downs but it is not a real problem. A few of the boys give me s—, saying, 'Take your tablets, mate.' Rhyce is the best for knowing how to deal with me. Mum and dad couldn't handle it."

This generation of Shaw brothers is four years apart in age but extremely close. They shared bunk beds—Rhyce on the bottom to avoid Heath kicking the top bunk—and until a month or so back, they shared a house.

"When I first moved out of home, I lived by myself for a while and Heath used to come over all the time and stay," Rhyce says. "And when he didn't have his tablets, he was just a muck-up—he couldn't sit still, he just used to keep talking and annoy the s— out of you. But when he had his tablets, he would clean my house from top to bottom. He wouldn't stop until everything was clean and everything was in the right order, like the cornflakes packet had to be facing a certain way, and he wouldn't talk to me for hours; he would just keep cleaning.

"I know it drives Shane Wakelin and Simon Prestigiacomo mad because they are the two guys that cop it the most from Heath. Wakes and Presty give it back—they have like a love-hate thing going on."

The family wasn't surprised when the ADD diagnosis came through.

"I was not really the golden child," Heath says. "Rhyce and Laine were the golden children—I was always in trouble. It was hard to be the golden child when you kept getting sent to your room.

"When I found out I had ADD in about year 9, I said, 'Mum, that's why I was always in trouble, you were picking on me and I have got a disease,'" he laughs.

"I think Rhyce was adopted—he looks nothing like us. My sister has olive skin and blonde hair, I have red hair and pale skin and Rhyce has black hair and dark skin, so I think we were all taken from our families when we were younger."

Not an academic type, father Ray admits he was surprised and impressed when, at high school, Heath began asking to be taken on a Saturday for extra study.

"We found out later he was on Saturday detentions. We just thought he was being enthusiastic for a change. He had heaps of them and because they were so regular, we didn't twig."

Self-deprecating, Heath Shaw laughs easily and often. He is still called Hughesy by teammates for his resemblance to Dave Hughes the comedian. He has a similar confidence.

The ADD means he is perfectly attuned for the frenzy of the modern game, but not the attendant meetings that consume days between games.

"I sometimes get a bit crazy around [coach] Mick [Malthouse] but he handles it well. I don't know if he realises I have ADD but he probably has a fair idea by now because I can be a bit hypo and a pain in the a—.

"You have got to pick your moments and tone it down in important meetings. A couple of times, I have been kicked by guys telling me to shut up because I am talking away when I shouldn't be. But it is a bit of fun."

He bought a Valiant Charger recently that he hopes to restore. It was an ambitious project, given that he admits to little mechanical knowledge, and thus far has managed only to pull the car apart and has little idea how to put it back together.

"I am not mechanically really any good, but I was really good at ripping everything out of it. I probably should go into demolition or something. I get a bit sidetracked."

Growing up a Shaw meant many things. Firstly, survival demands a confidence to fight your corner. Losing is unacceptable—particularly to your brother, father or uncle—and diving for a ball in Nan's backyard was a dangerous business.

Ray warned that Sunday cricket matches at his parents said much about all in the family. "The old man used to bury things in the backyard, so you would dive for a catch and Dad had buried a mattress for some reason, and you'd bounce. One day, someone tripped over behind the stumps, and the dog had died and Dad had buried it in the backyard. The soil is pretty hard in Reservoir, so Dad had buried the dog upside down and the bloody dog's paws were sticking up and they had come up out of the ground. There were no easy runs in backyard cricket."

Heath, a left-handed batsman and right-handed bowler, was capable, according to Ray, of playing cricket at a very high level. Sensing his young brother needed to be put in his place, Rhyce sorted Heath out at the nets.

"I came steaming in and hit him in the rib cage with a cricket ball, and he has thrown the bat at me a hundred miles an hour and walked back home with his pads and everything on, crying and cracking the s—s, and he wouldn't come back—I had to carry the rest of the gear home," Rhyce said.

Heath laughs that the matches prepared him for anything that could be said on the field: "We had some monster cricket matches. I am tipping there would have been a couple of worse things said than the Selwood situation."

The competitiveness of the younger Shaw to meet and beat his older brother has been a significant factor in developing the back flanker into a senior AFL player. Rhyce is renowned as one of the hardest workers at the club. Naturally, that means Heath must work harder.

This sibling rivalry boiled over in round three in an animated fight between the pair in the middle of the MCG against Richmond. It startled teammates and opponents, but not either Shaw boy.

Heath is not as quick as Rhyce, but is deceptively fast, despite a Shaw waddle. He won the Gavin Brown Trophy last year for the player best at tackling and other more incidental skills known as one-percenters. Former captain and premiership player Brown enthuses at the young defender's potential.

"He is almost the complete player, really," Brown says. "He is a beautiful kick; he reads the game as good as anyone. He is also a very good one-on-one player, which was the reason he got into the side in the first place—that and his kicking ability. He is getting better and better every year and not just incrementally but in big amounts."

After 32 games, Heath Shaw's greatest ambition is not to overtake his brother, father or uncle Tony in number of games played. His greatest ambition is to beat the least known of his Collingwood playing relatives, Neville. "I just want to get to 44 because my Uncle Neville played 43 and he always gives it to dad and Uncle Tony, saying, 'You played 146, you played 300 and whatever, but I played 43 good ones, so that is all that counts.'"

Perhaps, for the boy with ADD, it is about not trying to concentrate on too many things at once. Keeping it simple, for there is little doubting the desire to knock off big brother, dad and Uncle Tony. That is a life's work.

And he will certainly tell them about it.

The Age 25 April 2007

FACING UP TO LIFE'S REAL TESTS

Michael Gleeson

THE PHONE RANG. MICHAEL HURLEY checked the screen. It was his sister Brigid. It was 8am. On a Sunday. He ignored the call. She rang again. He ignored it. Third call. He'd better answer.

"She was a wreck. She was all over the place. She finally told me Xavier had passed away. I was speechless. It was tough," Hurley said.

Xavier was the four-month-old son of his older brother Dan. He had gone to sleep one night and simply not woken. Xavier died from Sudden Infant Death Syndrome mid last year. Michael was stunned, his close Irish-Catholic family shattered. Michael is the youngest of five children, his brother Daniel seven years older, and he looked up to him in the way a younger brother does. Dan had left home to try life in far north Queensland when Michael was in his late teens. The little brother sorely missed him.

"I got off the phone to Bridge and called dad and that was horrible. To hear your father crying is always tough. I went home and the family got together and it was a tough 24–48 hours and when I finally got up to Cairns to my brother, it was even harder with Dan and Kirsty [Dan's wife]. Particularly being my big brother and to see him so fragile," Michael said.

"Growing up, I always looked up to him, so it was pretty tough when he left and that made it even harder. And when he is so far away, you feel like you can't sort of help him at all. It [the death] just comes out of the blue—he just went to bed one night."

The Essendon Football Club gave Michael time off, he flew to Cairns to be with his brother and attend Xavier's funeral and flew back in time to play in the game against the Bulldogs.

"It was good to get out there and be among friends, but it was tough and there was a lot going on, a lot going through my mind. Once you are out there, it is a bit of a sanctuary and you can try to focus on one thing, but I struggled that day, I hardly got a kick," he said.

Hurley had been enduring what had already been a challenging 12 months. A young and enormously talented key position player at Essendon, his world had been on a steady and impressive trajectory when he got drunk at a *Footy Show* after-party and got in a fight with a taxi driver. That led to a heavy fine in court and a club suspension. Perhaps as painfully, it thrust his face onto the TV news bulletins and his name onto the pages of newspapers.

"It was a tough year. I missed the first few rounds through suspension and so it was a pretty big rollercoaster year, but I have learnt from that situation and moved on," he said.

Damian Hurley, Michael's father, said the past 18 months had forced his son to mature quickly. Before Xavier's death and his legal trouble, Michael's mother, Andrea, had been diagnosed with breast cancer.

"It's not something we go into too much, but in terms of the impact over a period of time it was another thing that was happening and then Michael got himself in strife," Damian said. Mrs Hurley has completed her treatment and is now in remission.

"Certainly no question it was difficult for Michael [the taxi driver fight] but also no question Michael did the wrong thing and he has learnt a lesson. It was certainly out of character and it was almost unbelievable from where we stood that Michael would do something like that and so it was a very difficult lesson, but a lesson to be learnt about responsible use of alcohol.

"I suppose Mick has had to grow up quickly with a number of things that happened in a short period of time, to see his mother's life threatened and with Dan. He was a real model to Mick. He looked up to him and he admired the way he played football and he was always around him. We only lived down the road from the football oval so Mick would always be down there with Dan. He was a mentor and role model to him, so to see the pain his brother was in was very difficult for him.

"Xavier dying was just so hard for everyone, but particularly the parents of course. SIDS is so sudden and it is not just the death but the impact, it is such an enormous trauma. It's inexplicable and just so counter-intuitive that young people die like that. With elderly people there is a sense of natural progression that this happens when you get older, but with a young child it is just inexplicable. Emotionally it turns you upside down. Certainly for the parents it is just traumatic, there are so many hopes and expectations and the promise and potential associated with the birth of a child and that is just gone."

It is trite in these circumstances to say the incidents put the importance of football in perspective, but it did give Michael a greater perspective on his family.

"It was a tight family but I think the situation with Dan and Xavier made us even tighter," Damian said.

Michael Hurley has urged people to donate to the Red Nose Day appeal to raise money for SIDS research by buying a red nose or calling 1300 1 Red Nose to donate.

"It is a big thing for me and I am pleased Essendon has got behind the cause . . . Every child is different and every case of SIDS is different, so whatever research we can do into it the better."

The Age 24 June 2011

A DOG'S NEW LIFE

Emma Quayle

On November 7, Sam Reid turned 20. He began his third pre-season on the couch, after intricate, painful groin surgery, but he wanted this to be his best summer yet and felt certain that it could be. He had played four games for the Western Bulldogs in 2009—only just missing out on the finals side—and he desperately wanted to play more of them. He craved a place in this year's senior team. He knew what the coaches wanted him to be—hard and tough, determined and diligent—and he knew that once he had his spot, he wouldn't give it up for anyone. "I wanted this pre-season to be massive," he said. "I wanted it to be huge."

Something wasn't right, though. Reid had his operation on the Monday before the grand final, and in the five weeks after that, he lost about eight kilograms. "Geez," his dad greeted him, when he went home to Echuca on his birthday weekend. "Where have you gone?" Reid's mouth was dry and he was drinking constantly, six litres of juice in a day. He was going to the toilet 20 times a day, and waking five or six times a night. On the Monday after his birthday, he weighed 79 kilograms and that worried him—he hadn't been under 80 in ages. A few days later, he got on the scales again. This time he weighed 74 kilograms, the same weight he'd been when he arrived at the club almost two years earlier.

"You don't look too good," Andrew McKenzie, the club's medical services manager, told him. Reid didn't feel sick, but he didn't feel particularly good, either. What the hell was going on? He saw the club doctor, he had his blood tested. Watching TV that weekend, his eyes went blurry and he couldn't read the words scrolling across the bottom of the screen. "I got a bit panicky then," he said this week, "but I could still find reasons for everything." He'd had surgery, so he'd lost a bit of weight. He was thirsty, so he was drinking heaps, so he was going to the toilet more. "I didn't feel weak and I still had energy, but I was losing so much weight and I was just starting to wonder about it, wonder what was going on," Reid said. "My brother realised it before I did. He said, 'You realise you've got weight loss, blurred vision and you're going to the toilet all the time.' He said, 'You know those are the three main points of diabetes.'"

He was right. At the club on Monday morning, Reid was sent straight back to see the doctor. Arriving at work that morning, Jake Landsberger had learnt that the midfielder's blood sugar levels were 40, dangerously high. A normal reading is about six—in another 24 hours Reid would have been unconscious, and if his levels weren't reduced in the next six to eight hours, he would have become very sick. "You have type 1 diabetes," Landsberger told him. Reid was shocked, had no idea what to say, and then wondered if he could still play football.

Assured that he could, he went straight to the diabetes centre at the Western Hospital. Ben Griffin, the club's rehabilitation coordinator, went along to keep him company, convinced this kid was going to break down or ask "why me?" at some point. At the hospital, Reid met a diabetes educator and for the next four hours had a crash course on his own new life. She told him what was happening to his body—that his pancreas wasn't producing insulin and that, instead of being converted into energy, the sugar he consumed was building up in his bloodstream. She taught him how to prick his finger for blood, how to test his blood sugar levels using a small machine, how to tell how much insulin he needed and how to inject it into his stomach.

She told him he would have "hypos"—that he would become hypoglycaemic when his blood sugar dipped too low—and that he would learn how they came on and what he needed to do to get his levels back to where they should be. "Nah . . . I don't want to do it . . ." Reid had grimaced, holding the needle away from him on his first try, but by the time he left he could do it on his own and Griffin still hadn't seen him look upset or flustered, or anything but attentive. "I was feeling staggered by it all," he said, "but Sam just sat and listened."

Reid rang his dad, Jeff, who went silent. He told his girlfriend, Elissa, and housemates Jarrad Grant and Jarrad Boumann. He went home, turned on the shower and sat under it for an hour, thinking. "My head was ready to explode," he said, "because I'd listened to so much stuff. I just sat there and wondered what it was going to be like." Then he went to bed, slept, woke up, pricked his finger, tested his blood, jabbed himself with his insulin pen and ate breakfast.

The club gave him two weeks off, to get used to everything and reset his body. He sat down with Louise Falzon, the club's dietitian, to figure out what he should and couldn't eat. He met James Gomes, his endocrinologist; the next step is for Falzon and Gomes to meet and map out a compromised diet for him, bearing in mind his needs as a footballer and his medical requirements.

"I'm coming to see the specialist with you," Jeff Reid told his son. "No you're not!" Sam said, but he rang his dad before going in, to find out what questions he wanted him to ask. "I knew how worried dad was, and I didn't want him to be. I didn't want to show him or Elissa or my brother that I was stressing out about it," he said. "That would have made them feel worse, and I didn't want them feeling like that. I wanted to do it on my own, rather than have people babying me and looking after me. I knew it was something I'd have to do for the rest of my life and I knew I just had to get used to it."

There was a lot to get used to. Reid had to work out how much insulin he needed before breakfast, lunch and dinner and remember to take his fourth dose before bed. If he was eating pasta, he had to inject a different amount than if he were eating steak. The first time he went to the supermarket with Elissa, they walked down the aisles looking at everything he used to buy, thinking "can't have that . . . can't have that". He tested his blood before and after eating certain things, experimenting, to see the effect. The first time he had a "hypo" was at home one night. The air-conditioner was on, but Reid was sweating. He felt irritable, hungry, sapped of energy and then his hands started shaking. Elissa got him some ice-cream, and a few minutes later he was fine.

Another night, home alone, he woke up shaking, and that was more frightening. "That one was a pretty big scare," Reid said. "My hands kept shaking and I was trying to do stuff, trying to eat and do the test and I kept dropping things and getting really frustrated. It was two o'clock in the morning, I was trying to butter toast and I was thinking, 'What is going on here?'

"I sort of like to do things by myself, and I was getting pretty annoyed for the first few weeks when people kept trying to help me. I'd just snap really quickly and it was weird. I'd get angry at the smallest little things, and it didn't feel like me."

Back at the club, Reid worried that people would look at him differently, like he wasn't the same person, and at first they did. "They weren't joking around with me, everyone was being so serious, and that was exactly what I didn't want to happen," he said. "For the first few days at the club, I didn't want to be there. I hadn't been there for two weeks, and I just wanted to leave again straightaway. It was weird even walking in, because I knew people were going to ask questions. I knew they'd only be worried, but I just didn't want it."

Before too long, his tension eased. The players were all filled in, told that if Reid seemed a little woozy or disoriented, like he was drunk, to check that he was OK or if he needed sugar. They were shocked—the leadership group looked at Landsberger with what-are-we-meant-to-do? faces—as did all the trainers, but they figured out how to cope.

"I think once everyone saw me back at training and saw that I was normal, they felt all right about it," Reid said. "When I'm on the bike now, they come past joking, saying, 'You're riding crooked, you're all wonky, you must need sugar.'" Every trainer at the club carries lollies with them, and every person at the club knows that if Reid sprints off the track midway through a session, he's feeling like his blood sugars are low and will be inside testing them. Everyone at Williamstown, the Bulldogs' VFL affiliate club, will be filled in next. "It's been an education for every single person at the footy club," said Landsberger. The whole club's along for the ride, football manager James Fantasia promised Jeff Reid over the phone, further easing his worried mind.

Reid is learning as he goes. During one session he felt light-headed, went inside and found that his levels were at three. Eat a few jelly beans, Landsberger told him over the phone, and ring me back. Less than two minutes later, he was back up to nine, and able to head straight off for a swimming session. "I remember saying, 'Sam, this is one of the best things that could have happened. You've had a hypo, you've eaten a few jelly beans, you've gone from dangerously low to nine in a few minutes and you haven't missed a beat,'" said the doctor.

"It was good for him to see how quickly he could get back to normal. It was a big moment for him, and he's just been brilliant." His specialist thinks so, too—his only complaint is that Reid hasn't been calling him enough—and so does his dad.

Jeff Reid freaked out the first time he saw Sam inject himself, but Sam told him to get used to it. "He said, 'Dad, if I don't do this you'll have one son instead of two,' and that made me stop and think. I was in panic mode, I didn't know how he was going to accept things, but he's just grabbed hold of it. I've done nothing, he's got me and his brother through it, and I'm so proud of him. The first thing he said to me was, 'I reckon I could help kids out with this,' and what do you say to that? I just reckon it's great."

Griffin has almost stopped looking for cracks, too. "I've been waiting, looking at him thinking he's going to crumble any day now, but he hasn't," he said. "I'm not sure he will. He's just such a resilient kid. Not many players at our club would have coped the way Sam's coped with this."

There will be hiccups. Reid will have hypos and get his insulin dosages wrong from time to time. His diet and dosages will need to change once he starts full training in two weeks—remember that major groin surgery?—and they'll need to be altered again when he starts playing games and during the off-season, depending on how much energy he's burning. If he gets a throat infection, he'll need to be on antibiotics longer than most people. If he gets a cut, it will take longer than usual to heal.

He'll have to test his blood before and after games, in the rooms and even on the bench. He'll need to be absolutely vigilant, every day, for the rest of his life, and he knows that. When he was diagnosed, Reid was told to carry some sort of identification on him all the time, in case he has a hypo while out somewhere on his own. On Christmas Eve, he had the words "Type 1 Diabetes" tattooed on the inside of his right wrist. Not long after, he had a dartboard tattooed on his stomach. "Why would you do that? You've got that forever," wondered Will Minson when he saw it. "Yeah, but, Will,' Reid said, "I've got diabetes forever."

"I had to lighten the mood somehow," Reid smiled. "People were being too serious."

He has to pay attention to tiny details, make sure he has enough strips to test his blood, take his little equipment bag everywhere, write his levels into his booklet four times a day. When the two Jarrads come home with pizza and chocolate, you won't be able to eat it, Landsberger told him, and that's going to be pretty tough. "I know," Reid nodded, "that's fine. I know it's a massive thing, but I think it might actually help me with my football," he said. "It's going to make me into a more organised person. I'm going to need to know every little thing about my body."

At the start of November, Reid was a 20-year-old, five-game AFL player. He was highly regarded by his coaches, he wanted to have a big pre-season, he wanted to find a spot in the Western Bulldogs' team and he wanted to stay there. He still plans to do all those things. "I know this is a pretty big thing that's happened. It's full on, but from what I've learnt in the last two months, I can still be the same person I always was and do the same things I always wanted to do," he said. "This is here for my whole life, but it's not going to ruin my life. It's something I'm always going to have to deal with, but that's the only thing I have to do, deal with it. I'm going to cope with it and I'm going to be fine."

Diabetics in the AFL

Dale Weightman played 274 games for Richmond between 1978 and 1983, captained the club, played for Victoria 20 times, won two best-and-fairests and made three All-Australian sides.

Nathan Bassett was diagnosed with type 1 diabetes while on the Melbourne rookie list in 1997. He was traded back to Adelaide, where he played 210 games from 1998 to 2008, making the All-Australian team in 2006.

TYPE 1 DIABETES

What is it?

Type 1 diabetes occurs when the pancreas produces little or no insulin and is most commonly diagnosed from early childhood to the late 30s. Although the causes are not entirely known, type 1 diabetes is believed to be caused by the immune system mistakenly turning on itself, destroying beta cells within the pancreas and removing the body's ability to produce insulin. Insulin allows the body to process sugar to create energy. Without insulin, the body literally starves as it cannot process food.

What is the treatment?

People with type 1 diabetes must test their blood sugar by pricking a finger at least four times a day and inject insulin several times daily or receive a constant supply of insulin through a pump. The goal is to keep blood glucose levels as close to the normal range as possible. They must be constantly prepared for potential hypoglycaemic (low blood sugar) and hyperglycaemic (high blood sugar) reactions as both can be life threatening.

What are the long-term complications?

Eyesight, the kidneys, heart and circulatory system can all be affected.

Information taken from the Juvenile Diabetes Research Foundation (www.jdrf.org.au). Western Bulldogs director Susan Alberti, whose daughter died after complications arising from type 1 diabetes, is the driving force of the world-renowned foundation.

The Sunday Age 24 January 2010

THE PACT

ST KILDA v GEELONG

Martin Blake

"We quite often talk about our plans. We've said to each other that we're going to take the club somewhere and be successful. We often discuss it at home."

Nick Riewoldt The Age 30 July 2003

St Kilda's current captain and inspiration, Nick Riewoldt, was sharing a house with his big-name teammate Justin Koschitzke in Brighton when he spoke these words in an interview. Leigh Montagna, not such a public figure then but an All-Australian now, also lived in the house, and they are the words that encapsulate everything that has taken St Kilda to the cusp of a premiership six years on. They are the words that make it clear that The Pact is real.

It may not be formalised in the written word. But the stars of St Kilda's grand final team have all agreed to accept lower financial inducements from the club to stay and grab the ultimate success. Which today is all about, of course.

Over the years 1998 to 2002 St Kilda pieced together the core of its current team as it floundered on the field, employing the national draft to good effect. But aside from the fact that they brought the likes of Riewoldt, Koschitzke, Lenny Hayes, Luke Ball, Nick Dal Santo and Brendon Goddard to Moorabbin in that period, it is the club's ability to keep them that is significant.

St Kilda has a history of losing its best players to other clubs, dating back to the start of the last century. If you ask people who know about the club's history why St Kilda has been so spectacularly unsuccessful, it is this fact that they will mention first. It defines St Kilda as a poorly run club over its full history.

Roy Cazaly, the man with the famous leap, was a St Kilda player who defected to South Melbourne in 1921. Dave McNamara, one of the greatest kicks the game has seen, fell out with St Kilda and went playing in the VFA. Carl Ditterich quit and went to Melbourne, came back and then left again. Ian Stewart had won two Brownlow Medals when he was traded to Richmond for a fading Billy Barrott in 1970, and the Saints watched as Stewart won a third medal. Just as they had to look on as Tony Lockett kicked truckloads of goals for Sydney, and Barry Hall lifted a premiership cup in Swans' colours in 2005.

Quietly, that history is changing, regardless of the result today.

We want to follow the Brisbane trend and if it was good enough for the other guys to do it, it was good enough for me. I love the boys and love the environment we have created here and I am pleased I was here when we were on the bottom of the ladder.

Justin Koschitzke, signing a new deal with St Kilda, 2005

Nick Riewoldt and Justin Koschitzke were recruited with the No. 1 and No. 2 picks in the 2000 national draft, the former from Queensland and the latter from country NSW. It followed that they moved in together to board in a house with a benevolent St Kilda supporter in Brighton.

A year or so later, they moved into their own rented accommodation with Montagna. Nowadays, they live separately, but their close bond remains. When Koschitzke was asked this week what he felt about Riewoldt's current form, he said: "I'll certainly be telling my friends I played with Nick Riewoldt."

St Kilda had finished last under Tim Watson's coaching in 2000, giving it a priority pick. Under a combination of Malcolm Blight and Grant Thomas in 2001, the Saints were 15th, giving them the second pick until Carlton was banned from the draft for salary cap infractions. The prized top pick handed them Brendon Goddard.

The following year they would take Nick Dal Santo from Bendigo with the No. 13 pick, and a less conspicuous success, Xavier Clarke, with the No. 5 selection. Clarke probably would have been in the team today had he not ripped a knee open this season, requiring surgery. His brother Raphael will be.

In 1998 St Kilda had taken Lenny Hayes, a Sydney boy, from under the Swans' noses with a No. 11 pick (the Swans had three picks before that but ignored Hayes). Instructively, Hayes, Riewoldt and Dal Santo were the best three players in the victory over Western Bulldogs last weekend. All three were named All-Australians this year, as well as Goddard.

The early picks were widely viewed as carte blanche to a premiership, a notion scotched when St Kilda was eliminated in preliminary finals under Thomas in 2004 and 2005. It merely reinforced the players' idea that they had to stay and finish what they had started.

Riewoldt had first re-signed in 2002; he has this year committed to the end of 2013. "We can build the club, shape what it's going to become," he said in 2003. "Other young guys might get drafted to clubs and play finals straight away but we're going to feel a sense of ownership when we get there. In a sense, we will own what we create."

It was through that period under Thomas's coaching that The Pact was done. "There's no doubt that core group made a commitment to each other to stay the journey," said one source who would not be named this week. "It's an unwritten thing that's between them."

Thomas would not comment this week, saying he preferred to leave the limelight to the current coaches and players. But former player Austinn Jones, who retired in 2005, was aware of The Pact. "It was about a year after I left," he said. "I think you can throw [Luke] Ball and Dal Santo into that group who just made a commitment to stay with the club. If it's true, then it's a credit to those guys because obviously there's money available. You don't see it happening at clubs who are struggling."

Former club chief executive Brian Waldron remembers a feeling that St Kilda was setting up for something special in the early 2000s. "There was a philosophical belief that they were on a journey with Grant in charge," said Waldron. "For unfortunate reasons, they weren't able to sustain it with that group, and it's evolved now to be with another group of senior players that Ross has brought in.

"It's not like there's a group saying: 'Hey, we're the Magnificent Seven.' But there was always a belief amongst them that there was a job to do and they wanted to complete that job."

I want to stand for something. I'm a loyal person and I think at the end of my career it will be great to look back and know that I'm a St Kilda person for life.

Nick Riewoldt, 2009, signing a four-year deal

What Thomas had done was convince the players to invest in their future. One by one, they re-signed with St Kilda when bigger money was on offer elsewhere, even after his acrimonious departure at the end of 2006. As they run on to the ground today, Riewoldt, Koschitzke, Hayes and Dal Santo are all locked up on contracts. Only Ball is out at season's end. Thus far, no one has broken the code.

Australian footballers are loyal by nature; they don't need that much cajoling to stay when they know that a club is on the cusp of something big. Even after Thomas's sacking by his once-close mate Rod Butterss, when the club teetered through an unstable period, the players held firm. The Butterss regime was tossed out by a group headed by trucking magnate Greg Westaway in 2007, and Ross Lyon arrived with a new game plan and philosophy. Still they stuck.

As recently as midway through 2008, when the Saints stumbled to 5–7 after a round-12 loss to Sydney, there was a crisis meeting of sorts. What came out of it was an embracement of the Lyon way; defensive intensity and accountability and team-first ethos. This was the time that Dal Santo and Stephen Milne were dropped for reasons that have never been specified. It was a time when the club could have disintegrated, but it did not. Dal Santo has since referred to it as a "wake-up call" for both he and Milne.

"We made some decisions as a group halfway through last year and from there, we've really started to work at what we want and the pre-season's really helped this year," said Montagna. "[It's] not so much them getting dropped. We met as a group and spoke about what we needed to do to become a great side. It was moreso as a group and what we wanted to achieve, and from that, came some consequences for players."

For St Kilda, it is the new way.

The Age 26 September 2009

OUT OF AFRICA, INTO THE TEAM

Peter Hanlon

WHEN MAJAK DAW FIRST PLAYED Australian football, the friends from school who had encouraged him to have a go made the first team, while he was shunted down the grades. "I thought to myself, 'I'm pathetic, I'm not good at this.'"

What worried him most was the prospect of walking this foreign path alone. "I thought I wasn't going to make any friends in the under-14Ds, but I didn't know how football works—you make friends wherever you go, wherever you play footy."

Just four years on from those first, tentative steps in the game, Majak Daw finds himself in the TAC Cup goal square, playing full-forward for the Western Jets. He is realistic about his prospects—"It hasn't come across to me that, 'I'll get drafted!' or anything like that. I'll just keep playing footy, and when the opportunity comes, take it."

Yet his progression shows what is possible, and what is surely on the horizon—the appearance of an African name on an AFL list. And then another, and another, and another.

"Five to 10 years there will be an African at the MCG," says Ahmed Dini, a 22-year-old Somalian refugee working as a youth advocate in the Flemington area.

"Inside the next five years," says Kim Kershaw, formerly of Richmond and Hawthorn, latterly coach of Flemington juniors, and of Team Africa in last year's International Cup. "These kids are very, very talented."

"Three, four years," says Daw. He is content that it might not be him, but knows many more will follow—kids who have played the game longer, learnt more, and are ready to shine.

Nick Hatzoglou endorses the shorter time-frame, and it's a day the head of the AFL's multicultural arm will rejoice in. Almost as much as April 13, 2005, when he started in a pioneering post at league headquarters. The son of Greek migrants, his pride at taking the game he grew up loving to a vast new audience is immense.

Football hasn't always been so ready to embrace, but like Daw's fledgling career, things are improving fast. Says the league's game development manager, David Matthews: "The next major investment the AFL will make in development will be in multiculturalism."

Six clubs now employ multicultural officers and, last year, 1300 AFL staffers and volunteers undertook training to increase cross-cultural awareness, and leave them better armed to interact, extend a welcoming hand, and use football as a means of helping newcomers to belong. People like Majak Daw, the face of footy in fast forward.

Daw was born 18 years ago in the Sudanese capital of Khartoum, the third of what has become nine children. The family moved to Egypt for three years, and arrived in Melbourne in 2003. His upbringing was different to anything his new friends could know, "but I had a better childhood than others, those who experienced war", he says.

His native tongue is Majak, like his name, but he had little English. He attended a language centre, and one day a tutor and his wife took him to the MCG as Collingwood played Fremantle. "So many people going to watch a game of footy . . ." he recalls. A fire was lit.

From Taylors Lakes to Keilor Downs, and eventually Werribee, where the Daws' house was across the street from Wyndamvale footy ground. He wandered over one pre-season evening, remembers standing by himself for a short time, "then the coaches approached me and introduced me to all the other guys. They welcomed me very well."

One new teammate was Joey Halloran, who can still see Majak's big hands trying to get hold of the ball. "To tell you the truth, he was hopeless."

Now, Joey drives Majak to Western Jets training, and they are part of a group so tight that Joey changed schools to McKillop College this year to be with his mates.

Halloran sees his friend as a pioneer. "At Wyndamvale, there are a lot of Sudanese kids now, and they all look up to him like he's some sort of superstar. Probably in every Wyndamvale (junior) team, you'll see one, and they all want to be like Majak."

The AFL stresses that the "talent outcomes" will be a by-product of the groundwork Hatzoglou's team is putting in, but the major focus is on football helping refugee and migrant families to assimilate. "We've got a really good demonstrated track record of using the game as a vehicle for broader social outcomes—education, self-esteem, building communities," says Matthews. It's about investing in the whole village, Hatzoglou says, not just the child.

Daw has seen what Bachar Houli's appearance in red and black has done for the Lebanese and broader Muslim community, and sensed the excitement in Nick Naitanui's debut for West Coast last weekend. He knows people are looking for a trailblazer, feels the weight on his broadening shoulders, but is bearing it well.

"The role model thing, everyone says I have it . . . I just want to be like other footballers, Bachar Houli and the like—go out there and encourage others to join the sport."

Ahmed Dini has watched the change come like a wave. At Debney Park, below the Racecourse Road flats, footballs spin through the air where a blink ago there was only soccer. "There's a huge shift from soccer to football. In Flemington, there's not a soccer team any more. Young men are playing football, all for established clubs—juniors at Flemington, seniors at Glen Eira, Moonee Valley, Maribyrnong Park.

"I'm surprised, as a young person who grew up with soccer. But the best way we can connect easily is to take part in what Australians love."

The Glen Eira experience has been telling. Dini relays the story of Scott Diamond, a teacher at Debney Park Secondary College, who a couple of years ago asked some students if they wanted to play football. Now they drive across town to train and play, and Glen Eira's senior team boasts several Africans.

Kershaw coached them as juniors, then at the International Cup, and says Glen Eira is doing "amazing things with African men". Men like best-and-fairest runner-up Mahad "The General" Farah. And Said Elmi, who Ahmed Dini likens to Leon Davis. And the brothers Kershaw says were known simply as B01 and B02. "Great footballers."

Kevin Ryan, the sports master at McKillop College, agrees Daw's progression has been jaw-dropping—from barely making the team in year 9, to winning the school association's award last year in year 11. At 195 centimetres (and growing), and 90 kilograms, he has no trouble meeting modern football's premium on athleticism.

What he wants is footy smarts, a knack for knowing what to do without thinking. "Every centre bounce he gets the tap, he can take a mark, but there are times he hesitates, just because he hasn't got that really long football background," Ryan says.

Daw doesn't hesitate to agree. "Reading the game, how it unfolds . . . I haven't had the experience of playing from under-9s to under-18s."

Yet those African kids who have joined Wyndamvale will have. Kids like Majak's little brother, who is playing his first game of football this weekend. "I've sort of brainwashed him," Majak says.

His father and older brothers once ribbed him: "Why are you playing this sport? Why don't you play soccer like the rest of us?" He replied that he was just trying something new.

He visits the gym with Halloran three times a week and, as a second-year Jet, is revelling in doing more around the ground, changing in the ruck, feeling his skills and touch mature. "I'm a more important player for the team now."

Ryan says it would be a huge gamble for an AFL club to draft him, but a rookie-list spot might appeal to a team that likes a flutter. Whatever, football is only part of the equation. From Ahmed Dini, to Kim Kershaw, to the women in the McKillop College front office, there is a resounding theme—this is a young man to be proud of.

Football has played its part. "It's helped me to fit into Australian society," Daw says, noting that the Sudanese kids who play soccer tend to stick to their own. "I'm one of the Sudanese who interact with other Australians."

Joey Halloran says the relationship works both ways; like all mates, they have learned much from each other. "He used to be just an African kid who played footy, now he really fits in. Footy hasn't got everything to do with it, but it's helped."

FROM A FOREIGN FIELD

While the AFL/VFL has long boasted players from diverse ethnic backgrounds, some have become emblematic of football's ability to speak all languages.

Players such as Alex Jesaulenko (Ukrainian heritage), Jim Stynes (Irish), Serge Silvagni (Italian) and Peter Bell (South Korean) have shown that

Australia's immigrant history can also be reflected on the footy field. And while the AFL has yet to see a Vietnamese player make an impact at AFL senior level, more recently Essendon's Bachar Houli has sparked greater interest from the Lebanese community as the AFL's first "devout" Muslim player.

The Sunday Age 21 June 2009

I'M PROUD OF HER: DAD'S TRIBUTE TO BABY LUELLA

Michael Cowley

JARRAD MCVEIGH LEANS FORWARD ON the couch, offering his phone for shared viewing. As he flicks through the photos of his daughter, Luella, you can hear the pride in his voice—punctuated by a gulp of emotion—and see the love painted across his face as his fingertip scrolls from one picture to the next.

Every father's photos are special, but these, and the accompanying memories—many so very painful—are all the Sydney Swans AFL co-captain and his wife, Clementine, have of their baby girl.

Last August, after a brave, month-long battle with a heart condition, Luella died.

McVeigh admits his emotions travel to both ends of the spectrum looking at pictures of his daughter's month-long life. It was a similar story as he spoke for the first time about Luella, and also revealed that Clementine is pregnant again. Their baby, a girl, is due in July.

"Sometimes I just find myself just looking at them and maybe cry, or I'm happy," he says of the photos. "I think after every game I played at the end of the year, I'd go and sit in the toilet and just look at my phone. Yeah, it can be both happy and sad.

"It does make me feel better talking about it, because I'm proud of her. She's touched a lot of people here at the club, a lot of people who never met her, even though she was here for a short time, which made us proud. It's hard, but it does help.

"There was a little spirit in her that I think everyone who saw her could feel. She was a very strong little girl. She went through a lot of trauma with four operations, and to keep fighting back?"

The first most people knew of McVeigh and Clementine's tragedy came on Saturday, August 27, last year, three days after Luella's death.

Wearing black armbands, the Swans stunned Geelong in the upset of the season, ending the Cats' 29-game winning streak at their home ground, Skilled Stadium.

The emotion of the moment was lost on no one and personified by the sight of McVeigh's close friend and co-captain Adam Goodes in tears after the game.

"Yeah, we watched that game," McVeigh says. "We sat down and watched it.

"I think that's the first game Clementine has watched fully. That [win] put a smile on our faces."

The club allowed McVeigh to decide when he would return to football, and he chose to get back on to the park the following week. He was among the Swans' best in their remaining games of the 2011 season.

When McVeigh and Clementine went for the three-month scan in January last year, their excitement was swallowed by anxiety when it was discovered their first baby had fluid around her heart. It meant a trip to Westmead every fortnight for scans and, while doctors knew the baby would require an operation, they wouldn't know exactly what it would entail until after the birth.

"From January to July, that was the hardest part—not knowing what the actual issue was; can it be fixed? what's going to happen? going out to Westmead every other week; stressing the whole way out there; not sure what today is going to bring," McVeigh says.

"The whole pregnancy went really well. We didn't have any complications with anything else, which we thought was weird. We stayed positive the whole time, although sometimes you would break down. But Clementine had a natural birth and they had said she mightn't be able to, she [Luella] was a good size, they said she would have to be on a number of drugs straight after to keep her alive, but they didn't need to do that, so we were quite positive.

"One of the hardest parts for Clementine was as soon as Luella was born, she only got to hold her—every mother wants to hold their baby—for about two minutes before they took her away to put her into an ICU."

The McVeighs moved into a flat across the road from the hospital, and would spend every moment they could with their daughter. McVeigh would drive to the city for the main training session each week but admits now it was "just a blur".

"I'd still be thinking about her, I was fairly useless at training, but I just tried to do something," McVeigh says. "There was only so many hours you can sit beside a bed before you go crazy. You want to spend 24 hours a day there but we knew it was going to be a long process, so we had to stay strong for each other and sometimes did different shifts.

"I spoke to Horse [Swans coach John Longmire] throughout the year. The team [apart from close friends such as Goodes and Jude Bolton] didn't know anything really. Horse was great and gave me a lot of time off and I could always speak to him openly and there were a few tears, but he understood, he's got children and everything else comes second."

Countless heart and brain scans were carried out in the first few days of Luella's life. Doctors found the left side of her heart was half the size of the right and scheduled an operation.

"We walked her to the surgery area, and at this point it was quite hard for her to open her eyes a lot of the time because she was on a lot of drugs and newborn and, just before she went in, she opened her eyes to us, just to say, 'I'll be all right.' The operation was meant to be from 8am, four to five hours, and they gave us a pager to let us know when to come back.

"The hours passed and we didn't get a call on our pager. It was the worst day ever. Every thought goes through your head: 'Is no news good news, is it bad news?' We walked over there and waited, and the surgeons came out at 6pm. The first operation was a great success but, as they were closing her up, they found her circulation was all back to front and they had to perform a second operation and they said she was a minute by minute thing to dying. Slowly that got to hour by hour, then they moved her into the ICU, where we could go and see her, but they had six or seven doctors beside her 24 hours a day. Her chest was still open at this point and, the first time I saw her, from how she was beforehand, I actually couldn't look. Seeing her chest open and the heart beating, just with a bandage over it, it was just too hard for me at first.

"She had so much fluid through her body from the operation, that's why they couldn't close her chest because that would mean too much pressure on the heart, and she wouldn't survive. They gave her drugs and it was up to her to get rid of the fluid, and we ended up massaging her for up to 10 hours a day trying to get it out—myself, Clementine, her mum, my mum, Clementine's sister, all rubbing her, and she seemed to respond well to that, and this went on for a whole month."

Doctors would try twice more to close her chest but couldn't, and Luella's condition deteriorated.

"We didn't know at that point [that the end was near] but I think they did. We were trying to stay positive and they closed it a bit and then we found out her right lung was half the size of the left, and that was why she couldn't get the fluid out."

The trauma of multiple operations had left Luella with severe brain damage and, after almost a month, despite trying numerous drugs, no fluid was coming out. The doctors told the McVeighs Luella would tell them when she couldn't take any more, "and it came to a point where there was nothing anyone could do". The hospital gave them one last night together as a family.

"They put us in a room with her on the Tuesday night and gave us a double bed. They took as many of the wires and stuff off her as they could, for us to be able to hold her and cuddle her, and that was the first time we bathed her that night. She really liked the water. She opened her eyes, she was really receptive to us and our voices, which they said doesn't happen a lot, but she would open her eyes and stare at us. We got to spend a night with her, then the next day that was it—then the whole world changes.

"It was us as a little family holding her, before she passed away. She opened her eyes to us, and then looked at us, before she went away, which is something we can hold with us for a long time," McVeigh says, surrendering to his emotions as his voice breaks and eyes well with tears.

Adam Goodes was among a small group of the couple's friends who visited Luella that day.

"We went out and saw Luella—it may have been 12 hours before she passed—and we all said our goodbyes," Goodes says. "It was quite a sombre drive back from Westmead to the eastern suburbs, and then the next couple of days you are just shaking your head saying how the hell does this happen to two fantastic people and you just ask so many questions."

That was August 24, and McVeigh needed to get through a few more weeks of football before the season was over. Once it was, the couple needed to get away, and planned a two-month trip to Europe and America. For McVeigh, football had provided a brief respite in that trying time, but Clementine didn't have "that bit of a release".

"Both our families and our friends were always there to support us. We were never really alone at any point for two months after, which was good for us. But when we were, it kind of hit you again and you would go up to bed, and your mind goes crazy. To get away from everything, to spend time together and heal together, was very important for us."

The couple asked themselves a range of questions, but sat down and decided there was nothing to be gained by such thoughts.

"There was nothing more we could have tried or done to make the outcome better, and we can sleep at night knowing we tried everything. We went through a stage saying things happen for a reason, but I thought I don't really like saying that because why? What's the reason why she has been taken away?"

About a month after Luella died, Clementine said to McVeigh that as soon as she was ready, she would like to try again. "You can either sit back and be depressed and not want to move forward, but we're the type of people who didn't want to do that. We went overseas and to fall pregnant while we were in Italy was a really special moment for us."

He admits it's been good to get back into the routine of football again, although he is "very very nervous" when they go for scans. Each has been positive. "It's good to try and get back into normal life, and prepare for another baby, and we can put all our effort into that and give her a good life."

"But it doesn't stop. Everything we do, we still think about Luella every day. We won't forget her. She will still be a part of us and part of our family.

"Because it was always there in the back of your mind what if this doesn't turn out good [that] we treasured every moment, and spent as much time as we could with her, and did whatever we could to help her.

"Among the sadness, we do have some good memories. Just when she looked at us. They kept telling us she hasn't woken up much, but as soon as we would go in there she would somehow wake up—just that look, and how she would squeeze our hands all the time, that was the best."

A new life begins amid flood chaos. Ask Jarrad McVeigh about the day he and Clementine discovered they were having another baby, and his eyes roll, the head shakes, and he simply says: "What a day!"

It was always going to be emotional, coming just two months after their daughter Luella had died, but neither expected what they got in Italy last October.

"We were in Cinque Terre. We woke up, it was pouring rain and, after taking four or five pregnancy tests, we found out," Jarrad recalls. "It was a bit sad as well. We were upset but happy, and asked ourselves if we were doing the right thing. 'We're not forgetting her [Luella]. Are we forgetting her?' But we realised it wasn't about that."

The couple thought they would go for a walk along some of the cliff-side trails for which the area is so famous but the torrential rain cruelled the plan.

"It turned out to be the Monterosso floods, where whole villages got washed away and around 10 people died, and we were in the eye of the storm, and would end up stuck there with no food and water for four days," McVeigh says.

Soon their hotel, on the top of a cliff, was taking on water and the footy star says he thought, "Geez we're in a bit of trouble here with landslides and those things." The couple's hosts were not so worried. "The Italians were like, 'It will be right.'"

McVeigh says he and a fellow Australian tourist spent six or seven hours brushing water out of their hotel. He started to worry about how he and Clementine would escape.

"It's one way in, one way out, and there were cars washed out into the ocean. We had parked a kilometre up the road so we didn't know if our car was still there. Three days later we got to our car and it was under mud—it was gone."

Some locals told the tourists that a train would leave soon, so they set out for the station.

"There were about 20 Aussie ladies, over 50, on a tour and [to get to the train] we had to go through the water and mud and they all had their big bags, so myself and another Aussie guy had to go back and forth, carrying their bags and we only had half an hour to get to the train. We all got there safely, only to be told there was no train for three days, and no food anywhere."

They waited for four hours trying to work out what could be done, before news spread that a nearby boat was leaving for safety at 3.30pm. About 100 people fled for the boat, only to arrive and find out it had left at 3pm.

"A couple of the Aussies were yelling, 'Get us a boat, we want to get out of here,' and two hours later a boat came and we all got on, and went to a place called La Spezia, an hour away, got a hotel, then caught a train to Venice and then to Rome. It was an adventurous four or five days, but it's a good story to tell the new baby one day."

www.smh.com.au [5 February 2012]

THE GOOD, THE BAD AND THE UGLY

Football has a way of dominating the media landscape, particularly in its heartland of Melbourne, and a big story can transfix the city. The AFL throws up news stories on a daily basis—and there have been some big ones since the turn of the century. Perhaps none bigger than Wayne Carey's affair with the wife of teammate Anthony Stevens that would force arguably the greatest player in the history of the game to leave North Melbourne in disgrace. A decade on, relationships are still strained.

Ben Cousins, like Carey, dominated headlines for his off-field activities, so, too, did Brendan Fevola. "Fevola's is a sorry tale, of his own doing but one involving so many willing and often irresponsible participants," *Age* chief football writer Caroline Wilson wrote. Then there have been the loveable rogues, such as Geelong's Cameron Mooney. Before the Cats achieved greatness, Mooney, when explaining his rash of suspensions to Samantha Lane, commented: "I don't think there's anything that anyone can do except me really. It's just me getting control of myself. To stop being a dickhead."

Barry Hall also had control issues, but said he had learnt from his mistakes. "Everything happens for a reason, whether they are good or bad," he said upon retiring.

While there have been many troubling stories, the AFL is also full of good news stories. Peter Hanlon recalls Michael Barlow's tale of perseverance, but it's the stars of the game who really excite and entertain—and sometimes frustrate. The AFL has been fortunate to have the likes of Chris Judd, Gary Ablett, James Hird, Matthew Richardson, Andrew McLeod and Lance Franklin in recent years; while the late Jim Stynes, once a hero on the field in his days at Melbourne, will be remembered equally for his work in saving his club that was on the financial brink when he took charge as president in 2008. Stynes' influence was also felt in charitable work, and Garry Lyon, his long-time friend, provides a heartfelt tribute to his former teammate who lost his battle with cancer in 2012.

HE'S FOOTY ROYALTY BUT . . . A BLUEBLOOD?

Greg Baum

CHRIS JUDD IS SITTING IN THE Carlton boardroom beneath a portrait of the Carlton team of the century, wearing a Carlton shirt, with 199 games to his name and at least one of everything football has to offer metaphorically in his pocket.

For Judd and the Blues, it is the perfect picture, except in one detail.

The 2006 premiership is still his most cherished achievement in 10 exceptional years in AFL football, but it was with another club. "Because I know how special it [a premiership] is, I feel if I don't achieve that here, I'll retire a West Coast player," he says.

Contradicting himself, but only slightly, Judd says a revitalised Carlton's self-validation will not necessarily be a premiership, but a place in the top four. From there, many factors come into play, including fluke. He uses St Kilda as an example: accursed these last two years, but to his mind successful.

"To me, a successful club is a top-four club," he says. "To really live as a footballer—not just survive—you've got to be at a top-four club, playing every week and uninjured.

"I think I'll get that chance. I've got more energy now than I've ever had since I've been here." The gleam in his eye matches his words. Of course, first Carlton must win a final, a feat it last achieved before Judd was an AFL player.

Judd at Carlton subverts a football paradigm. As a native Victorian playing for West Coast, he was universally admired in Victoria; he was the best player in the AFL. But the sense always was that he would come home, and that when he did join a Victorian club, fans of other Victorian clubs would lose their affection for him. But the esteem for him is undiminished.

Instead of hardening their hearts to him, he has softened them—a little—towards Carlton.

Yet Judd's decision to go to Carlton was strictly and unemotionally a business one. It was about money: not his, but the club's. "It's very hard to be a successful club if you can't spend money on the football department," he says. "Our spend is in the top three Melbourne clubs. What do they call it? Showbiz, not show-fun.

"You can't separate money from successful sporting teams."

Judd's other reason to pick the Blues was nobler. He wanted to develop with a premiership team, not gatecrash one. "I didn't want to just jump on the coat-tails of another group of players," he says. West Coast had been bottom four the two years before he was drafted. So was Carlton when he arrived.

When Judd played his first game in 2002, he thought 200 would do.

He looked at West Coast greats who barely reached that mark, or didn't: John Worsfold (209), Chris Mainwaring (201), Brett Heady (156). He was on his own cognisance a kid, but an anointed kid, who paraded an impossibly slim model girlfriend as he blithely won a Brownlow at 21 and starred in grand finals the next two years.

Then, he couldn't see very far forward. Now, he doesn't bother looking back. "I don't sit around and reminisce about the good old days when I had long hair and lived on the other side of the country," he says.

"What's going on here right now is pretty exciting."

At 27, he says he is as dedicated as ever to football, but there is a difference.

"Every decision I've made in my life, from 18 to now, is based around that three hours on a Saturday afternoon," he says. "That hasn't changed.

"I've always been incredibly passionate about football. I just haven't been as passionate about being a footballer, if that makes sense." In other words, he could do without the ephemera.

Tonight, Judd will play against David Swallow, perhaps this decade's Judd. The original's advice to the new model would be to remember always what it was that attracted him to football—and it wasn't that he didn't have to line up at nightclubs. "There's a lot of young players now who almost want the lifestyle more than they do to be a successful player," he says.

Upon winning his second Brownlow Medal last year, Judd made an impromptu speech in which he said that football was "make-believe . . . a self-indulgent past-time", whose "heroes" cannot compare with, for instance, Jim Stynes, a guest that night.

Elaborating, he says: "That's the way I've always felt about it. It doesn't mean I care less about the game than the next bloke, but it is important to realise that it is just a game." He says reporters and fans should keep that sense of proportion, too.

Previously, Judd had spoken out against the idealisation of footballers, saying children's role models should be people who are real to them. Since, and again this week, he has said he accepts that children cannot rationalise their hero-worship, and that he is comfortable in their adulation. "I'd still encourage them to look up to someone they know," he says. "Just because you see someone on the telly doesn't mean you know them."

An impression is growing of Judd as statesman and philosopher. He demurs, saying it is merely that a man grows and learns much from 21 to 27. The model girlfriend is now his wife and soon will be the mother of his child, and he admits that impending parenthood already has modified his world view. And, yes, he will miss round 22 to be at the birth if it comes to that.

Judd has learnt from many on his journey. An early tutor was Ben Cousins. "The main thing I learnt is to take control of your own footballing program," he says. "A lot of players get their weekly schedule and think: 'That's what I've got to do this week'.

"Cuz, there'd be no point giving him a schedule. He'd already have what he wanted to do through the week. If he didn't want to do something, he'd tell the fitness guy pretty forcefully."

The irony, of course, is that Judd took control, Cousins lost it. Contemporary legend has it that they were never close, but Judd says that they talk twice a year at least, usually over breakfast. "Mutual friends in Perth, the Eagles," he says. "We don't sit there analysing stoppages."

Cousins was, well, unmistakeable. So was Brendan Fevola, whose name did not crop up: it has become taboo at Carlton. "I've played with a lot of blokes who've been loveable rogues," Judd says. "There's not really much place for loveable rogues in footy any more. Pretty much all our blokes are solid citizens."

Judd is redgum solid. Off-field he has been impeccable, no mean feat in the era of the camera phone. On-field, there have been notable exceptions. He laughs them off. Campbell Brown and eye-gouging?

"It was a stupid thing to do," he says, "but it wasn't eye-gouging." Michael Rischitelli and a lame excuse about a wrestling manoeuvre? "[Wryly] That was well handled, wasn't it?" Matthew Pavlich and a split eyebrow? "It was an accident. It got seen in that light."

There was also a head-on collision with Matthew Lloyd at the MCG that floored both players. There was no suggestion of wrongdoing—quite the opposite—but Judd played out that match with concussion, which makes it topical again now. "I fibbed to our club doctor," Judd says. "He was dirty on me because I was telling porkies."

Now there is a new rule mandating the substitution of concussed players. Recently, Judd said that under it there would be no more concussions; all players would lie. He was seen to be a smart-arse, but defends himself. "That's the natural reaction of a player: to pretend you don't have concussion, wouldn't you think?" he asks rhetorically. "Was it being cynical, or was it speaking the truth? Many people just say it's a good rule and leave it at that."

Also new this season is the three-man interchange bench. One match's worth of experience has given Judd pause for thought. "I had stronger views a week ago," he says. He is not as vehemently opposed as, say, Essendon's Jobe Watson, who proposed a player protest.

Tired teams will set sloppier zones, says Judd, space will open up, and the team that is prepared to "grind"—his word—will find it. "The game's going to open up a bit, late, which I think is good to watch," he says. But he sees a flaw in the idea that the new bench will ameliorate the unbalancing effect of injury. "If you get one injury, it's less of a disadvantage than last year," he says. "But if you get two: good luck!" Judd, at last, is injury-free. "My groins are a million dollars," he says (each, he might have added), "and have been for a couple of years now."

He freely admits that he played better football for West Coast than he has yet for Carlton. He has lost pace, which he puts down to age and the cumulative effect of the buffeting he gets. He hopes rather than expects that it will come back.

The game has changed nearly out of all recognition, too. "When I first started, if you were at a stoppage as a midfielder, and you broke past your direct opponent, or one or two players in front of you, generally you had 20 or 30 metres of free space, where you could have a bounce and do something creative," he says.

"But with the full ground press, that space gets chewed up really quickly."

There, in a nutshell, is the difference between images of Judd at West Coast and Carlton.

Seemingly, this is intelligent design, meant specifically to curb Judd's powers of evasion and acceleration.

Certainly, it means he has to play his role differently. But he demurs at the idea that one player can no longer dominate. "I don't think that's true," he says.

Carlton was at a low ebb when Judd arrived. He remembers a match it lost by 50 points and the crowd—grateful that it was not 100—clapped the team off. "The club had been on its knees for so long," he says. "That changed a year or two later. The expectations are high now, and so they should be."

He disagrees that he is critical to the Blues' advance. He says his role has changed as the team has strengthened. "Whether I'm the best player here or the 20th best, it's really exciting," he says. He feels he has a last burst in him, coinciding with Carlton's projected peak.

The careers of Judd and Gary Ablett began a week apart in 2002. For the best part of 10 years, they—with Jonathan Brown—have been the best players in the competition. In a symmetrical twist, Judd will play his 200th against Ablett (as it happens, on Brown's home ground). Judd plays it down. "We're playing Gold Coast, and he's their best player, but we're not playing Gary Ablett," he says.

Nonetheless, their contest will personify this match, a milestone for Judd, a landmark for the game.

JUDD ON . . .
The key to winning premierships
"It's very hard to be a successful club if you can't spend enough money on the football department. You can't separate money from successful sporting teams."

Carlton
"The club and the list is getting pretty close. It's exciting."

The new interchange bench
"I had stronger views a week ago. The game's going to open up a bit, late, which I think is good to watch."

The new concussion rule

"The natural reaction of a player is to pretend you don't have concussion, wouldn't you think?"

Invasive media

"At the captains' day last year, there was a journo who'd been sent by his boss to find out which footballers were gay. The invasion of privacy is greater. But footballers still have options. If it bothers you that much, you don't have to play football."

Footballers as role models

"I understand kids don't analyse who [they] should or shouldn't look up to. They just do. If kids look up to me, I'm comfortable with that. If I was a parent encouraging my kid to look up to someone, I'd still encourage them to look up to someone they know."

A sense of proportion

"The game is important, but keeping that in mind, it is just a game."

Advice to draftees

"Remember what you're there for. It's not so you don't have to line up at nightclubs."

The CBA

"Anyone you ask thinks the players should get a fair chunk of the revenue, and if that revenue is more than forecast, they should get a fair chunk of the increase. That's my view, the AFL's view and the AFLPA view."

THE JUDD LOWDOWN	
Born	September 8, 1983
Recruited from	Caulfield Grammar/Sandringham U18 (2001 draft—priority selection, No 3 overall)
To	West Coast
AFL debut	Round 2, 2002

THE JUDD LOWDOWN	
Traded to Carlton	2007 draft, for Josh Kennedy, No. 3 and No. 20 draft picks
Games	199 (134 and 65)
Goals	180 (42 and 38)
Honours	Brownlow medallist 2004, 2010 West Coast premiership 2006 Grand finals 2005, 2006 Best-and-fairest 2004, 2006, 2008, 2010 Norm Smith medallist 2005 All-Australian 2004, 2006, 2008 (captain), 2009 (vice-captain), 2010 Eagles captain 2006–07 Blues captain since 2008 AFLPA MVP 2006

The Age 2 April 2011

BUCKS STOPS

Michael Gleeson

FOR A PLAYER WHO WON everything and nothing, Nathan Buckley leaves with no regrets. A premiership or three would not have been unwelcome or undeserved for one who had been so achingly close, but he accepts he could do no more.

The Collingwood captain, the lauded player of a black and white generation, the man with more Copeland trophies than any other and arguably the best player the club has produced, only now will have the time to reflect on a career and the game, for playing did not offer that luxury playing it Buckley's way.

At the moment of his retirement yesterday, Buckley recalled a recent conversation where fellow retiring Brownlow medallist James Hird reflected on the rare chance in games when things fell so well it allowed the indulgence of enjoying the moment.

"I thought about it and, to be honest, I don't think I've ever felt like that," Buckley said with a tone not of regret, but of dawning self-realisation.

"I've always played football red-lining. Fair enough, I get in the zone every now and then, but I've worked as hard as I possibly could 100 per cent of the time.

"Everything that I've done in football, I've done because I've worked hard . . . whatever I've achieved, whatever I've failed at, it hasn't been for lack of effort."

Which is a true observation of his effort but an understated and inaccurate depiction of his talent.

"Two or three [premierships] would have been better [but] I don't have any regrets."

The cruel irony of Buckley's career is that the single-mindedness was only understood later in life and the rewards—beyond the personal with a Brownlow Medal and six Copeland trophies—proved elusive. Typically, when Collingwood fell five points short of Geelong in the preliminary final, Buckley injured his hamstring in the dying moments, meaning he would not have played in the grand final, regardless of whether his team did.

"I did have visions throughout the year that at some stage I will be sitting behind the fence when Collingwood wins a flag, I was hoping it was going to be this year but it will be some time in the future, no doubt."

It was at that moment when his ragged hamstrings gave way again that Buckley realised the body that had carried him through 15 seasons and 280 games had given up on him.

"My body is just not ready to go, I will never not want to play the game—that will remain with me for the rest of my life—[but] I just can't trust my body any more," he said.

Those repeated hamstring strains already had tested his resolve for he admitted to nearly retiring late in the year before coaxing his body into one last tilt, which yielded five wonderful, unexpected games.

"I am glad I stuck it out because that last little bit was a fair ride," he said. "I think it made it easier [the last injury] to know I made the right decision . . . I can't with all good intentions and faith put my hand up to go again because I have no idea what my body will do."

Life for Buckley and for Collingwood will not be the same again. For Buckley, it means finding a job and while inevitably he will seek to be a senior coach, that will come after a year or two in the media and studying management courses here or abroad, then an assistant coach apprenticeship somewhere.

It will mean he steps away from Collingwood, for the sake of him and the club. For now.

For the club, it means it will confront life without the dominant figure of a generation. It does so with a team missing his obvious heir in James Clement and no obvious candidate, save the short-term option of Scott Burns, to assume leadership.

Coach Mick Malthouse says the club will not be rushed into a replacement, probably making a decision in March. "How do you measure up against Nathan?" he sympathised in advance with the successor. "I know there is life after him but we have to be cautious, we have to be methodical in our approach . . ."

The spectre of confronting the force of personality that was Buckley was one Malthouse met on arrival at Collingwood. There was a strength of will in the captain the coach had to break for his own authority. Consequently, he was deliberately contrary to create conflicts where none should exist with Buckley, to force him to bow to his will.

"My first couple of years with Nathan hurt me more than at any other time with a player . . . but he went into a position of beyond captain . . . something else that is not tangible," Malthouse said.

Evasive on where he would place his captain in football's pantheon, he would admit only to a ranking somewhere close to the greatest he had seen in Wayne Carey and Leigh Matthews.

His president, Eddie McGuire, who makes sport of his personal infatuation with the club's captain, was not exaggerating when he sought to figure Buckley in Collingwood's history.

"Jock McHale said that Bob Rose was the greatest Collingwood player he ever saw and Bob Rose said Nathan Buckley was the greatest footballer he ever saw. And that, basically, is the history of the Collingwood Football Club," McGuire said.

BUCKLEY'S BRILLIANT CAREER	
July 26, 1972	Born to Ray and Karen Buckley in Adelaide. The young Nathan moves around the country with his family, including a stint in the Northern Territory.
1990	Plays for Port Adelaide under-19s in the SANFL before playing for Southern Districts in the NT summer season.
1991	Makes his debut for Port Adelaide seniors.
1992	Wins the Magarey Medal, the SANFL's best-and-fairest award, and is part of Port Adelaide's premiership side.
1993	Makes his AFL debut for Brisbane. He plays 20 games in his only season with the club and is the inaugural winner of the Rising Star Award.
1994	Goes to Collingwood and ties for the Copeland Trophy, the club's best-and-fairest. It is the first of six Copeland trophies for Buckley.

BUCKLEY'S BRILLIANT CAREER

1996	Selected in the All-Australian team for the first time. He goes on to win six more caps for the representative team (1997–2001, 2003), including three as vice-captain (1999, 2000, 2003).
1997	Picked on half-back flank in the Collingwood team of the century. Captains the Allies side in the state-of-origin series, winning the Jesaulenko Medal for the side's best player.
1998	Represents Australia in the international rules competition against Ireland. A year later, he captains the team.
1999	Appointed Collingwood captain under coach Tony Shaw, but suffers a serious jaw injury against Carlton in round two. It keeps him out for six weeks. Buckley captains the side in its final match at Victoria Park.
2001	Picks up 32 kicks and 16 handballs in Collingwood's round-two defeat of Fremantle at Telstra Dome.
2002	Suspended for a week after wiping his blood on the jumper of Geelong's Cameron Ling in round 15. Later that year, he captains Collingwood in the grand final. He picks up 32 possessions and wins the Norm Smith Medal but the Pies lose to the Brisbane Lions by nine points. Buckley marries Tania Minnici in a New Year's Eve wedding.
2003	Wins Brownlow Medal, tying with Adam Goodes and Mark Ricciuto, and later that week captains Collingwood in another grand final defeat against the Brisbane Lions.
2005	Is forced to have surgery on a hamstring. The injury limits him to 11 games for the season.
2006	Becomes the record-holder for matches as Collingwood captain, eclipsing Syd Coventry. Later that year, he becomes a father with the birth of Jett Charles.
2007	A recurring hamstring injury restricts him to only five games for Collingwood, including three finals, before announcing his retirement.

BUCKLEY'S BRILLIANT CAREER	
Games	280
Goals	284
Honours	Captain 1999–2007 (161 games)
	All-Australian 1996–2001, 2003 (vice-captain 1999, 2000, 2003)
	International rules 1998–1999 (captain 1999)
	Brownlow Medal 2003
	Norm Smith Medal 2002
	Copeland Trophy 1994, 1996, 1998–2000, 2003
	Magarey Medal 1992
	AFL Rising Star 1993
	Jesaulenko Medal 1997

The Age 6 October 2007

RICHO: A TIGER WHO EARNED HIS STRIPES

Martin Flanagan

WHEN I STARTED WRITING A book with Matthew Richardson, a Richmond supporter called George Halkias, who is also the coach of the Australian Homeless World Cup Soccer team, said to me, "What a great subject." "Why?" I asked. "Because everybody has a view of him."

I have since found this to be true. Everyone with any knowledge of Australian football has a view of "Richo". Other players have become household names over the past 17 years, but none in the way that Richo did. The careers of players like Michael Voss and James Hird amount to a sort of sporting perfection. Richo was manifestly imperfect. He was fallible. He was like us.

Richo's father, Alan "Bull" Richardson, played in Richmond's 1967 premiership team, the first of five premierships the club won in 13 years. The last of these grand final wins, in 1980, was also the first game of football Richo remembers seeing. To his five-year-old mind, football and the Richmond Football Club were one and the same.

The irony, one of many in his career, was that the first game Richo saw, the one that gave him his passion for the club, also marked the end of its great era. The Tigers would make the grand final again in 1982 but then slip from football's First World to Third World. It would be Richo's destiny to carry the flag for this once proud and mighty club during its years of ignominy.

One of the words commonly used in relation to Richo is paradox. Here is one example: in football, Richo is regarded as a great individualist, but he is someone who sees no point in individual sports. For Richo, the team's the thing. Last year he flatly refused to believe allegations that players were tanking. The best thing in footy, he says, is the feeling you have for 30 minutes after a win. "You feel so shit after a loss. No one would willingly inflict that feeling upon themselves."

Richo played with his emotions bare for all to see. This included moments early in his career when he expressed displeasure towards teammates when leads were ignored or passes went astray. He was considered truculent and, some said, selfish. For most of his career, there was someone somewhere saying that Richmond would be better off without him, that his singular style of play was too disruptive to the game plan.

Jack Dyer, the greatest of all Richmond figures, played for 18 seasons. Richo played for 17, beginning when he was 18 years old. His record is amazing for the fact that, given his dominance within the club, he won its best-and-fairest only once. The Jack Dyer Medal even failed to come his way in 2008, the year he nearly won the Brownlow.

And while most people know that Richo had a career-long problem with his kicking, few know he kicked 800 goals and stands second only to Jack "Skinny" Titus as Richmond's all-time highest goal scorer.

One of the best articles I have read on Richo appeared without a byline on a website called PuntingAce.com in 2008, and was written by an extremely erudite rugby league supporter. The writer is in a club somewhere when a Richmond game comes on.

"When Matthew Richardson hits the screen, a nasty polarisation sweeps the room . . . some take delight in highlighting, without invitation, that they enjoy watching Richo play as he will inevitably cost Richmond dearly. Others, who claim to have a knowledge of the sport . . . rattle off inaccurate and ill-considered diatribes about Richo's petulance and selfishness and assert that he, among other things, has cost the Tigers at least two wins a season. His goalkicking is mocked, his pride is questioned, his attitude slammed and his achievements derided. The focus is on his flaws. These fools who get their kicks from cheap attacks on Richo can't see the forest for the trees.

"There is no doubt that Richo has his flaws, like nearly all of us. He has a tendency to get a little nervous from set shots and occasionally his heart-on-the-sleeve behaviour can be misconstrued. But these are nothing more than blips on his radar of greatness and they certainly don't define Richo the man or Richo the footballer. That is because Richo is the personification of heart.

No player has the phenomenal ticker that Richo has. He runs all day and then runs some more."

Away from the game, Richo is a humble, polite man whose second love is music. He is also someone with a deep regard for the history of his club and the game. Judith Donnelly, the Tigers' media manager, called him her "go-to man". If there was a need for a player to make a hospital visit to see a member of a Richmond family, he was the one who would always do it. Mike Perry, the president of the Richmond Old Players' Association, says, "Richo gives and then he gives some more."

One reason for the public's change of heart towards Richo was the sheer longevity of his career. Football followers watched Richo grow up. And then there was his bravery. In one famous match against Essendon at the MCG, he played with a broken nose and two black eyes, kicked the winning goal and had it taken off him by an umpire's ruling. It seemed to sum up the luckless nature of his career.

Richo never got to play in a grand final. His reward was in the hearts of Richmond followers and football followers generally, along with the respect of other players.

I was at Alice Springs airport when I got the message that Richo had, in his words, "pulled the pin". A moment later, I chanced upon Liam Jurrah and did what I have done with many people over the past six months, I asked him what he thought of Richo. "A great player," he said. "Why?", I asked. Liam does not waste words. "He was good for that long time," he said.

The Age 14 November 2009

A SORRY TALE THAT HAS TORN A TEAM APART

Caroline Wilson

THE STORY THAT HAS REWRITTEN and ended Wayne Carey's golden career at the Kangaroos began much earlier but reached its lowest point four nights ago at a party in Warrandyte, at the home of Carey's teammate, Glenn Archer.

It was wife Lisa Archer's 30th birthday and while the band played on the tennis court, the action that counted took place inside. Wayne and Sally Carey had been among the first to arrive, along with Carey's vice-captain and close friend Anthony Stevens and his wife Kellie. Both couples had been childhood sweethearts.

Only a week earlier, Stevens and Carey had shared a lane at the North Melbourne pool, joking between laps. And Stevens had promoted the virtues of fatherhood at a Kangaroos fund-raiser, saying he wished he had started having children earlier.

But all that changed last Sunday night following an incident that took place at the party, involving Carey and Kellie Stevens.

By all reports, Archer tried to break up the angry altercation that followed between the North captain and Stevens and ended up getting hit himself. Three strong men who have fought so many valiant campaigns and won two flags together, alcohol-fuelled and tearing each other apart— it was a terrible sight.

So the party that witnessed the end of the Kangaroos as we know them did not end all that late. Stevens and Archer, however, sat up most of the night and did not make it the next day to the Labour Day morning training session.

By the time the Kangaroos' football manager, Geoff Walsh, found the pair, the strong feeling was that they could no longer play football alongside Carey. It was also on Monday that Stevens learned that an extra-marital relationship between his wife and Carey had begun last year.

Struggling to hold himself and his young family together (Anthony and Kellie Stevens have a baby daughter Ayva) Stevens was consoled by club management, but was asked to keep himself together to the extent that he attend training—Stevens is weeks away from making a comeback from serious knee injury—on Tuesday afternoon.

Geoff Walsh met coach Denis Pagan and held talks with North's new chief executive, Michael Easy, who has been battling to keep the club financially afloat since joining it last September.

Sally Carey, whose wedding took place in Wagga just over 12 months ago, was hospitalised earlier this week and placed under sedation.

Even early on Tuesday, there was a determination that the team could ride out the crisis. Stevens made it to training. That night, the 1999 best-and-fairest winner and popular clubman was still being consoled by friends and trying to make sense of his upside-down life.

By yesterday morning, it was clear to all at the club that this was one indiscretion it could not cover up. In fact, Carey appeared to be one of the few remaining who thought the incident could be overcome for the good of the team.

Not his teammates. It came down to the captain or the club and the club won, although in truth there has been no winner in this dreadful saga. Carey's fellow players voted him out.

For three hours yesterday afternoon, Walsh, Easy and chairman Allen Aylett held talks with Carey's manager, Ricky Nixon, and Nixon's new colleague, Greg Miller. The meeting stretched out partly because Carey still did not accept the club's verdict and negotiations went back and forward.

It appears to have been Nixon who told Carey that his career at North was finished, although the club, according to the AFL's collective bargaining agreement, will have to honour his million-dollar contract.

Several staff wept last night in the Kangaroos' temporary administrative offices in Boundary Road when told by Easy that Carey was gone.

And then an hour later, at 6pm, Aylett and Walsh addressed the players at Arden Street. Pagan attended the meeting but did not speak. Carey told friends that it had been his choice to resign.

Surely this is the AFL's greatest scandal. Football's first million-dollar man, its biggest name, is today in disgrace, forced out of the team he led and made famous for a decade.

Betrayed is not a word used often in football but there is no better one to describe the emotion that engulfs North Melbourne Football Club today.

CAREY ON STEVENS:

On the eve of Stevens' 200th game: "He's the heart and soul of the club . . . he doesn't get the recognition from the general public, but he does from those who see him every week and he doesn't get underrated from the opposition. He is a bit like my dog, Oscar—you just throw a ball and watch him run at it."

In early 2000, after Stevens' neck was slashed by a shard of falling glass outside a North Melbourne pub: "He is one of my best mates. I'm shattered. I went in to visit him in hospital and I didn't want to leave. I wanted to sit with him all day. He's such a good fella."

At a 200 Club dinner in 1999, talking about life after football: "I look forward to attending [the function] in three years when I'll drive down from Wagga, pick up 'Stevo' in Shepparton on the way, and make a big night of it."

STEVENS ON CAREY:

After Carey played his 200th AFL game in 1999: "He is just a fantastic bloke. I don't think people get to see the actual Wayne Carey—after training nights he stands out and signs autographs for all the kids."

The Age 14 March 2002

DARK SIDE OF THE MOONEY

Samantha Lane

IT WOULD BE EASIER FOR Cameron Mooney to say he'd worked out why, in 2006, he was, in his words, such "a dickhead". Easier still for him to make a solemn eve-of-new-season vow that he is reformed.

But if he's honest—and the Geelong utility is a refreshingly straight talker—Mooney cannot explain why, in the space of one year, he became the most suspended footballer in the history of the game.

The bit of self-examination that he has done since then has led him to believe that it's not external factors that push him over the edge.

Mooney's tendency to short-circuit, he thinks, is due entirely to his internal wiring. He snaps. And last year Ben Holland, Josh Mahoney, Daniel Pratt and Amon Buchanan were, well, duly snapped.

"At the end of the day it's just that mentally I'm just, I think, weak in that area because I lash out and I haven't got control over it," Mooney says, gazing into a cup of coffee as Geelong's off-season of discontent draws to an end.

"I don't think there's anything that anyone can do except me really. It's just me getting control of myself. To stop being a dickhead.

"It's not ever because someone's stirred me up or anything like that . . . I believe, just talking to a few people, that it's just a reaction I have."

And, history proves, a reaction that he has had over and over again.

Even when discussing, with serious face, the multiple suspensions he incurred last year, Mooney throws in a quip that it's "fun" hitting blokes. Presumably, he can't help it. And, perhaps more seriously, no one to date has been able to help him. And so the pattern has inevitably gone: offence, suspension, pained private remorse (from Mooney), a docking of pay (from club), a public tut-tutting (from official/ teammate/coach), until his return.

Which would be followed, sure enough, by offence . . .

Mooney tracks his fiery streak back to his mum, Lyn. He was the youngest of three hell-raising boys who grew up on a farm near Wagga and who was forever having to hold his own against a couple of "pretty physical kind of guys", namely brothers Jason, a 129-game player for Sydney and Geelong, and Heath."

"All we had was each other, really, so we'd just run around and belt the living shit out of each other."

But Cameron Mooney was no enforcer then.

"I was a sook. I was the baby. I used to cry if I got pinched."

He did, however, develop means of fighting back.

"I would be screaming, crying my eyes out, but chasing Jason with a butcher's knife around the house wanting to kill him," he says.

Mooney didn't finish school and left home at 16 to play footy.

Cats coach Mark Thompson chose fairly measured words on the occasions he discussed Mooney's first three suspensions last year.

But when Mooney whacked Sydney little man Buchanan in the ribs in round 20 and disqualified himself from Geelong's last two matches of last season—at the time the Cats were still some chance to make the finals—Thompson vented this: "You just have to know the rules. Ninety-nine per cent of the players adapt to it and you have got one that doesn't. Well, it's his responsibility to change."

At the time, Thompson said he'd seen Mooney as a potential skipper of the club. But after the fourth suspension it was inconceivable.

"We are going to have a program which is ongoing, a management program to try and get him to control himself," Thompson said back in round 20, 2006.

Mooney, who lives in a Melbourne bayside suburb and is expecting a child with long-time partner Seona, never did any anger management. He also says that he didn't realise just how much he was hurting his club. Because, in his view, no one told him straight. It's a rather incredible assertion but one that, when questioned again about it, Mooney stands by.

"This is the problem we've had at the club: we've never been really good at confrontation with each other," he said. "At the time I thought, 'They've got the shits,' but not really. I didn't really take it to heart.

"Not until they sat down with me and all looked me in the eye and said, 'You're being an idiot.' That's when it hit home. During the year it never really came across that way."

What would seem an overdue moment of truth came late last December when Geelong enlisted the help of a leadership expert, Gerard Murphy, who has run hour-long peer assessment sessions with the club's players and coaches, among other things. Groups of eight dissect personality and performance. Mooney describes his assessment as "brutal".

"It was the first time they've actually sat down and told me exactly how they feel.

"It just shits them to tears that I'm letting them all down. They've basically said that they need me out there and the fact that I'm not out there due to a stupid little incident, it really frustrates them. And that hurt, that really hurt actually, hearing that from all of them."

It emerged he was a figure many of his teammates found difficult to confront. That the young players especially found him intimidating. Which goes some way to explaining why the lashings Mooney received in public felt fiercer than any he received in private.

"During the season it wasn't a joke but it came across as a joke to me. Because they didn't really want to stand there and go, 'Oh, Moons, you f—ing idiot.' It was more like, 'Oh, geez, you've gone again,' stuff like that."

A 195-centimetre, 99-kilogram presence can come in handy. It has also meant Mooney—who administrative staff at Geelong regard as a gentle giant— has consistently been prejudged.

"I've been to parties where people have thought I was going to trash their parties and destroy it. By the time I've walked out, we were best mates.

"I've been called a caveman by some bloke once. That was a bit harsh, I thought," he said with a smile.

Mooney's image couldn't be more contrasting to that of new Geelong skipper Tom Harley, who is ever-diplomatic, eloquent and presentable—the football equivalent of a school prefect.

"He's exactly that," Mooney said with a laugh.

And, as it happened, Mooney's peer assessment was done right after Harley's.

"I was just the stupid little bum behind him that got sprayed.

"Tommy's was fine. Tommy's was f—ing perfect.

"Mine? Geez . . ."

Mooney did, however, retain his position in the club's leadership group—King and Matthew Scarlett pulled themselves out, Max Rooke was voted in.

"I know I couldn't have done what he's doing right now," Mooney said of Harley.

The work sitting square on Mooney's plate this year is of a more personal nature. "I've had my teammates sit down and look me in the eye and tell me it's not good enough, and that they're extremely pissed off with me. I don't particularly want to sit down in front of them again and have them say that," Mooney said.

He won't be fully marked on his task until the final siren of Geelong's final game. And until then, like any addict, he'll be viewed as being just a messy 24 hours away from relapse.

CAMERON MOONEY'S HONOUR BOARD
Number of charges: 11
Times guilty: 9
Total matches suspended: 13
Career matches: 119

2006—Four times guilty
- Round 6: Contact to face of Ben Holland (Melbourne), 1 match. Thompson: "The act itself was not the smartest thing in the world to do."
- Round 15: Striking Josh Mahoney (Port Adelaide), 1 match. Thompson: "We'd like him to just curb it a little bit, but we'd still like Cameron Mooney to be the Cameron Mooney that he is. That's tough and hard and a little bit scary. The two times he's been reported they were only minor incidents, and that tells me he's improved a fair bit since three years ago."
- Round 17: Charging Daniel Pratt (Kangaroos), 1 match. Thompson: "He might not necessarily come straight back in. We love Cam. We think he's passionate. We think he's improved as a footballer. He's controlled himself a lot more. He's been reported for three silly things this year and copped a week each time that we're not happy about."
- Round 20: Striking Amon Buchanan (Sydney), 2 matches. Thompson: "You just know the rules and 99 per cent of the players adapt to it, and, well, when you've got one that doesn't, it's his responsibility to change. You

can get all the professional advice, but the thing is there's not much that will actually change apart from just constantly mentoring and coaching him on what's acceptable behaviour and what's not."

The Age 3 March 2007

BUDDY: AN AUDIENCE WITH
LANCE FRANKLIN

Samantha Lane

"I'M NERVOUS WITH THAT THING," Lance Franklin says, pointing to the device that will record his voice for the next 90 minutes. Yet during the sitting, the man known variously as Buddy, Bud, Franco and Emu is far from an awkward or unobliging subject. Even if he does show he is an unpractised interviewee.

In the courtyard of a Glenferrie Road cafe that has been picked as the meeting spot because it is empty, the young Hawthorn superstar speaks with his skinny latte sitting on the table untouched for 20 minutes because he is so focused on the task of giving detailed answers. Upon realising, Franklin gives himself a self-deprecating reminder to drink up, grabs the glass and, in one enthusiastic gulp, swills half of it back. Later, in a brief break in proceedings, he admits he's dying to go to the bathroom and is profusely apologetic as he excuses himself.

Franklin the footballer may be blessed with talents that cause AFL legends to go ga-ga and have an on-field presence in the league of Wayne Carey's, but Franklin the young man presents as a rather different package: polite, gentle-natured and at times endearingly childlike.

He knows the purpose of the conversation is to cover personal terrain for a magazine profile that will appear in the June edition of *Sport&Style* magazine—out in *The Age* on Monday—and he does that with a surprising amount of passion. When it comes to football, it quickly becomes evident that Franklin has a pet topic: Jarryd Roughead, one of his closest mates, a fellow 2004 draftee and erstwhile second banana in Hawthorn's forward line, and who in the first half of this season has regularly taken the No. 1 billing.

"There's no doubt in my mind that Roughy's just as good as me," Franklin says.

"His confidence is up, he's got a great set of hands on him and it's good to have another big power forward up there that you can work with. It takes the pressure off me a little bit, too, so we work off each other.

"I'd love Roughy to win a Coleman Medal . . . he's a great footballer and I've got no doubt he'll get 100 [goals] one year. No doubt. Maybe we can both kick 100 in a year."

Franklin chuckles as he articulates the fantasy. Rival clubs would not be so amused by the thought.

If Hawthorn's hierarchy hasn't got just a hint of perverse pleasure from listening to the Franklin-related commentary this year then it would have at least noticed the change of key.

Leigh Matthews is one of a handful of football sages who has questioned whether the 22-year-old is lacking condition. It was for that reason that Hawks captain Sam Mitchell found himself in the unusual position of talking up a teammate whom he is more accustomed to hosing down when he sat on a couch to talk footy on television recently.

Internally, the club has found the criticism of Franklin's shape laughable. The spearhead is 1.5 kilograms heavier than last year, but the Hawks says his skinfold levels are unchanged. Strictly speaking, Franklin's 2009 statistics show he has not been as dominant a forward compared with last year—he is averaging 3.4 goals compared with 4.5 per match last year, is down on score assists, disposals, marks and disposal inside the forward 50—but he is winning considerably more ball in the midfield (41.2 per cent compared with 28.7 per cent in 2008).

Franklin is also tackling more, and where he missed the goals completely almost once a match last season, this year he has failed to register a score from a scoring shot just twice.

Franklin's assessment of Hawthorn's position as the 2009 season reached its mid-point could just as well have been a statement about himself: "We're not thinking too far ahead . . . but we're reasonably confident in our ability . . . I think things will come together."

The 2008 Coleman medallist had thumb and shoulder surgery after winning the flag last season and, while on the topic, happily clears up one of many rumours about him by saying that, contrary to tabloid reports, his hand did not become infected because he was surfing during his holiday in Bali. In fact, he takes pleasure in clarifying, he didn't jump on a board once.

In recent outings on-field Franklin hasn't clasped onto the ball as he would have liked and he admits his hands aren't 100 per cent yet. This is the main area of his game he has been working on and, in aid of the cause, the club's forwards coach boots the ball hard and direct into his hands up to 40 times a training session.

"I've done a lot of work on my hands. Not so much over summer, because I couldn't really do much with my thumb and my shoulder, but the last six or seven weeks I've really been concentrating on . . . trying to get them right because I reckon that's the main tool you need as a forward. Your hands have got to be rock solid," he says.

When quizzed about an element of his game that has deserted him spectacularly at times and vexed football fans of all persuasions—his goalkicking accuracy—Franklin has a good-natured laugh.

In cracking the ton last year, he also kicked 88 behinds and registered bags of six and seven points in a total of six matches. It gave him an accuracy ranking of 47th in the AFL's top 50 goalkickers (56.2 per cent). This year, with his tally at 31 goals 16, Franklin is ranked 24th (55.2 per cent).

He denies that he has avoided taking set shots on occasion—in round four against Port Adelaide it looked like he did—but Franklin says he simply made some wrong decisions to play on.

"I reckon my general shots weren't too bad really last year. I got . . . 90 points but I reckon 50 of them were in general play, just snaps and that, so I think my goalkicking isn't too bad," he said.

"It doesn't help [my accuracy] if I'm just having snaps in general play.

"I'm not nervous at all, I'm pretty confident within my set shot . . . I suppose I've still got to work on it and I am still working on it, but I don't think it's as bad as people actually think."

Just how many hours a week he puts into perfecting his unorthodox method of goal scoring, Franklin can't say. On Tuesdays and Thursdays the Hawks' forwards usually have about 30 shots at goal before training and, by Franklin's reckoning, would have about 50 all up by the time those sessions are done.

After receiving advice from club legend and former superboot Jason Dunstall, Franklin tinkered with his goalkicking technique late in the 2007 season by straightening his run-up rather than beginning with his trademark hook to the left. Reprogrammed, Franklin went out and kicked two goals

11 behinds in a game against the Western Bulldogs. The fact that Franklin actually counts that match among his best rather than one he'd rather forget is an insight into how Hawthorn handled the episode.

"I would have thought that was one of my better games because I had so many shots. I was still getting the ball, it was just a matter of converting," he says.

A fortnight later Franklin was the stunning match-winner in the Hawks' elimination final against Adelaide when he booted seven goals two.

The only element of his goalkicking routine that he has modified this year with David Rath, Hawthorn's resident expert on such things, is the distance of his run-up.

"I've probably been kicking off two or three steps this year in a six-to-seven metres run-up. That's been a little bit better," he says.

The game has always come naturally to him, and if there was a lesson in the Dunstall experiment it was that, perhaps, in some areas, Franklin is best left to his natural devices.

"But that can be a bad thing, too, because it can make you lazy and think that it's going to come easy. It can be a negative more than a positive sometimes, I reckon, being more naturally talented," he says.

"I've learnt that being at the club; they've taught me to work hard and that things can't come naturally. They can come naturally on the field, but you've still got to work hard for it."

Messages such as these were impressed upon him by his AFL club from day one. Soon after Franklin was drafted, Hawthorn's entire list and coaching staff completed the Kokoda Trail. Franklin, who with his born-to-do-it air instantly became the Pied Piper among the kids, ate his daily food rations in one early lunch sitting. It meant his teammates had to share what they had saved with him at dinner time. Unbeknown to Franklin, they also put stones in his backpack (coach Alastair Clarkson knew and approved). Unsurprisingly, the trek got harder for Franklin from there and the moral of the story was eventually explained to him.

Now, even when he hits the kind of sweet form that saw him boot eight goals in a final last year, Franklin insists the game doesn't ever feel easy. He does at least say that when it is like that it does feel particularly good.

"You just feel confident," he said. "It goes so quickly you don't realise. I suppose once you're in that zone you just keep trying to get the ball in your hands, you've just got so much confidence you just want the ball kicked to you all the time, so it's a good place to be in."

Nathan Buckley last year declared Franklin as "the most sublimely talented player in the AFL" even before he played a game in a season that saw him win Coleman and premiership medals, an All-Australian guernsey and his first club best-and-fairest. But regardless of whether he perfects the art of goal-kicking and marking, Franklin does not think he will ever win the league's highest individual honour.

"I can't see a forward or a backman winning it," he says of the Brownlow Medal. "I think it is a midfielder's game, votes-wise anyway. They're on the ball and getting all the touches and they're right in the umpires' faces. As long as I'm playing good football and the team's having a win, I don't really care where I sit with anyone."

Within his club, Franklin is considered an emerging leader with largely untapped power and yet he says he can't imagine himself ever being captain.

"With leadership I think some people are born with it and I don't think I'm actually born with it, I think I've got to actually learn.

"It would be great to be in the leadership group in a couple of years, but I'm still just learning and taking it all in," he says.

When asked who the best player in the league is, Franklin doesn't hesitate: "Gary Ablett definitely. So fast. He's got everything. He's amazing. He's by far the best I reckon."

Pushed to choose second and third, Franklin nominates Brisbane Lions captain Jonathan Brown, who last year said Franklin was the best athlete the game had seen since Gary Ablett senior, and Carlton's Chris Judd. He can't separate the competition's best key defenders and so splits the honours between West Coast's Darren Glass, St Kilda's Max Hudghton—"He's the glove, he's just really tight on you, which can give you the shits after a while!"—and Geelong's Matthew Scarlett.

He pre-empts the next question: "You're not going to ask me where I'd put myself. No, I'm not going to say. I don't know, I wouldn't have a clue. I'd be happy to be in the top 50."

It's the only time that Franklin looks like he wants to turn off the voice recorder that didn't really seem to make him nervous.

FROM THE LIPS OF LANCE

Jarryd Roughead

"He's a great footballer and I've got no doubt he'll get 100 (goals) one year."

The Brownlow

"I can't see a forward or a backman winning it."

Captaincy

"With leadership I think some people are born with it and I don't think I'm actually born with it."

The AFL'S best player

"Gary Ablett definitely. So fast. He's got everything. He's amazing."

Where he rates

"I wouldn't have a clue. I'd be happy to be in the top 50."

The Age 30 May 2009

LET THE LIGHT SHINE

Martin Blake

Robert Harvey, who breaks St Kilda's games record tonight, first appeared at Moorabbin when he was 15.

"I was at Seaford playing juniors and I was happy. I came up for a few games and I just didn't get a look-in. I was on the bench most of the time, and it wasn't a really enjoyable experience."

Robert Harvey played league football at 16, a babe-in-the-woods situation that could never happen under today's rules. But St Kilda had spent nearly two years getting a reluctant Harvey to that point.

Recruiting manager John Beveridge, who plucked him from Seaford juniors and John Paul College, brought Harvey to Moorabbin in 1987 to play for Nepean in the under-15 school titles. There was no draft back then, merely geographical zones, and Harvey was slap bang in St Kilda's homeland.

Beveridge, one of Australia's best spotters by repute, saw talent. "Blind Freddie could see that he could find the ball and get through traffic, plus he could run and run."

But he also saw some indifference. "It didn't really mean an enormous amount to him early on to let his light shine as a potential AFL player. He liked playing with his mates and coming in to an unfamiliar situation was difficult for him."

Harvey, who was also in the state age cricket squads and playing district cricket as a left-arm fast bowler, confirms that he owes Beveridge much for his diligence. "It really had to be forced out a few years later to come down,"

Harvey said. "And I thank Johnny and my parents, who really pushed me to have a go at it, which I wasn't really keen to do."

When Harvey returned to play under-19s for the Saints in 1988, aged 16, Beveridge recalls that he had to fight to get him included on the bench for the opening round, the coach feeling he was too light, and too young. But St Kilda nominated him for the Victorian Teal Cup squad that year. "I remember sitting with his mother [Marilyn] at Waverley at a practice match one day, and I said, 'We've got to go out and try to get him to get the ball a bit.' He was so unselfish. It didn't mean anything to him and he didn't let his light shine."

Ultimately, Harvey would make the Victorian team and play in the national under-17 titles in Canberra, winning all-Australian selection alongside the likes of Wayne Carey. "I think it was probably then that he realised he could play," says Beveridge.

"I know it was the Western Oval and I know we got beaten by a lot and I got the first kick of the game. I remember the build-up of the week. I was still doing year 11 at school, and I was 16. The buzz around school was great and I was pretty popular that week."

St Kilda had a dreadful year in 1988 under the legendary Darrel Baldock. Late in the season, Baldock dispensed with caution and began elevating kids from the under-19 team. Nathan Burke was one, and in round 19 at the Western Oval, Harvey was another, that first kick symbolic of a career in which the football would follow him.

Near the start of the 1989 season, Tony Lockett's 10 goals against Carlton secured one momentous triumph for St Kilda. "I still have a tape of that game," says Beveridge. "Robert's wearing No. 52 and it's quite remarkable when you watch it, how many times he is the next person to get the ball. He had a remarkable ability to get himself in the line of vision of the person who was about to get the football."

St Kilda plainly had a good one on its hands, even if the club itself was a rabble.

"I don't even know how I do it. I used to watch Timmy Watson really closely as a kid. If you see footage of him, he does it all the time. I watched him and Essendon so closely that I've mimicked him. It's an unconscious thing that I do."

Robert Harvey was an Essendon supporter as a boy and it left him with his most familiar pose. Every AFL follower knows it only too well—the half-crouch at a stoppage, hands grabbing the hem of his shorts. He looks spent, as though he cannot go another step. Then the umpire pounds the ball down and he is gone again. That pose, and the step around a lunging opponent, became his trademarks.

At the height of his career, around 1997 and '98, teams despaired at how to stop him, for no one could run with him. They tried rotating taggers on him and Adelaide, under Malcolm Blight, effectively gave up. Blight played Mark Ricciuto on him, figuring that Harvey was going to get his 30 touches anyway, so the Crows might as well have a decent player in the middle.

"He's pretty much like those wind-up toys," says Grant Thomas. "You just turn that key on the back a few times, kick them up the bum . . . and away he goes. When it runs out, you wind it up again. He doesn't run out too often."

"Actually, playing is what you love. All pre-season you think, 'Maybe I could live without footy,' and then you get back and play your first intra-club game and you think how much you love it and how much you'd miss it if you didn't have it."

Grant Thomas says Robert Harvey is "an extraordinarily driven person".

It's a matter of public record that not long after he turned 30, Harvey had to be told—more than once—to tone down the level and intensity of his training. As the model professional, he was breaking himself down.

Harvey learned. "I'm in a good routine with my body and, arguably, I'm feeling actually younger."

When he received a partial tear of the plantar facia tendon in the base of a foot last season, he deliberately tore it by jumping around in his backyard. "All the doctors basically said, 'Just keep playing and do what you do and eventually it'll snap in a game and you'll find it'll get better after that.' So I just wanted to hurry the process along. At that stage I didn't know how many games I had left in me. So I didn't want to waste time with niggling injuries."

Harvey never craved the spotlight of *The Footy Show* or other distractions, despite the suggestion that he has been slightly undervalued by the public as a result. "I haven't been one that likes the centre of attention and it's never changed. I'm a footballer and I've always seen myself that way, and that's the way I go about it."

Ultimately, he would sit comfortably among the greats of his era—Carey, Michael Voss, James Hird and Nathan Buckley. "Harves is gifted from a skill perspective, but you wouldn't put him at the absolute top of the tops," says

Thomas. "It's more about his work rate and his mental toughness and his ability to endure pain and continue on.

"He reads the play very well and he knows where the ball's going to go, but I think they're the intangibles and if we all had that courage, there'd be a lot more Robert Harveys around. But for one reason or another, most of us mere mortals decide enough's enough, and we haven't been able to push through that barrier."

"From my point of view, I'm at round seven now. Round 22 is like three years away for me. That's the way I feel. That's the way it's got to be. I'm most unlikely to be playing next year, but I just don't know."

On form, Robert Harvey might well do a Craig Bradley and play on beyond 35, pushing into 2007. He has had some outstanding games in 2006 and his performance in St Kilda's winning final in Adelaide just last season will go down as one of his finest.

"When I play, physically I feel like I can't do things I used to do, but I've been able to manage that by just adjusting my game a little bit to what needs to be done in those areas," he says. "I've obviously lost a bit of pace, and that happens to everyone. I've been able to use my experience to make that not as much of a factor. I don't carry the ball as much as I used to, for instance. That's just something that has to happen as you get older."

At St Kilda, Thomas and others suspect a premiership might round it off just nicely. "That's up to him entirely," says Thomas. "If he plays how he's been playing and he wants to continue on, we'll sit and have a chat about it. But it's one thing for that to happen; it's another thing for the mind to be able to cope with the rigours of another year, which is very, very intense. It's not something we'd decide on now. Quite obviously if he achieves some of the goals he's after, that may make a decision for him."

"The mind and motivation I don't think will be a problem, but I don't want to hang around too long either. Maybe I've already done that."

Not likely, most of the footy world would say.

The Age 12 May 2006

ABLETT THE YOUNGER MAKES HIS OWN MARK

Greg Baum

GARY ABLETT HAS SPENT A lifetime growing into his name, and outgrowing it. When he was with the Geelong Falcons in the under 18s, 200 turned up to see him one day at Warrnambool. On learning that he had missed the bus, all but a handful left.

Ablett grew up at the edge of the limelight, so its glare now is not as blinding as might be presumed.

"The reality of Gary Ablett's life is that he has been in the spotlight for more than three years," said Geelong chief executive Brian Cook. "He had to get used to it a long time ago."

He and brother Nathan went to training and games with their famous and enigmatic father, and sometimes he absent-mindedly left them behind.

Many Geelong players remember the mini-Abletts as barefooted pests in the rooms, and Tim McGrath and Garry Hocking have told of how they drilled kicks at their heads to try to drive them out. The junior Abletts caught the balls and laughed.

The Abletts were comfortable with their name. Player/manager Ricky Nixon, speaking on *Fox Footy* recently, told how the boys would get their father to sign football cards, then sell them at school for $70 apiece, until Gary snr stopped it.

Ted Whitten jnr, one of the few who has successfully followed in the footsteps of a legendary footballing father, said fame was not so alarming. Once asked if he wished he had a different Christian name, Ablett jnr matter-of-factly replied: "I'd still be his son."

Ablett grew up and lives still with his mother, Sue, in Jan Juc, a beach town not given to fuss. "Everyone knew he was Gary Ablett's son, and people did treat him differently, but not differently bad," said Josh Rudd, a teenage friend and teammate at the Falcons, who tomorrow plays for Port Melbourne in the VFL grand final. "He was just Gaz, you know.

"Jan Juc's a bit of suburbia. It's not like walking down Bourke Street. It's a surfie town. There are a lot of young people, and a few don't have an interest in footy. If he lived in Belmont, it might be different."

"When you grow up with your dad playing footy, and you're at the club day and night from when you were born, it's not that hard," he said. "You get used to people looking at you and knowing who you are."

"A lot of our life was footy," he said. "Any time we got the chance, we'd kick the footy together. Footy and surfing—that's what Torquay's all about."

Ablett still surfs, as coast kids must. When he began in the AFL, his unruly hair was a teenage surfer's careless effect. Now a Geelong salon claims to style it that way for him. Ablett snr left long ago, and Sue understandably has guarded her privacy so rigorously that few even at Geelong footy club know her.

She has left Gary jnr to his own footballing devices. He idolised his father and remains close, but when his dad retired, Ablett became fascinated with Robert Harvey. Ablett had his father's name, but his own ideas.

Falcons general manager Michael Turner, a Geelong legend and contemporary of Gary snr, said other parents grumbled about nepotism when Gary jnr was picked out by the feeder club at 15. Turner was unfussed because he could see an exceptional footballer.

"He will be more like Garry Hocking than Gary Ablett," he told Geelong at the time. "He's so creative with his hands." Hocking, a contemporary of Ablett snr, won four best-and-fairests at Geelong.

Others have seen in Ablett an image of the prepubescent Michael Voss. Ablett has had to live up to many names. But always there was one.

"He's got the Gary Ablett gene," said Billy Brownless, an accomplished and much-loved teammate of Ablett snr. "Only one other's got it. It's something different. If you could, you'd clone him."

Andrew Bews, another much-decorated peer of Ablett snr, hears the father in the way the son laughs.

Ablett jnr worried then, and does still, about undue privilege "He's very anxious about the fact that people do things for him," said Alan McConnell, until last year an assistant coach at Geelong, and chauffeur to Ablett before he got his licence. "He doesn't want too much of a fuss."

This consciousness led to an overdeveloped team ethic. Damian Christensen, Ablett's coach at the Falcons, said Ablett had to be taught to be selfish.

McConnell said: "One criticism early was that he handballed too much, almost to the point where it was ridiculous."

The 2001 draft was the richest yet. Nine Falcons were taken, and Ablett was a bargain for Geelong at No. 40 under the father–son rule. He was 17 and rough-edged. He sometimes borrowed clothes without returning them, though this soon stopped. But he won people with his guileless nature. Gary snr negotiated with the club on his son's behalf about media and training. He feared inquisition and overexposure from the media, and burn-out on the training track. He also asked his own manager, Michael Baker, to handle Ablett jnr's affairs.

Ablett snr realised his son had a privilege denied to him in his footballing youth—control of his own destiny. "If I had someone like yourself, I probably could have done a lot more than what I've done," he said to Baker. But Ablett snr had enjoyed a privilege his son did not—his name had been his own to make. Young Ablett initially preferred the club's new spa to the gym. He kept a wary distance from the media. Brownless interviewed young Ablett and the other draftees for *The Footy Show* one night at Kardinia Park, but only after Ablett snr had rung Brownless to ask him to go easy on Ablett jnr. Ablett snr waited in a nearby cafe.

Ablett jnr was suspicious of people until they earned his trust. One was Gary Harrison, a friend of coach Mark Thompson and his clipboard man until a recent fall left him in a wheelchair. There was a poignant moment at the end of last Saturday's semi-final, the first game Harrison had attended since his accident. He and Ablett embraced, and Ablett spent a long time kneeling by his chair.

Ablett has never been less than proud of his father and his football heritage. "If I'm half as good as my father, I'll be very happy indeed," he said in a rare public utterance in his first season. He displayed more social graces than his father, who had always been a remote figure at the club.

"He wasn't the next Gary Ablett," said Warwick Hadfield, then media manager. "Except he was."

Ablett began the year in the seniors and finished it in the reserves, usual for a rookie. The interest he excited then was enormous.

By the second year, Ablett was accustomed to the rigours of AFL life. A club official was astonished early that season to see Ablett with a group of new draftees in the club restaurant. "No chips," he cautioned one. "Have salad."

He began to speak up at team meetings. His football blossomed. Kevin Sheedy called him the best young footballer in the competition. Ablett finished fourth in the club's best-and-fairest award.

This year has been Ablett's coming of football age. He is bigger and stronger. He has made sticky positions his specialty. He leads the league in contested possessions. He leads Geelong in tackles. Two-thirds of all his possessions are classified as "hard"—the average across the league is one-third. Turner has seen him strip the ball from opponents in the thick of packs, as he saw him do in the under 18s, but not again until this year.

He is third among Geelong's goalscorers, first for scoring assists. McConnell highlighted a moment in last week's semi-final when he marked, played on and weighted a pass into a space that he knew would soon be filled by Paul Chapman. It was, said McConnell, the play of the natural.

Ablett jnr has managed all this despite a continuing battle with osteitis pubis that watchers say has obviously limited his preparation all season.

McConnell said Ablett's progress was a tribute to coach Mark Thompson's delicate handling of all of his generation over three seasons. Thompson has not rushed and ruined any of them, but nursed them in and out of the team, accepting short-term defeat and the fans' opprobrium for the gain that has ensued.

"People don't understand how well he has managed that," he said. McConnell explained this was why Ablett was not played on the ball sooner, and was not always played there now. It is clear now that father and son are different people from different generations, playing in different Geelong teams and in different roles. Ablett jnr chose not to wear his father's No. 5 guernsey, but the next that came out of the bag. Now, said Cook, his No. 29 is the guernsey most demanded by Geelong fans.

Ablett gets more emails than any other player. At clinics, half the kids want to be in his line. At matches, the older crowd thrills to the romance of Ablett reincarnate, seemingly without the torment this time.

Turner had seen previously how one player could fill Skilled Stadium, and did not believe it would happen again. "But it's getting to that stage again with Junior," he said.

Ablett is thriving in all ways. He owns two blocks of land in Torquay and is building a house on one, and has just bought a $60,000 car. He has thawed a little towards the media. He is completing year 11 with the help of a tutor at the club.

"He knows where he wants to go in life," said Baker. "He's gained a lot more confidence in himself, not only in footy, but in his personal life."

Cook said Ablett was obliging with sponsors and coteries, and open with supporters, "in particular those who seem to be in need".

Associates describe Ablett as polite, courteous and good-natured, but cherubic only in appearance.

"He's had his moments," said McConnell. "No one's suggesting that he's an angel. He's a knockabout kid. His name happens to be Gary Ablett."

Rudd, watching from a distance, said he felt relieved that Ablett was making it on his own terms. "It's like, there you go, he's done it himself," he said.

Ablett jnr is 20, but has played 50 games already. His father did not begin at Geelong until he was 22. That does not mean that Gary jnr will be an even better player, just that he has grown up in another time and another system. He is his own person and his own player, in his own time, and it is now.

The Age 18 Septemer 2004

IN THE TWILIGHT, SUN SETS ON ESSENDON ERA

Greg Baum

MELBOURNE BADE FAREWELL TO Kevin Sheedy and James Hird at twilight. It was the right light for the occasion, glorious while it lasted, but ultimately fading to blackness. For the Sheedy/Hird era at Essendon, grand as it has been, there will be no last railing against that fading light.

The night began with a stagy entrance, the two of them alone, greeted thunderously by nearly 90,000. Arriving fans had mingled with those departing a Jehovah's Witnesses convention at Melbourne Park, adding to the evangelical feel. All that was missing were the hallelujahs.

Both causes célèbres were, frankly, discomfited. It seemed like putting the end at the beginning. They had said all along that this was, before anything else, another match there for the winning: a finale, but not—if they could help it—final. As soon as dignity allowed, they gestured for the team to join them to shred the banner. They did not so much stand on ceremony as stomp on it.

It finished with fireworks, a lap of honour and a guard of same, too, formed by players from both clubs. Sheedy and Hird walked their laps in opposite directions, embracing when they met halfway. It symbolised their years together at Essendon, each going his own way, but ultimately finishing in the same place.

Both said they were profoundly grateful to the club and the fans, and would cherish the memories forever. But arch-competitors that they are, both were a little rueful that it had to end this downbeat way. A club official put it bluntly: "We'd rather have the four points."

On this night, they did not get them, nor deserve them. Hird won a free kick within 20 seconds of the first bounce, and kicked a goal on the quarter-time siren to put the Bombers two in front. But thereafter, he and they declined like the setting sun.

Hird ranged up and down the ground, and every now and then darted across it, still searching for angles; in this, he was like the many who have paid tribute to him latterly. He was as creative as ever when in the play, but unable to bend this match, unlike so many others, to his will. Still, Richmond watched him hawkishly, knowing the inspiration he might provide if allowed to cut loose.

Hird spent the last quarter on the forward line, from which redoubt he so often has proved heroic before. But, save for one last mark and goal, he could make no impact. Mostly, the action was at the other end of the ground. Finally, he inserted himself at a centre bounce, but again the play washed around him and away towards Richmond's goals.

Hird said he played the closing moments in a daze. Defeat hurt now as much as ever, perhaps more, for, as he said later, he will never have the chance to redress it; he will never again play for a place in the finals.

The match rose to no heights. The vast crowd and the sense of occasion could not disguise a sober truth, that neither side had it within itself to scale pinnacles. It has been a wretched season for Richmond and a muddling one for Essendon. This night, the Tigers at least could count a win, precious for its rarity this season. Essendon had no consolation. Sheedy, still the coach, was succinct. "We don't deserve to be in the eight," he said. "Simple as that."

The final siren was an anticlimax. At first, no one approached Hird, then at length Andrew Lovett, then a bunch of Richmond players, who could now afford to be gracious. One handed him the match ball, which he bounced disconsolately a couple of times, then kicked to a trainer. His playing days on the MCG finished to strains of the Richmond theme song. "It's been an amazing ride. But I'm spent, I'm tired and I'm gone," he said later.

Soon enough, though, he, Sheedy and the massed Bomber faithful gathered themselves up, for this was not about one unfulfilled night, but a many-splendoured era. Their lap was truly an honour; the fans made it so. "Once the siren goes, you've got to get on with it," said Sheedy. "I enjoyed the moment." Slowly, the weight of defeat lifted from the moment.

Essendon's dressing room was less gloomy than is customary for losers. Partly, that was because the warm-up area had become a de facto creche, ringing to the shouts of players' children who, in their innocence, had no thought other than for the next kick. No one had the heart to growl, nor now any cause.

Hird's priorities were plain: media, yes, but before that, one last kick on the ground with his children. He had said that he would be chasing a kick to the last siren. In fact, he was still in pursuit an hour afterwards. It is the mark of the man.

Sheedy admitted that he had felt a lump in his throat upon leaving the arena. Later, he appeared red-eyed. One eye anyway had been figuratively blackened this night by Richmond, making at least for an agreeable colour scheme. This is the eternal way of football.

One match remains, in faraway Perth. For most of its course, the Sheedy/ Hird era has been a fairytale. All that remains now is the ending.

The Age 27 August 2007

THE CONTENDER

Peter Hanlon

THE FAIRYTALE OF MICHAEL BARLOW has given the football cognoscenti a shake, planting a rare seed of self-doubt: what if we don't know best after all? Yet his greatest lesson speaks to us all—no matter how many times you get knocked down, don't stop getting back up, don't ever lose sight of the dream.

Barlow's is a very Australian story, with a central character who would not have been out of place on a different field, in another time, fighting a battle more cutthroat even than AFL football in 2010. Dig for the root of this resilience, and you'll unearth the crossheads of a nation's history—immigration, goldrush, war, toil of an unforgiving land by hard men and even stronger women and, above all, persistence.

Michael is the middle of Herb and Jenny Barlow's five children, the third of four boys. His father—the third in four consecutive generations of Herb Barlows—is a Cobram dentist who grew up at Rushworth, where his grandfather, the pioneer of this magnificent moniker, alighted from England. He soon decided running a butcher shop had greater prospects than digging for gold, laying the foundations for his sons to make a life on the land.

"Dad got tuberculosis on the way home from the war," Herb says of the second Herb Barlow. "My two older sisters were born, and he spent about four of the first five years of his marriage in Heidelberg repat."

"They couldn't even sit on their dad's lap because he was infectious," Jenny says, adding how old Herb had marvelled at his wife, Julie, who spent the post-war years lugging a suitcase and her children between their Rushworth farm and hospital in Melbourne. "They were amazing people really. Herb had major, major health issues, but they just got on with it. Julie used to always just say, 'He'll be right.'" And he was. Herb left hospital minus five ribs and a lung, and with his spine surgically mended from skull to base.

"That was the early '50s," Herb says of his father. "And he died in 1995."

Jenny's father, Pat Beirne, was from Drogheda, County Louth; he contested the Northern Ireland championships in the 220-yard sprint. As Michael's catalogue of AFL rejection grew, she'd try to soften the blows by chipping him: "Have you told them your grandfather's Irish? They're going over there getting kids all the time!"

Long before laser treatment, her dad had a shamrock tattoo removed so he could join the Royal Air Force, leaving a dimpled square of tortured skin on his arm. Come peace-time, he sought a better life in Australia, leaving behind three sisters who would never marry because they couldn't afford a dowry. "Dad always wanted to make something of himself," Jenny says.

Her mother knew what she wanted, too. "She chased him rather more vigorously than he chased her," says Jenny.

Encouraged by his wife to finish the studies denied him by the war, Pat became a teacher, moved the family to Canada, then on to Coventry in the English Midlands. It was there that Herb and Jenny would become more than the friends they'd been at Melbourne Uni where they initially met. And it was there that their eldest children, Herb No. 4 and Domenic, were born.

An exploration of the Barlow family tree is pertinent because it lays bare Michael's DNA. Ray Carroll, who coached the Barlow boys—including their 1972 school best-and-fairest winner Herb—at Kilmore's Assumption College, puts it plainly. "This is a family of the highest character."

Their bond is heart-warming.

Asked what she misses most about Michael since he moved to Perth, 18-year-old Maisie says: "I miss all my brothers. It's just good having them all together, because they're a lot of fun to be around."

We're almost up to Michael, but a sketch of his siblings fills out the picture. Herb, 25, studied pharmaceutical science and lives in Port Fairy, having returned from a working holiday in England during which his father says "he became very proficient at darts and drinking beer". Dom, a year younger, is in Adelaide studying dentistry, having switched from physiotherapy, and before that mechanical engineering.

"Talk about resilience," Jenny says. "This is his seventh year of studying."

Maisie is working through her gap year before studying science at Monash, starring on the netball court for Shepparton Swans, a source of great pride for Jenny, a Goulburn Valley netball legend who represented Warwickshire and trialled for England. And then there's Declan, who has been amusing his family for most of his 20 years.

"We don't talk about Dec," Herb laughs. "He just exists." Maisie calls him "very witty"; Jenny says he's "a trick, always joking", and has always been clever. Come school awards nights, Dec would tell his parents, "You'd better bring the wheelbarrow!" then be mortified when he picked up only one gong.

Playing footy, he'd tell Herb all the way home in the car how well he'd gone. "I'd reckon I must have been at a different game," says Herb.

Yet beneath the bluff is that Barlow persistence. Three years ago, when Michael was starring for Shepparton United, Declan was struggling to get a game in the under-18s. Against undermanned Rochester one week, he volunteered to change sides to make up the numbers, then asked his parents if he could make the switch permanent.

A couple of weeks later, they played Shepparton, and Declan lined up at centre half-back against one of the opposition's guns. Herb turned to Jenny and said: "This is going to be a long couple of hours." But the kid who jokingly talked a better game than he played, who just wanted to be out there having a go, played the game of his life. "I didn't in my wildest dreams think he had that in him," Herb says. "To this day, that's the best day at the footy I've ever had."

Herb and Jenny Barlow have had some pretty amazing days and nights at the football in recent months, which brings us to the equal second favourite for the 2010 Brownlow Medal, 22-year-old Michael John Barlow. If his forebears have given him the tools to pen his chapter in the family's tale, he has done them proud.

Jenny says Michael knows what not to take too seriously in life. His prominent nose has long been a source of amusement. The possibility that he was only recruited by Fremantle to make Matthew Pavlich feel better has been raised in the Barlow household.

Herb notes that Michael "sometimes struggles with the English language", laughing as he reels off examples of comical mispronunciation. Freo's "entertainment co-ordinator", David Mundy, recently asked Michael what he thought about holding a quiz on away trips. "Michael said, 'Good idea,' and David said, 'Righto, you're in charge of the quiz then.'" Michael thinks Mundy is a good delegator. Herb thinks there will be some pretty strange questions in the quiz.

Mention football's conventional pathway and Herb shakes his head—not out of bitterness that Michael missed the ride, but because "the system" convinces kids that if they don't make it at 18, they never will.

"That's terribly sad for a kid," he says.

He has seen too many either say "stuff it" or go bush for money. Neither tends to produce a healthy outcome.

He has never seen Michael so dejected as when he was cut from the Goulburn Valley under-15 schoolboys squad. "He was going to Assumption the next year, and their first match of the season was against GV schoolboys," Herb says. "I asked him, 'What happens now?' He said, 'I'll just have to wait another year to show them how good I am.'" He said, after he had 35 possessions against the team that rejected him.

And on it went. Not deemed good enough for Murray Bushrangers' TAC Cup team, he matched Shane Crawford's possessions haul at Assumption. Prime to shine for Vic Country in 2007 while starring for Shepparton United, he was the last man cut from the squad. "He always had someone who could beat him along the way," Herb says.

By now he was studying urban planning at Melbourne Uni, and travelling home on weekends with Dom to play for United. Their father laughs every time he crosses the Goulburn Valley Channel near Murchison, at the memory of them breaking down on the way back to the city one Sunday, and killing time by stripping down and doing their rehab, standing in the freezing water watching the traffic pass by.

Jenny says you need someone to believe in you, and for Barlow that was Craig Blizzard. United's then footy manager called his old mate John Beveridge, St Kilda's veteran recruiter, and told him he should come for a drive. "How good?" Beveridge asked. "You're not going to like what you see," Blizzard told him, "but what's inside is unbelievable."

Beveridge stood behind the goals with his notepad and pen, a plea from Blizzard—"Look past the wounded-duck run, don't take what you see as gospel"—ringing in his ears. At quarter-time, Beveridge said: "He's taller than I thought, he looks slow . . ." By game's end, he'd counted 43 possessions and nine tackles.

"He was running down people who were faster than him," Beveridge told

Blizzard. "His mind's either quicker than his body, or he just knows what to do." The pace question is interesting. Barlow did the 2008 pre-season at St Kilda, and was beaten only by Robert Eddy in three-kilometre time trials.

Endurance is his pet subject, yet at the state screening trials that year, the "wounded duck" ranked in the top 5 per cent over 20 metres.

The Saints decided he wasn't what they were after, taking Eljay Connors from Echuca instead, but Herb says Michael was by now emboldened.

Impressed by coach Simon Atkins knocking on his door, he moved to Werribee and continued his education. At the end of a stellar 2008, Jenny recalls Atkins saying to him: "I don't know what they're looking for, I don't know why you didn't get drafted, but you're coming back next year and we'll try something else. And I can promise you, you'll be on a list at the end of the year."

By last November's draft, fresh from inclusion in a second VFL team of the year and Werribee's best-and-fairest, he'd talked to six clubs. His mates in Melbourne floated the idea of a draft celebration barbecue, but his parents cautioned patience—just in case. Again, his name wasn't read out.

Jenny told her devastated son: "You've achieved hugely, Mikey, but maybe this is the level you'll play at, and you're a gun. That's very credible, very substantial." He looked at her and said what he'd said every other time his heart had been ripped out: "But, mum, I just know I could do it." The next day, he was running 200s around the Cobram footy ground. "He'd just pick up his bag and off he'd go," Jenny says. He trained with Essendon for a week before the rookie draft, and when the Bombers chose Kyle Hardingham, who'd been targeted by Fremantle, the Dockers picked Barlow. Herb still wonders if there was spite at play, but so be it.

In Shepparton, Blizzard's phone rang. "Your boy's just been picked up," Beveridge told him. "You know, I've got a funny feeling he's going to break all the rules, and he's going to be great. I just hope a kid like that shakes the system." Thirteen rounds into his debut AFL season, he's done that and then some.

The Barlow brothers have been backing Michael for most possessions every week, initially at big odds, and he has filled their wallets five times. Jenny asked young Herb if he'd put money on him for the Ross Glendinning Medal, and received a text message back saying: "Mum, I don't know why people wouldn't back him!" An aunty had $50 on him for the Brownlow at 1000–1.

Declan has taken to declaring: "Cash cow, Jenny, cash cow!" Asked if achieving such an all-consuming goal has changed him, Jenny says, "He's trying awfully hard to be Michael, because he likes who he is." After a Dockers clinic in Templestowe last Sunday, he hooked up with Melbourne mates and raised a glass or two and, after a night back in his own bed, he was sweating it out in Cobram. "He does the time when he's done the crime," she says.

Before flying west again, he dropped in at Shepparton's Deakin Reserve and took a few drills at training. Blizzard said he hadn't made it five steps onto the ground "before six blokes had had a crack at him". It won't soon be forgotten that he boarded a plane in Perth recently with his keyless-ignition car still running in the long-term car park.

Driving around "doing a few jobs" with Jenny on Tuesday, he got hold of her iPhone and replaced a screen-saver picture of Maisie with a madly grinning Michael Barlow self-portrait. After he'd gone (having forgotten his runners and phone charger), he sent Jenny a text message which she calls "the essential Mikey".

"Just want them to know that I'm still just Mike Barlow. Love you Mum, and sad I'm heading back. But loving what I'm doing."

THE GAP YEARS	
What Michael Barlow did from age 17 to 22	
2005	Assumption College school football: won Peter Crimmins Medal for best-and-fairest and Laurie Bakewell Award for academic, conduct and sporting excellence.
2006	Shepparton United in the Goulburn Valley Football League: runner-up best-and-fairest.
2007	Shepparton United, GVFL: best-and-fairest winner.
2008	Werribee FC, VFL: VFL team of the year, fourth in the best-and-fairest.
2009	Werribee FC, VFL: VFL team of year, best-and-fairest winner.

The Sunday Age 27 June 2010

McLEOD'S SILVER LINING

Martin Flanagan

I RANG MALCOLM BLIGHT THIS week and said I wanted to talk to him about Andrew McLeod the footballer. "Ah," Blight replied. "What a lovely project." Blight coached Adelaide to back-to-back premierships in 1997 and 1998. McLeod won the Norm Smith Medal in both grand finals.

When I met McLeod on Thursday, I asked him what he remembered of the 1997 grand final against St Kilda. His first memory is running out and realising there were more people at the MCG than there were in the whole of Darwin. "I freaked right out," said McLeod, who hails from Darwin. He has a slightly slow way of speaking, the edge of a Territory drawl.

Darwin's home, he tells me.

Always will be.

When I push him a little further, he does give me one other memory from the '97 grand final. It's Blight saying to him at three-quarter-time: "Have you got another one in you?" That's the end of the story.

You have to imagine the rest.

I imagine Blight is saying: "Do you have another quarter in you like your first three?" I sat with Bernie Sheehy that day, a canny observer of the game. I thought McLeod deserved the Norm Smith Medal and so did Bernie. "He was good when they weren't," Bernie said. He meant Adelaide wasn't good early but McLeod was. And by the end of the game, he was doing more than playing well—he was 21 years old and controlling a grand final.

The next year, against a Wayne Carey-led North Melbourne, his mastery was even more pronounced, particularly after half-time.

As Blight described it: "Every time he touched the ball, or nearly every time, we scored a goal. It was unbelievable. He gave people such clear possession." That's what I remember about the 1998 grand final—the acres of space that started appearing around Adelaide players after half-time.

By good fortune, I happened to stand beside McLeod's father, Jock, at the press conference after the game. I asked him how he compared his son's two grand final performances.

He thought about it and then said: "Last year, he dominated. This year, he created." Jock confirmed that his son played the second grand final with an injured knee.

Jock's father spent time in the Northern Territory but Jock was born in Sydney and grew up in Melbourne. He went to the Territory "about 40 years ago" and played footy with the Buffaloes, Darwin's famous Aboriginal club. Andrew's mother, Marie, is an AhMat, one of the major Darwin Aboriginal families. Andrew McLeod has both Aboriginal and Torres Strait Island heritage and asked what it means to be indigenous, he said simply: "It's who I am."

As a kid, he played all sports and was drawn to rugby league as much as footy. He says he just played for fun and to be with his mates who called him "Bunji", a local Aboriginal word for brother. He says most of Adelaide calls him that now.

He went to Port Adelaide in the SANFL and fell to Fremantle in the AFL draft. In one of the most infamous football transfers of all time, Fremantle, then coached by Gerard Neesham, traded him to Adelaide for a player whose name has long since disappeared into the mist. But playing AFL football was not something McLeod had aspired to. He just played for fun. "I suppose football got serious when I was traded to Adelaide," he said.

Blight said he could see the talent in McLeod when he arrived as coach of the club but was unsure of how to release it.

"We played him half-forward, he did OK, but it wasn't quite happening for either Andrew or the team." Blight rang Stephen Williams, McLeod's coach at Port Adelaide in the SANFL."

"Well," Williams said, "we recruited him as a half-back."

And from that day onwards, says Blight, McLeod's career blossomed.

That same year, 1997, McLeod won the club best-and-fairest from half-back. In the course of the year, Blight also tried him on the ball. That worked very well, too. But Blight didn't leave him there. In the coach's words, "we put that one back in the pocket". As a result, Blight says, "the tagging of him never happened. No one knew him and it set us up."

I put McLeod's two grand final performances up with those of Michael Long in 1993 and Gary Ablett in 1989 as the great individual performances I have witnessed, but in terms of McLeod's career, they are now a long time ago. The story of the intervening years is one of continued success, the only significant individual honour to have eluded him being the Brownlow. In 2001, McLeod lost to Jason Akermanis, the joker in the pack, after a final round in which McLeod had 37 possessions and didn't poll a single vote.

Blight describes McLeod's career as "brilliance and durability" but there was a period around 2004 when he nearly lost his way. He had marital problems and moved in with then best friend Lleyton Hewitt, a friendship that later fell apart over Hewitt's plan to publish film of places McLeod had taken him on traditional Aboriginal land in the Northern Territory without permission from the traditional owners of the land.

McLeod is now back with his wife. This unsettled period in his life made him the property of the tabloid press, which he clearly found most distasteful.

"I'm a pretty private person."

Of the overall period, he says: "I like to think I've become a better person from those experiences."

What happened to Andrew McLeod, the footballer, is that he woke up one morning and didn't know why he was playing the game any more. Something had gone. He still finds it difficult to describe exactly what happened but in the end, he says: "You can get away from why you actually do things." He credits his former captain and premiership teammate Mark Bickley for giving him "tools" with which to handle some of the pressures that befell him.

Bickley, now a presenter with Channel Nine in Adelaide, remembers McLeod being "flat".

The incident that put McLeod back on track was going to watch his son play footy with his father, Jock. "I saw why my son plays footy.

"He loves it. And I was standing there with my old man. That's what it's all about." And he did something he doesn't normally do—he watched a replay. "I'm not one to watch footy. I don't watch replays. I don't like to read about myself."

Nonetheless, he watched a replay of the 1997 grand final and found he enjoyed reliving the game. "It ignited that passion again."

Ask Bickley what makes McLeod a great player and he says, jokingly: "What? You can't see for yourself?" When Victorians list great players of the past five years, they usually nominate Nathan Buckley, James Hird and Michael Voss.

This is not the South Australian view. Bickley says what distinguishes the best players is "brilliance over a long period".

McLeod's met that criteria.

Blight says McLeod is one of the best five players he's ever seen. I ask Blight if he would compare McLeod to Gary Ablett senior.

"Yes," he says. "They both thrilled you nine times out of 10."

Bickley says a characteristic of McLeod's career is that he has always produced in big games, pointing to the individual honours he has won in representative matches.

I confess to Bickley a slight feeling of disappointment about McLeod's career in that having seen him perform so well in two grand finals, I always wanted to see him in a third. Three Norm Smith Medals would make him unique. Bickley disagrees. "He had two opportunities and he took them. Some players, like Brad Johnson, don't even get one opportunity."

When asked the highlights of his career, McLeod says grand finals are "the ultimate".

After that, he says, is playing for Australia. McLeod toured Ireland in 2005 and got to room with Hird. "I know I shouldn't swear, but I was thinking, 'How f—ing good is this?'"

McLeod says you make "special bonds with other people" out of representative games.

"I really want to play with 'Buddy' Franklin and Matthew Pavlich," he says. Every player wants state of origin because it's the opportunity to play with the best, McLeod says. If you play the game for the reasons McLeod does, that's what you naturally want to do.

After the 2005 tour, Jim Stynes said it was the indigenous players in the Australian team who got the most out of Ireland, and specifically named McLeod.

When I mention that, McLeod tells me of entering a 700-year-old castle. Watching his face, I could see him recall the moment the great age of the stone walls closed around him. "The passion Aboriginal people have for their land and their country is similar to the Irish."

Stynes told him of how his uncle jumped the fence at Dublin's Croke Park the day the British soldiers opened fire on the crowd in 1920.

"I love those stories," he says with a grin. "They get me going." McLeod has a Torres Strait warrior headdress tattooed on his right shoulder and is described to me by one who knows him well as a very proud man.

After playing for his country, he lists his next highlight as playing for the Aboriginal All-Stars. I ask him who his footy heroes were growing up. "The Territory blokes," he says. Maurice Rioli and Michael Long but first and foremost Michael "Magic" McLean. "Magic's No. 1 in my eyes."

At the age of 31, McLeod says the biggest thrill he gets out of footy is going into indigenous communities and spending time with kids. Adelaide's football operations manager, John Reid, not a sentimental type, describes what McLeod does for the Aboriginal kids who come to watch the Crows train. "He puts a smile on their face for three weeks," Reid says.

McLeod says he no longer takes the game for granted. A match such as the one to be staged tonight, he says, is an opportunity to represent his family, his state, his home town, his people and his club.

In fact, he's representing everyone but Victoria. Finally, I ask McLeod what he thinks of Blight. "I loved him as a coach. He gave me so much confidence as a young bloke. He said, 'Let yourself go. Play the game your way.'"

The Age 10 May 2008

CAPTAIN FANTASTIC:
THE LEGEND OF ROO

Emma Quayle

MARK RICCIUTO WAS READY TO GO. He had his first footy jumper, a pair of shorts and new boots for his five-year-old feet.

For weeks, he had been begging his father, Murray, for a berth in the under-10 team he coached each Saturday morning on Waikerie's riverside oval. Finally named for his first game, Mark yanked up his black and white socks and knotted his laces. He jumped out of the car, took one look at the milling group of mean, snarling nine-year-olds and decided there was no way he was playing football.

"He got a bit scared. I think he thought, 'Hang on, I need a bit more time here,'" Murray Ricciuto recalled. "He didn't play at all that year. But after that, you couldn't stop him."

Ricciuto has not backed down from much since. When he left his orange-tinted country town, the self-proclaimed citrus capital of South Australia, he was a 16-year-old premiership player not the least bit frightened of bigger, tougher bodies.

Errol Matschoss, a Ricciuto family friend who watched every Waikerie game from a fallen log with Murray, Mark's uncle Ralph and a communal bottle of brandy, remembers the teenager being moved from a forward pocket to the middle early in the 1991 decider.

Six goals down late in the first quarter, Waikerie won its first flag in 17 seasons. "Mark just turned everything upside down. He won the game," Matschoss said. "He got in there and said, 'Enough of this, I'm taking these blokes on.'"

Adelaide's captain is still as strong-willed and decisive as ever, not just on the ground. Teammate Ken McGregor says Ricciuto will not merely suggest that a teammate do something with more devotion—he will demand it. "There aren't any mix-ups with Roo," he said. "You know when he's serious."

Ricciuto's ability to deliver a blunt message is something his predecessor, Mark Bickley, has envied. "If someone had to be pulled into line, I'd get them alone, talk to them and massage them a bit," Bickley said. "Mark would just march right up and say, 'Listen, this is the way it should be done.' He's very forthright, and he's not as emotional as I was.

"I start crying at the drop of a hat, so at different stages, I'd get up in front of the boys and start bawling. When we'd run out on the training track, Roo would say, 'Bloody hell, Bicks, you're hopeless. What's the world coming to?'"

But if Ricciuto is direct and demanding, he does not distance himself. Rather, people are drawn to him, and have been ever since he would party at the Waikerie disco, then lead a crowd to the local bakery for a freshly baked 3am pie.

Most who toured Ireland with the Australian team last October wanted to have a drink with Roo; if there is fun to be had, McGregor said, the skipper is "right at the middle of it". "He knows where it is, actually. Everyone follows him there."

Bickley suspects Ricciuto has a bit of everyone in him. Or can find something to do with anyone. "He loves to have a beer and he loves to have a punt. He's a pretty good card player," Bickley said. "It's the country upbringing, I reckon. You're always inventing ways to have fun in the country. He's probably a pinball wizard who's good at eight ball and can throw a mean dart. He'd find fun doing anything."

Ricciuto likes to be surrounded, too. First, by the family of which he is intensely proud. An action picture of him covers the fridge door in Waikerie, but Mark shares wall space with his sister Lisa and her family, and older brother Craig, who runs a car yard with Ricciuto.

As a kid, Ricciuto involved himself. In the middle of many a card game with Murray and Ralph, Matschoss would turn to find a pint-sized Mark sitting at his elbow. "He was a card sharp," he said. "He was a sharp kid, an alert little kid. He knew where he needed to be."

Disregarding the debut game that wasn't, he always wanted to be bigger, too. Matschoss had the 11-year-old in his passenger seat on a yabbying trip when his car clipped a rock and the steering wheel spun. "My elbow flicked up and he copped it right in the jaw," he said. "There was a bit of a whimper. There might have been a tear. But he wanted to be one of the gang, one of the blokes, so he kept it in. He was pretty tough."

Determined, too. The Matschosses lived across the road from the Ricciutos when they ran the family property outside town; if Mark was not playing (insert any sport) with his brother and their two boys, he created competition for himself.

Joy Matschoss can remember looking out her window and watching Mark stand at the bottom of the hilly street, kicking his footy uphill, gathering it on the roll-back, and doing it all again. "He'd do it for half an hour solid," she said. "There was just that determination about him. He was always going to have success."

That he has. But Ricciuto's Brownlow Medal, premiership medallion, multiple club champion awards and eight All-Australian spots, says Bickley, have drawn more people to him, not elevated him even higher above them.

"People are attracted to successful people, and Mark's hugely successful," Bickley said. "If a young footballer came down to Adelaide and said, 'I want to be like Roo and I'm going to mimic him,' they'd be right on track. He's dedicated and he trains hard, he takes his team to war every week. And he's a good fella, too."

Adelaide's players are encouraged to emulate their leader even if they are physically incapable. One of the Crows' pre-season activities, the "Ricciuto Run", is based on what he does in a quarter. The players might sprint for 10 seconds, stride for 30, jog for 10, then stand up and lie down to finish. Then, they repeat it, 29 times.

"By the end, you're absolutely knackered," says McGregor. Ricciuto, incidentally, lists the run on his website "fan file" as his least-favoured form of exertion. "You'd think he'd be used to it," said his teammate. "He does it four times every week."

Ricciuto wants those around him to grow from his actions, a quality he has always had. Bev Nitschke, Waikerie's president in that premiership season, taught a mulleted but by no means big-headed Mark through his middle years of high school.

She remembers him as generous and accepting (and writing a particularly good poem about trees), but never using his powers for evil.

"He was a ringleader, but not in a bad way," she said. "He gave people confidence. People wanted to be around Mark because he made them feel good."

The Ricciuto book, however, has never been completely open. Murray Ricciuto drove Mark to Adelaide and back three times a week when he started at West Adelaide, and can still see him sitting in the back seat with a $20 bucket of KFC, doing his year 12 homework by torchlight but never saying much.

Carol Ricciuto considers her son low-key and contained. "He keeps himself pretty well hidden," she said. "I see the most of him when he kicks a goal, really."

Twice, she has seen him more completely exposed. The first time was when a groin injury kept Ricciuto from the Crows' 1997 premiership side, a disappointment he wiped only when they won again the next year.

The second time was more devastating: as he celebrated his Brownlow win two years ago, Ricciuto was grappling with the death from deep vein thrombosis, two weeks earlier, of his second cousin and great friend, Joe De Vito. The pair had grown up together; they were what Errol Matschoss describes as "little Godfathers". For a long time, says Carol Ricciuto, he struggled to balance his achievement with what he had lost. "It really hurt him," his mother said. "That took a toll on him. He went to Melbourne, and he had to celebrate, but he was really hurting inside. You knew how much it hurt because he doesn't normally show that much."

That said, Ricciuto's final footballing goal is easy to pick. Should he become Mark Ricciuto, premiership captain, on the MCG next week, expect something to spill over.

"It's the one thing he really wants. You can just sense this real burning desire," Bickley said. "I've got no doubt that's a real driving force and it would be the crowning glory, really. It's the only thing he hasn't achieved."

CARRYING THE FAMILY MARK
Mark Ricciuto's tattooed back is not the result of a whim. The 30-year-old deeply researched his Italian and Australian families' heritage before having the names Ricciuto and Light, and their crests, drawn on his right shoulder. On his left shoulder, Ricciuto wears what his father Murray describes as a "family tree".

Ricciuto's grandfather moved to Australia from southern Italy when he was 18, with a cousin. The pair worked among the Queensland sugar cane, went home to Italy to marry, and returned to Melbourne, where they opened a fruit store.

During the depression, Ricciuto's grandfather moved to the Adelaide Hills and his cousin went to Waikerie, in the Riverland, where the pair were eventually reunited.

Murray Ricciuto, the only boy in a family of five children, brought his family up on the property, outside town, his parents ran but has lived closer to town with his wife, Carol, for the past nine years.

Carol's father, Bruce Light, perhaps had a hand in Ricciuto's football ability. He ran the wings for Port Adelaide in the SANFL, playing 215 games between 1967 and 1978.

THE RICCIUTO FILE	
Born	June 8, 1975
Recruited from	West Adelaide
First played	1993
Games	285
Goals	235
Finals	14
Premierships	1 (1998)
Brownlow medallist	2003
Career Brownlow votes	125
Adelaide best-and-fairest	1998, 2003, 2004
All-Australian	1994, 1997, 1998, 2000, 2002, 2003, 2004, 2005

LEADERS OF THE CROWS	
Chris McDermott	1991–94
Tony McGuinness	1995–96
Mark Bickley	1997–2000
Mark Ricciuto	2001–

The Age 17 September 2005

BRISBANE TO SACK FEVOLA

Caroline Wilson

BRISBANE LIONS WILL SACK TROUBLED footballer Brendan Fevola within the next few days. The Lions could make the official call as early as Monday, having held high-level talks yesterday at AFL headquarters.

Contrary to recent reports, the AFL yesterday confirmed it would use its discretion to relieve the club's salary-cap woes by spreading Fevola's seven-figure payout over two years, as it did with St Kilda last season when Andrew Lovett was sacked.

A Brisbane Lions contingent led by club chairman Angus Johnson, acting chief executive Steve Wright and football boss Dean Warren yesterday met AFL bosses, including Andrew Demetriou and Adrian Anderson. Although Fevola was not the only topic on the agenda, when the talks broke up no one was left in any doubt regarding Fevola's fate.

Fevola's manager, Alastair Lynch, said he had not received any official word from Brisbane but agreed that the longer the stalemate lasted the worse it appeared for Fevola, who remains in a rehabilitation facility and has no meeting scheduled with Lions coach Michael Voss or other club chiefs.

Lynch said Fevola would remain in care until he knew whether or not he had a future with the Lions—the club he joined last season after Carlton terminated its star full-forward, the 2006 and 2009 Coleman medallist. *The Age* understands that special arrangements would be put in place by Lynch's Velocity Sports to help Fevola rebuild his life after leaving Brisbane.

Under Fevola's generous three-year deal, he is due to earn at least $1 million this season from the Lions, along with $100,000 from Carlton. With the Lions looking to settle with Fevola to the tune of at least $1.2 million and potentially up to $1.5 million—he was contracted in 2012 for about $400,000—the AFL is believed to have approved spreading Fevola's payout over two seasons.

Anderson, the AFL's football operations boss, last night confirmed the league had discretionary powers to spread any termination settlement over more than one season, although he refused to discuss Fevola specifically.

With significant six-figure gambling debts, Fevola—a confessed gambling addict, depressive and binge drinker—is expected to return to Melbourne in a bid to rebuild his life.

The Lions board had reportedly planned to reach a decision on Fevola next Wednesday but was awaiting an official recommendation from Wright and new football boss Warren. Yesterday's talks are understood to have significantly speeded up the proceedings.

Fevola was suspended indefinitely by the club after being arrested for being drunk and disorderly in Brisbane in the early hours of New Year's Day, but even before that incident the club had looked at cutting its losses and terminating his contract.

It had hoped to release him at a less significant financial cost after a woman alleged he had exposed himself to her at a community function last September, but Fevola was cleared by police of those allegations.

Fevola then flew to China to join the club on a post-season tour which included an exhibition game against Melbourne, where his poor behaviour was witnessed by AFL officials.

The New Year's Day incident involving a clash with police proved to be the last straw for the turbulent but talented full-forward.

As costly as Fevola's payout will be, the decision to recruit him—led by Voss and his then football boss Graeme Allan—has already proved devastatingly expensive for the Lions. The decision was approved by now departed chairman Tony Kelly and then CEO Michael Bowers, who was exited from the club late last year. The decision never went before the board and led in part to the resignation of director David Liddy.

Premiership forward Daniel Bradshaw quit, disenchanted, for Sydney, and at the end of 2010 Michael Rischitelli and Jared Brennan left for bigger money at the Gold Coast.

Despite Fevola's increasingly highlighted off-field issues, the view from

Brisbane is that the club is not a rehabilitation facility and the fortunes of the Lions' playing group had to be placed ahead of Fevola the individual.

It was not a difficult decision. His mood swings were proving a massive distraction to the youth-led path Voss has been forced to take, and influences like Fevola—who can lead the pack on his charm as soon as shun it—were damaging. The club was also mindful that having sacked the errant Albert Proud, it would have been sending mixed messages by keeping Fevola.

The problem was that the latter was much costlier and layered with complexities. Lynch's comments regarding Fevola's well-being, desire to play again and his recommended need for the disciplined structure offered by football placed more pressure on the club. But in the end it was not enough to retain an unfit and unpredictable 30-year-old.

And with some finessing from the AFL, even the payout became a secondary concern. As costly as it will be to sack Fevola, the Lions knew it would have been costlier to keep him.

The Age 19 February 2011

HIGH AND DRY

Linda Pearce and Peter Hanlon

PETER EVERITT'S NOTEBOOK IS FILLING up, but not with motivational sayings, cryptic Malthouse-style philosophies or training reminders. Each time Everitt makes a bet that he can stay aboard the alcohol-free wagon until season's end, he adds a new incentive to his lengthening list.

It includes a promised evening at St Kilda board member Michael Gudinski's Docklands nightclub and an all-expenses-paid day out with mate John Mason, his partner in a Mornington Peninsula roller-door business. Yet the frivolities are incidental to Everitt's primary goal of completing a year he hopes will be a major improvement on the last.

So far, although his team has been struggling, the signs are exceptional. Off his beloved beer since the end of February, Everitt has shone in his revised role as a near-permanent forward. His massive height advantage has helped him to 20 goals from three rounds, and his pace and agility at ground level have long made big "Spider" particularly hard to match up.

Yet Everitt's resurgence is also timely in a personal sense. Last year was fouled by the Scott Chisholm racial vilification case, and although his genuine apology and self-imposed punishment of a $20,000 donation to an Aboriginal community scheme, four-game suspension and counselling sessions drew widespread praise, the stigma remains.

So, in a more practical sense, was his inactive period a costly break, with Everitt failing to work hard enough during his month on the sidelines. What he lost in match fitness he struggled to recover, playing out the year at a level far below his All-Australian form of 1997 and '98. "I look back and try to learn from it. Those four weeks I could have trained a lot, lot harder and not just thought it would all just happen anyway."

Not that the Chisholm business has been the sole black mark against the ever-colourful Everitt name. Spider is the first to admit he is a Saint only in nickname. After famous misdemeanours that have included a pub stoush with an off-duty policeman and several traffic offences—the last of which brought a licence cancellation and suspended jail sentence—he is keenly aware that the public has been left with a less-than-flattering perception.

"People see me probably as a person who gets into a bit of strife, probably oversteps the line too many times," admits Everitt, a father of two, including 11-week-old Summer. "Good with kids, but oversteps the line, which ruins the whole concept of being a high-profile AFL player."

Is that a fair assessment? "Yeah, it's fair in the way that I love kids, I love working with them—my wife [Jodie] and I do a fair bit with OzChild, foster kids and all that—and it's just been an unfortunate fact that when I was growing up I wasn't the best 15- or 16-year-old kid around Crib Point.

"And when I've grown up, everything I've done in the last three or four years has been publicised, and pretty much I haven't done too much. Other than the racial vilification, what have I done? Driving without a licence and got into a pub fight. But unfortunately that all snowballs on to bigger and worse things."

For their part, the Saints have never considered Everitt a major behavioural concern; his mistakes "not deep, serious trouble", says president Andrew Plympton. "Peter's just a very active young man and he's had a few indiscretions, but he makes up for those with a hell of a lot of good things. He's critical [to St Kilda], not just for his football ability, but for his bravado, his cheek, he'll give anything a go. It's an old line, but I've never seen 20 Methodists win a bloody grand final."

Coach Tim Watson agrees, having himself "played alongside some blokes who were fairly trouble-prone", and stressing the importance of man management in drawing the best from players to benefit the team. "Spider obviously is a colourful personality, he'll be an enduring colourful personality when he finishes playing the game, and he's an intelligent fellow. In some ways he underutilises his own intelligence, but no one should take him as a fool."

Far from it. Everitt, he of the spiderweb headband stall, enjoys lucrative media work as a *Footy Show* regular and co-host of a Foxtel children's show with Shane Crawford and Nathan Buckley. His football alone would make him a highly marketable commodity. Toss in the blond dreadlocks ("If you'd seen my hair when I was young, you'd have picked I'd definitely have to do something"), the tattoos, nickname and gregarious personality, and the 25-year-old social animal from Hastings has become one of the stars of the game.

This year, one of the main changes has been to his on-field role. Everitt realised as soon as delisted pair Damian Monkhorst and Aaron Keating arrived at Moorabbin for pre-season training that the search for another ruckman was on. Even so, Monkhorst's presence means Everitt has spent even more time up forward (in what Watson says is a short-term measure) than he had expected.

Which is fine, Everitt says, although he enjoys the ruck and so is keen to maintain his endurance levels. That means an extra training session or two each week, but track slackness has not been an Everitt failing since the very early days of his 135-game career that continues today at the MCG against Melbourne.

This year has also brought the benefit of a stricter off-season, despite including a month's holiday in the US with teammates Austinn Jones and Tony Brown. "I probably let my hair down a little too much, you could say," Everitt said of past breaks.

"But by the time you're 24, 25, you start to learn that eight weeks off away from the club isn't just to see how much alcohol you can drink and how much shit food you can eat, you've still got to keep some form of fitness. Last year was obviously a tough year for myself and the club, not making the eight when we really should have been in the top five or six, as the media keep reminding us. The weeks we spent away from the club, Tim pretty much wanted us to come back in the same kind of shape."

Still, Everitt's full-on style means controversy often lurks close by. Last week it was a claim on *The Footy Show* (to which, incidentally, his involvement was initially delayed by almost a season while he proved to Plympton and chief executive Don Hanly that he could produce the performances to match the words) that morale was low at St Kilda due to limited social activities.

"I think he just got cornered on a subject; didn't think some of the consequences through," says Plympton. "Generally, his level of working out the morale and social interaction of people differs from others' level. He's imposing his own standards there. Peter's highly active in everything he does, and he needs to understand that not everybody around him can be like that."

Yet Everitt stands by his words. "I just said that the club wasn't real close.

Three years ago we had players with no kids and stuff and you'd go to the pub after a game, and now with kids and stuff we've found it a little bit hard. During the pre-season we probably let it lapse a little bit, which I think cost a little bit of team morale.

"We're back on track now, and it was heaps better at the weekend, but it was the way it was and everyone pretty much responded to it. A lot of players don't like that sort of stuff out in the public, but at least it's out there. The more people know about it the more you're gonna get things done."

Have no doubt, Spider is still out there, too. He remains a regular Sunday patron with his mates at the Frankston Hotel, even if soft drink has temporarily replaced beer as his beverage of choice. The only problem is that the main effect of his new grog-free lifestyle has been grumpiness born of the sudden end to his main form of relaxation.

"It was just a thing I decided to do myself, one of those mental challenges you set yourself," Everitt says. "You go through your whole footy career and a lot of people go off it and say it's good for you and a lot of people stay on it and say it doesn't make any difference. There's only one way to find out, I suppose, and I've enjoyed it."

Just as he will relish the spoils on that day in August or September when the ban is lifted and, he insists, the bets called in. "I'll make it. I will. I'm committed now, so I definitely will," Everitt says, grinning. "I can't wait for that first beer. It'll be interesting."

Of course it will. What else? Peter Everitt, for better or worse, has ensured we now expect nothing less.

MOORABBIN CULT FIGURES
Kevin Neale

"Cowboy" went up about 25 kilograms from the big kid who arrived at Moorabbin from South Warrnambool, but his size never matched the place he filled in St Kilda fans' hearts. When coach Allan Jeans conceded in a team address before the 1971 grand final that Hawthorn's Peter Hudson was bound to kick five or six goals, Neale was heard to mutter: "Not if he's unconscious." (A groggy Hudson duly fluffed several goalkicking record attempts after a brush with Neale's elbow.) "Cowboy" could play, too, four times leading the club's goalkicking (including five on that famous day in 1966), winning the 1973 best-and-fairest and playing a then club record 256 games.

Carl Ditterich

From blond and brilliant in the early sixties to headbanded and hated by the late seventies, "Big Carl" was one of the most feared ruckmen the game has known. Unique in having played for St Kilda then Melbourne, then back at St Kilda before finishing at Melbourne, he notched 203 of his 285 games for the Saints. He was also a Monday night regular at Harrison House and later VFL House, making 19 appearances before the tribunal for 11 guilty verdicts and 30 match suspensions. He was back in the news last September when, running as an independent, he almost won the National Party seat of Swan Hill in the Victorian election.

Robert Muir

Another Saint who had a tenuous grip on his halo, "Mad Dog" was the darling of Moorabbin's infamous "animal enclosure", the area between the social club and the players' races where opposition fans strayed at their peril. Blessed with electrifying skills, Muir also had a lightning temper that led to him missing 22 matches through suspension in his 68-game, three-stint career with the Saints. His last suspension, for 12 weeks, came after he abused a goal umpire, threatened a field umpire, headbutted Carlton's Bruce Doull and struck former teammate Val Perovic. He returned to relative obscurity in the country, and copped a two-year ban for striking two players and a goal umpire.

Tony Lockett

No question that "Plugger" could play, as 1357 goals, four Coleman Medals and a Brownlow testify. As far as Saints fans were concerned, the important thing was that he played for them. From the moment the big kid from North Ballarat sent his first kick through for a goal they couldn't get enough of him, on the field or off it, where he was immortalised by the Coodabeen Champions' "Massive from Moorabbin" and through his crutch-throwing, single-syllable relationship with the media. He even escaped the usual "traitor" tag after moving north to Sydney, with the St Kilda administration copping the brunt of blame for his 1995 transfer.

The Sunday Age 2 April 2000

THE EAGLE WHO CRASH-LANDED

Peter Wilmoth

THE IMAGE OF BEN COUSINS lying drunk at Southgate a fortnight ago was shocking only in the context of the rules of fame in the 21st century. If another 28-year-old had been photographed lying there, it would have been a ribbing at work. But when you are probably the most popular footballer to have ever played in Western Australia, a rich, glamorous icon with the world at your feet, a Brownlow Medal around your neck and a string of controversies to your name, the photograph takes on a sad, even sinister dimension.

Are any of those people in Perth who watch him play and thrill to his courage, persistence and leadership skills asking the question: what is Ben Cousins doing with his life?

Four days after Cousins was arrested at Southgate for being drunk in public following a verbal clash with police, leading to him spending four hours in jail, Andrew Demetriou came out firing—what turned out to be a popgun.

The AFL chief admitted the behaviour of Cousins was not a "great advertisement" for the game, and said "it's very important to make sure we deal with this professionally and that we send out a message."

So what kind of message would be sent out? The Eagles, Cousins' increasingly embarrassed employer, decided on this message: it would take no action towards its champion midfielder and one-time marquee name. "The club believes that Ben has already received sufficient punishment through the public scrutiny of his arrest," was its statement.

Not since Gary Ablett has the football world witnessed a flawed genius whose breathtaking feats on the field stand in such contrast to his poor and sometimes bizarre behaviour off it.

Cousins' extraordinary story can only be understood in the context of the culture of the West Coast Eagles and the role this powerful club plays in Western Australia. It's a story about wealth, power and the expectation and smothering attention of a two-team town. Cousins has been a huge star all his adult life. It's perhaps not surprising that cracks have appeared. His defenders are at pains to stress that he's just a bloke who plays football magnificently and stuffs up occasionally.

Cousins' reputation as the dark prince of West Australian football was confirmed in May last year when he and ruckman Michael Gardiner became embroiled in the investigation into a January shooting between bikie gang rivals at a popular Perth nightclub. Cousins and Gardiner both came under criticism from WA Police Commissioner Karl O'Callaghan for choosing not to answer certain questions about alleged phone conversations they had with one of two men charged over the shooting incident.

Cousins issued a statement. "As captain of the West Coast Eagles football club, I am extremely disappointed with the public perception of my continued association with people who are regarded by others as underworld figures. I have obviously let down a lot of people and I apologise to my family, friends and the football club, in particular my teammates, and the public of Western Australia."

Eagles chief executive Trevor Nisbett said Cousins and Gardiner were on their last chances.

In February this year, Cousins abandoned his $140,000 Mercedes near a booze bus and fled, reportedly trying to avoid police by jumping into the Canning River, disposing of his shirt and then ending up outside a locked door at the Bluewater Grill restaurant. He was later charged with traffic offences and eventually fined $900.

Several meetings took place between the club and Cousins before Cousins announced he was stepping down from the captaincy. It was not officially clear if he jumped or had been pushed.

The wagons circled quickly. Coach John Worsfold hastily defended Cousins, telling the ABC: "The countless hours that Ben has spent visiting sick children, personal requests to visit people he's never met, to visit hospitals, to spend time signing autographs is not covered, and as a role model in that regard, he'd be one of the outstanding members of the community."

He was outstanding again, for all the wrong reasons, earlier this month. A man who was "helping" Cousins decided to take a photo of the prone footballer. This is where celebrity bites. The awful image of Cousins lying at Southgate, clearly alcohol-affected, was hard to reconcile with those of him holding his Brownlow Medal in 2005 or standing with John Worsfold and Chris Judd, the man who reluctantly replaced him as captain, on the premiership dais just 10 weeks ago, encouraged to share the glory by his teammates for whom he remains the "spiritual leader".

With the incidents covered nation-wide—in Perth, *The West Australian* newspaper gave over its first five pages to Cousins' flight from the booze bus— some might have caved in, but Cousins is made of stronger stuff. Four months after the nightclub incident, he won the Brownlow Medal and led the Eagles to within a whisker of the premiership. This year, seven months after another humiliation, he was a premiership hero, earning All-Australian selection for the sixth time.

With this capacity to repeatedly bounce back from off-field embarrassment with stunning on-field achievement, there are tempting parallels with Shane Warne. But in Perth, Cousins is a one-off, a superstar and a publicity-magnet, almost universally feted and fawned over and, until Judd took over the captaincy, the bedrock of the Eagles' marketing campaign. All of which means that, according to some close observers of WA football, when he acts up, he is forgiven.

It would be hard to overstate Cousins' status in Western Australia. At 28, he is rich, a pin-up boy and, if not the best then probably the most popular footballer to have ever played football in the football-obsessed city. Local commentator Dennis Cometti once said you could sell 500 tickets to watch Cousins eat a chicken sandwich.

Accordingly, it will take more than a string of misdemeanours to dislodge local loyalty. Veteran sports commentator George Grljusich of radio 6PR says there is a small "prudish element in society, a righteous group of people" who feel a rage at what Cousins does. "Many normal supporters would regard him as one of them—they get around a barbecue and get pissed."

Compartmentalising his problems has become a famous skill. "He has a special quality," says Grljusich. "He can overcome his severe embarrassment. He comes from a good family and he would have been severely embarrassed. A lot of people would have dropped their bundle in those circumstances, but

Ben is able to continue to work as normal. When things like this happen, he feels the need to further prove himself. These things act as a catalyst."

Despite his off-field behaviour, Cousins enjoys extraordinary support in the west. During the weekend radio shows he hosts, Grljusich says that out of dozens of callers "99 per cent were supportive of Ben".

Former Eagles player Karl Langdon says he was surprised the Southgate incident received such wide coverage. "Running away from a booze bus and falling asleep on a bench in Southgate are poles apart," he says.

While conceding that Cousins has made some mistakes, Langdon says the footballer is a victim of the "guilt by association" that can dog footballers because they happen to attend nightclubs with insalubrious characters. "I've rubbed shoulders with the same people," Langdon says. "These people have a presence in nightclubs, they want to talk to you about footy, and then, when you do, suddenly you are mates of theirs." After everything, Langdon says, Cousins is still "regarded as a hero".

The top end of town, many of whom are influential Eagles supporters, have other ideas. Nigel Satterley, a Perth property developer and high-profile Eagles member, says he and others in the city's corporate world believe Cousins' behaviour was disappointing. "Most people wish he would conduct himself appropriately. It damages his personal brand and that's for him to work out." With a note of exasperation Satterley added: "If you or I get pissed, we go home. If you walk around and tell the cops you are Ben Cousins and you get arrested, we can't help that."

Cousins' brilliance on the field, and his willingness to run all day until he is literally sick, is well-documented.

Local observers believe his status has ensured a protective layer around him. The Eagles were quick to punish forward Quinten Lynch after a drink-driving escapade in 2004 (he was fined and suspended) and to sack ruckman and Cousins' friend Michael Gardiner after he smashed his car into two parked cars while over the legal limit earlier this year. The "trial by media" exoneration wasn't extended to the pair.

In Perth football circles, the view is that the Eagles moved on Lynch and Gardiner because they weren't of Cousins' calibre, and that Cousins is an untouchable. "He's a brilliant young player, a good-looking kid, he's got charm, he's the whole package," said Mark Duffield, of *The West Australian*, who has reported WA football for 15 years.

"He's been indulged all his life. Too few, apart from his family and the club, have been prepared to say to him, 'You shouldn't have done that.' He's basically had the run of the farm."

Cousins, the son of former West Australian star Bryan Cousins, who played 67 games for Geelong, started playing senior football at 17 and became a superstar in his early 20s in a city where the two AFL teams—the Eagles and the Fremantle Dockers—are bitter rivals who play it tough off the field. It's not always pleasant. "The one-on-one town breeds a nastier football culture than in a town of 10 clubs," says Duffield. "In Melbourne, you tend to be able to have well-rounded conversations about football. Over here, there's a nastiness to it."

Covering a two-team town can have its special challenges, as Duffield found out when, after the booze bus incident, he said Cousins should stand down from the captaincy or be relieved of it by the club. Many Eagles fans didn't like the media taking on a favourite son. Rather than criticise Cousins, some talkback callers blamed the police for setting up the booze bus and the media for its wide coverage.

Everywhere Duffield went—in the street, in taxis—he was deluged with pro-Cousins supporters to the point where he decided to stay out of circulation. "I went out twice in three months," the reporter says.

In trying to understand Cousins, it's helpful to consider the culture from which he sprang. He is a product of a club that is rich, powerful, used to success and intimidating. "A lot of the media are frightened to take them on," Duffield says of the Eagles. "You are not just taking on a football club, you are taking on the big end of town."

They are bred tough, from the coach down. In March 2006, as a media gathering prepared for a boundary-side conference with Fremantle assistant coach Michael Broadbridge, Worsfold ran 70 metres across Subiaco Oval to call the media "f—ing spastic". Worsfold was angry that reporters had breached an Eagles club directive that bans them from standing inside the fence, a move instigated after *The West Australian* reported Worsfold's dressing down of players after player Beau Waters was hit by a taxi in the early hours of the morning.

On another occasion, Worsfold turned on *West Australian* reporter Craig O'Donoghue. O'Donoghue approached Worsfold after a press conference, during which the coach had said he had no problem with Waters getting hit by the cab, even though he'd taken a harder line on the issue with the players. O'Donoghue told Worsfold he'd be reporting the coach's comments to the players.

"Half the team stood there watching," O'Donoghue remembers. "I got the famous Worsfold stare as he questioned my professionalism, morals and ethics over and over again. He reminded me that he worked for the West Coast Eagles and I worked for a 'shit newspaper'. It was confronting."

Says a media insider: "They attempt to paint anyone who goes against them as coming from the lunatic fringe. It's a typical stance of a body that knows they hold the balance of power. They could come out tomorrow and say 'the Earth is flat' and the next day, according to the Eagles, it would be officially flat."

The Eagles' tentacles spread wide in the west. After Gardiner's car crash in July, Nisbett suggested Gardiner was suffering from depression. Gardiner had never spoken of depression and his family were angry at the presumption. Duffield rang an ethicist to seek views on whether the club was out of line. The ethicist "tried to hose the story down" and then one hour later the Eagles were aware of Duffield's investigations.

"Obviously, loyalty to the Eagles overrode other considerations," Duffield says. "They are a powerful, well-run club, but the extent of their power in Perth is sometimes stretched to the point where it's unhealthy."

Footballers behaving badly is not a new phenomenon, and certainly not confined to the Wild West. The attention the young gods receive in the media is fine when things are sunny, but commensurately bad when they're not. After the Lynch incident, former WA Premier Geoff Gallop said there was "a lack of reality" in the lives of AFL players. "They're getting too much money, too quickly, without any relationship to the real world."

Both Ben Cousins and his father, Bryan, who is also Cousins' manager, declined to speak to *The Sunday Age*.

On top of everything else he has done for the Eagles, Cousins has now helped make them a punchline. "I saw the Eagles on TV last night," local stand-up comic Jeff Hewitt often tells his audience. "Did anyone else watch *Crimestoppers*?"

"That always goes down well," Hewitt says.

But not everyone's laughing. The Cousins story, like Ablett's and that of ex-Collingwood star Chris Tarrant, is salutary: superstars are forgiven a lot as long as they remain useful, but when their services are no longer required, it's a different story.

Contacted about Cousins, AFL chief Andrew Demetriou wouldn't be drawn but, through a spokesman, said: "As a general comment, the AFL's view is that AFL players must always conform to community expectations on behaviour. No AFL player, like any citizen, should ever believe they are above the law or not required to meet expected social standards."

Mark Duffield wrote earlier this month that people with Cousins in Melbourne say he was no more intoxicated than others there and that he was unlucky to be targeted by police. "[Cousins] has too many incidents to his name to claim bad luck as the sole source of his troubles. Sooner or later, a little skirmish is going to turn into an almighty collision if he can't get things right off the field."

THE GOOD, THE BAD AND THE UGLY: WEST COAST'S 2006

February: Ben Cousins causes a storm in Perth when he abandons his Mercedes near a booze bus and flees into the night, later charged with traffic offences and fined $900.

March: Eagles coach John Worsfold apologises to reporters and to the Cerebral Palsy Association of Western Australia after calling media assembled on Subiaco Oval "f—ing spastic".

July: 27-year-old ruckman Michael Gardiner crashes his Holden SS Commodore at high speed, causing more than $90,000 damage to three cars, including writing off his own $60,000 vehicle. Gardiner is fined the maximum $5000 and suspended indefinitely by the club. Eagles chief executive Trevor Nisbett said Gardiner would more than likely never play for the club again. He is later fined $800 and had his driver's licence suspended for four months after pleading guilty to drink driving.

September: The Eagles win the AFL Premiership by one point.

December: Cousins arrested at Southgate for being drunk in a public place.

The Sunday Age 17 December 2006

ONE TEST ENDS, A NEW, BIGGER ONE BEGINS

Jake Niall

FOOTBALL WILL BE ANOTHER HABIT that Ben Cousins will have to learn to live without. If this sounds trite, consider what might have happened to Cousins had Richmond not called out his name with the final choice in the 2008 pre-season draft.

Football preceded drugs in Cousins's life. Unlike the substances and lifestyle that almost destroyed him, football has been primarily positive for Cousins, especially over the past two years.

The game cared for Cousins. It gave him structure and meaning. When he found trouble, his club would intervene.

Teammates, officials and managers looked out for his welfare. When he fell—overdosed on sleeping pills, went AWOL or descended into an abyss— others would pick up the pieces.

Typically, addicts do not have the support network of an organisation with the nuturing power of an AFL club, which compelled Cousins to train, to attend meetings, to be involved in a collective cause that dragged him away from the throes of addiction.

Football urine-tested him three times a week. It forced him to stay clean, albeit only from certain substances. Legal substances—alcohol, prescription medication—are no less dangerous than cocaine when the person imbibing them cannot control his urges.

But the game also covered for him, because he was an exceptional footballer. It is arguable that football allowed Cousins to take liberties that others would never have been permitted.

Alternatively, his status as a good-looking champion meant that his addiction became one of the nation's most popular spectator sports—as the ratings for his documentary doubtless will attest.

Cousins had the misfortune to be Australia's first true celebrity drug addict. In the United States, dozens of Hollywood stars check in and out of rehab, in full public view.

We did not have anyone of Robert Downey jnr's ilk. We don't have a confessional culture; here, it is possible for public figures to deal with their addictive demons on the quiet.

Not Cousins. As a superstar in an obsessively followed sport, he couldn't avoid scrutiny. He filled the celebrity vacuum. We in the media will have to kick the Cousins habit, too.

Cousins' challenge is to find an outlet that keeps him focused, prevents him from keeping bad company, gives him control of his life.

His old manager, Ricky Nixon, said yesterday Cousins would need a calling that "kept his adrenalin pumping. You've got to find something in your life to get you out of bed each day," he added.

The cautionary examples of what can happen to a player with self-destructive tendencies are Wayne Carey and Gary Ablett snr. Cousins is a different beast to that pair, since his problems with substance abuse began much earlier.

He represents a significant challenge to the AFL Players' Association, which has been sympathetic to Cousins, without ever having to deal directly with his issues.

When he is retired, Richmond's responsibility ends, as West Coast's did when it cut him.

Perhaps for the first time in his adult life, Cousins will have to take responsibility for his actions himself. He will not be accountable to anyone, either. If he falters, he will not be letting anyone down but himself.

No teammates will be there to bring him into line. No coach or official will crack the whip.

Then, it will be up to Ben.

The Age 17 August 2010

CALLING TIME ON A BIG, BAD, BUSTLING CAREER

Martin Blake

FOR ONE OF THE LAST TIMES as a footballer, Barry Hall drew a crowd. The auditorium at Whitten Oval filled with the entire playing list and staff of Western Bulldogs and that was before the dozen or so television cameras and journalists filed in to hear him announce his retirement.

It was fitting, too. Hall's has been a career that you could scarcely turn an eye away from. He fell out with St Kilda, thrived in Sydney and lifted the premiership cup, belted a few opponents and fell out with Sydney and finally, turned back the clock for the Bulldogs.

The symmetry is good. As a boy growing up in Broadford, he barracked for the Doggies. Now, he said, he would be a Bulldog for life.

Hall had a big, diamond earring in his left ear and not a tear came to his eye and he told how grateful he was that the club had given him an opportunity to redeem himself. Make no mistake—this was the most significant point of his final two seasons at Whitten Oval.

Hall says his "resigning" from the Swans was the low point of his career, even deeper than the night he smashed a left fist into Brent Staker's face at Stadium Australia and brought a hellfire upon himself. But he had no choice but to leave. Paul Roos, the coach at the time, told him so and the players had turned against him too, having built a culture of strong discipline and seen their best player ignore it.

Hall was thrown out of the club he co-captained to a flag. It's not every day you see that. Which is why he planned his retirement announcement for this week, and why Sunday's game at the SCG becomes a Sydney farewell for big, bad, bustling Barry Hall—even though he will play out the season. "I've certainly done a lot in Sydney and I owe the fans a goodbye, I think—even though we're against them on Sunday. I think that's important."

The Sydney fans will surely forgive him his feeling that he is a Bulldog forever. "Everything happens for a reason, whether they're good or bad. Ironically I ended up with the Bulldogs and I'll certainly be supporting them long after my career's gone."

He was unequivocal on this point, the most interesting of his media conference. "I'm very proud of what I achieved there [in Sydney] but most footy clubs would say, you just move on from stuff. The couple of years I've had as a Bulldog have been memorable for me and that's something that's fresh in my memory. It's stuck with me."

Part of his attachment to Whitten Oval is the fact that coach Rodney Eade gave him the chance at all; a chance to ensure that he would be remembered as a great player and not just as a thug. Hall knew that when he departed Sydney at 32 his reputation was so stained that it was possible he was finished.

But Eade had coached one season at Sydney in 2002 when Hall arrived from St Kilda, living next door to the star recruit, "which was a bit of fun for a while, at night". He liked Hall and trusted him. The gravity of that decision seven years down the track, when Eade was in charge of the Bulldogs, was never lost on Hall. "They gave me a chance when probably no other club would. [They] put their head on the chopping block, they had their knockers and doubters."

In particular, Eade had a lot to lose. "They did take a risk," Hall said. "If there was an incident on-field, the first bloke that would be copping it would be him [Eade] and then me. It shows a lot of trust in me and I'm really glad it's worked out for the better."

His part of the bargain was to put away the aggression. "In my later years in Sydney, I was carrying injuries and all the rest of it, but I was still expecting myself to perform at the highest level. I had really high standards. Coming to the Bulldogs, they made sure that wasn't the case and I made a bit of a pact with myself that I needed to enjoy footy."

Hall has had injuries this year, in particular an aching ankle, but has kicked nine goals in the past two matches. Still sore on a Thursday after a game at the weekend, he knows his time has come—even though he will miss the camaraderie and the banter and "hiding in people's cars".

He is in a good place and it showed. "I'm really content with the decision I've made. I don't want to be a player that signs another year contract and then is going to really struggle to perform, could be dropped to reserve grade and finish that way."

He is already mapping out a future. He has written a book with *Sydney Morning Herald* journalist Michael Cowley, aptly called *Pulling No Punches*, which will be published in August. He enjoyed the chance to set certain records straight. "People see you on the footy field and get perceptions. The way I'm perceived is not how I actually am."

He is getting married in November to partner Sophie Raadschelders. "I'm looking forward to the next chapter of my life. It's going to be different to what I'm used to, but it's good. Change is good."

Almost certainly, the money will come for him to step into the boxing ring. Hall was a fine amateur pugilist, is a close friend of Danny Green's, and rejected a professional offer as recently as 2008.

But yesterday he was unsure. "I'm not going to rule it out. But in saying that, I've trained pretty hard for 16 years and my body needs a bit of a rest. I'm going to have to train just as hard if not harder for a boxing career. Whether I'm prepared to do that is another thing."

BARRY HALL'S AFL CAREER AT A GLANCE		
	Games	Goals
Career Totals	283	715
St Kilda	88	144
Sydney	162	467
Western Bulldogs	33	104
Honours	First VFL/AFL player to score 100 goals at three different clubs Premiership: 2005 Grand finals: 1997, 2005, 2006 Best-and-fairest: 2004 All-Australian: 2004, 2005, 2006, 2010 Leading AFL goalkicker: 2005 (80), 2010 (80) Leading club goalkicker: 1999 (41), 2001 (44), 2002 (55), 2003 (64), 2004 (74), 2005 (80), 2006 (78), 2007 (44), 2008 (41), 2010 (80) Club captain: 2006, 2007	

ON BARRY

Andrew Demetriou, AFL chief executive

"He deserves to go out of the game on a high."

Leo Barry, former Sydney full-back

"In the end I think Hally got a bit tired of the process in Sydney, and it needed change, just like his time at St Kilda. We were fortunate enough to get the best footy out of Hally and his impact was enormous in the time he was there."

Simon Garlick, Bulldogs chief executive

"From our perspective, what's stood out is he's a great football club person. That's something that externally a lot of people won't understand. By that I mean that he just gets it. He understands absolutely the meaning of the term 'team over individual', and all his actions with us have backed that up."

Rodney Eade, Bulldogs coach

"Everyone knows the events that led to him finishing up with the Swans. Barry spoke about that [to me] and I think he said publicly that he didn't want to end his career on that note and be remembered as that sort of person. I knew that he's not that sort of person."

Julia Gillard, Prime Minister

"It's lovely to hear Barry talk about how he remembers growing up in Broadford, racing home from school, kicking the ball around the back paddock, pretending he was Simon Beasley, getting handballs from Doug Hawkins."

Barry Hall

"I'm really content with the decision. I think my body's screaming out for it now. I'm glad my form's OK going out of the game. That's the way I wanted it to be."

The Age 20 July 2011

"I LOVED THE NATURE OF OUR FRIENDSHIP. IT WASN'T DEMANDING. IT WASN'T COMPLICATED. IT WAS STRONG AND LOYAL AND COMFORTING."

Garry Lyon

THERE WAS A TIME, NOT that long ago, that I joked with Jim Stynes that he needed to put me on retainer as his "tribute" man. There was the Brownlow Medal tribute, the 244 consecutive games tribute, the retirement tribute (that seemed to last almost as long as his career), his Australian of the Year tribute, his battle against cancer tribute.

As with most things when it came to our relationship, I tackled all these tasks with a perverse sense of humour, ensuring, in the great Australian way, that this extraordinary human being never got the sense that he was ever too big or perfect not to be brought down a peg or two.

The irony in that, of course, is that he was never in danger of getting caught up in his own self-importance, and that was clearly demonstrated in the way he selflessly went about his day-to-day life.

But that didn't stop me. I revelled in every opportunity to take the piss out of him whenever we caught up. He tried to counter with his own version of a cutting remark or a cheap shot, but the fact of the matter was, he was out of his league. Sledging came far easier and naturally to me, and I guess when it came down to it, he was too kind and had too generous a soul to really put his heart into it. Ultimately he would just look at me, shrug his shoulders and cop it on the chin and laugh along.

That was the basis on which a strong and profoundly respectful friendship developed over a 27-year period.

There were times, early on in his football career, when we clashed a bit and had differing opinions on the way we prepared and played, but as time passed, and our days as footballers came to an end, there was just a really comfortable understanding and acceptance between the two of us that I valued enormously.

And I loved the nature of our friendship. It wasn't demanding. It wasn't complicated. It was strong and loyal and comforting, knowing that our link to the past and the future would be preserved.

And even when he was first diagnosed with cancer, nothing really changed. Why would it have to? This was Big "Jimma" we're talking about. He was indestructible and this battle would just add another heroic chapter to an already heavily laden tome.

So I kept hanging shit on him, he kept laughing, and operation after operation, tumour after tumour, he would bounce back and we'd all shake our heads and marvel at what we already knew—that the bigger the challenge, the bigger the fight, the more unyielding he became.

Until it became apparent that victory was not assured. And it was over the past four or five months that I got to know Jimmy on a whole new level.

To just sit and talk with someone for hours at a time is foreign to me. But that's what we've been doing for the past few months and it has provided me with some of the most memorable and uplifting moments of my life. It was a true privilege to have had the time with him.

Humour remained my strong suit and we laughed often. But I also cried, which I hadn't done with him before.

We relived former glories, reminisced about trips away, dissected the personalities of most of our former teammates, critiqued the current list of our football club and argued and fought over the merits of modern-day football versus the old. Stuff I was really comfortable talking about. Stuff I thought I could educate him about.

But we also talked about family dynamics and relationships and children and marriage. And about vulnerability and honesty and affection and trust and self-awareness. Stuff he was really comfortable talking about. Stuff I knew he could educate me about.

We also fought and argued plenty. He had lost none of his competitiveness. His amazing wife, Sam, left me at the hospital one night to go home and check on the kids before returning later in the evening with the express instruction to make sure he was taking it easy.

Jimmy, in the meantime, wanted to stretch his legs, so we walked around the ward at 2am and stumbled across a mini pool table in the recreation area. Sam returned to find an empty hospital bed and, on hearing some yelling coming from down the corridor, went to investigate.

She walked in to find us in the middle of a heated argument over whether you could shoot backwards after receiving two free shots. Jimmy, connected to an IV machine, with his failing eyesight, having just got out of surgery less than 24 hours earlier, was refusing to give an inch. It was vintage Jim. And he beat me!

I was in awe of Jim, on so many levels. I was in awe of his capacity to spread himself around so generously. I was in awe of the unbelievable dignity he maintained while battling the most undignified of diseases. I was in awe of the relationship he grew and nurtured with his wife, Sam. I was in awe of the total lack of self-pity or victimisation he displayed when he had every right to feel such things.

I was simply in awe of the very, very good person Jim was.

A former coach once said to me you will make hundreds of mates out of football but only a very few truly great friends. It is so true.

I pay tribute to one of mine, Jim Stynes.

The Age 21 March 2012

MARN GROOK

Indigenous players have made a major contribution to football and several are among the game's greats. Adam Goodes has been one of the superstars of the past decade, while David Wirrpanda had a key role in the rise of the West Coast Eagles. Wirrpanda was a special talent—and so was his name. "First, there are six names, some of which even David occasionally forgets. But more importantly, we have been calling him the wrong name," Michael Gleeson wrote in 2005. However, adjusting to life in the AFL hasn't been easy for many indigenous players, many of whom are from remote areas, and this has been a challenge not only for players but for their clubs and administrators.

Michael Gleeson's news story in 2012 highlighted that there were still issues in the recruitment area, with his yarn leading to the axing of Adelaide recruiter Matt Rendell. Liam Jurrah's troubles of 2012, according to veteran columnist Martin Flanagan, would also bring to life troubling issues. "I'd heard the whispers before and, since Liam Jurrah's dramas of the past week, the whispers have grown louder—AFL clubs are starting to back away from recruiting indigenous players, Flanagan wrote. "They're 'too hard', it is said, 'too much trouble'. Recruiters are paid to deliver premierships, not racial harmony, the argument runs. Sponsors don't want their names associated with players breaking the law or offending community values." Only time will tell if this situation improves.

MUM MADE ME DO IT: HOW
ADAM GOODES BECAME A STAR

Michael Cowley

HE'S A GOOD BOY, THAT Adam Goodes. Well mannered, well spoken, and does precisely what his mother tells him. It may have been 14 years ago, but his mother, Lisa Sansbury, vividly remembers the trip she made with a teenage Adam from country Victoria to Melbourne airport, to send him to the Swans . . . and her instructions.

"At the airport, I said, 'Well, son, this is the start of great things to come and don't forget you are bringing mama home a Brownlow,'" Lisa recalls. "He goes: 'Oh mama, I haven't even got on the plane yet.' And I said: 'You'll be bringing one home for me my darling.'"

Adam listened, so intently that he brought his mother one in 2003 and another in 2006, and some are suggesting she may get another this year. But before that, Lisa and her two other boys will be at the MCG tonight watching Adam play his 300th game, which, had she not been so insistent, is 300 more than it might have been.

Lisa raised her boys, Adam, the eldest by two years to Jake, who is two years older than Brett, as a single mum, first in Adelaide before moving to Merbein in northern Victoria when Adam was 13. She always encouraged the boys to get involved in sport because it "gave them confidence and kept them out of mischief. They were all a bit cheeky, but no trouble and sport kept them off the streets."

"With us it was always about sport," Brett says. "When we were in Adelaide it was soccer and basketball. We would have a little goal set up somewhere and just mucked around as kids do, and we would have some great games when our cousins came around."

Jake says Adam "could have been a soccer star if he had kept at it", but when the family arrived in Merbein, the only soccer option was playing with much bigger seniors.

His mother suggested Adam give Aussie Rules a chance, and by season's end he had won best-and-fairest. It did not surprise her. "Whatever he puts his heart to, he conquers," she says.

There have been a plethora of moments of which Lisa could be proud. She was Adam's partner at the 2003 Brownlow, but she does not hesitate when asked if any moment stands above the others. "I will never forget the day in 1997 when he kicked six goals for the [North Ballarat] Rebels [in the TAC Cup final] and then a few weeks later got picked up by the Sydney Swans. That was one of the most important days of his life, all our lives. Yeah, his Brownlows were fantastic and the premiership was great, but the day he got drafted . . . I was just so over the moon and so proud of him."

While they were delighted Adam had a shot at the AFL, his absence was keenly felt. "Not having dad around from a younger age, you just took for granted how much Adam did and you did rely on him," Brett says. "When he did leave we were very excited for him, but once he had gone there was a bit of a void."

Adds Lisa: "We all missed him badly. He was like the man of the house and set a very good example for his brothers to follow and, thanks to Adam, they have turned out very well."

Adam was struck with homesickness when he arrived in Sydney and pleaded to come home. "He was missing us a lot and ringing almost every day, at times so homesick he was begging me to come home," Lisa says. "But I wouldn't have let him. I just kept saying: 'This is what you worked so hard for, you have done this, you have to suck it up and keep going.' And he did."

Jake and Brett continued to play football after Adam left, the younger Goodes more serious than the elder. When Jake was was 15, he left school and began an apprenticeship as a landscape gardener. He is now a park ranger at the Grampians.

Brett won two VFL premierships with North Ballarat. Like Adam, he had the AFL dream. He's still involved in football, working in player welfare with the Western Bulldogs, and playing with VFL affiliate Williamstown.

"I thought the AFL dream was over a few years ago," Brett says. "I'm working at the Bulldogs and very much enjoying my role at the club, plus I get to play with the younger guys on the weekend.

"The dream is always there, it probably will be until I'm 35 and hobbling around, but working in the AFL system and playing in the VFL, I'm pretty happy with that."

While at times it's not easy living up to being the brother of Adam Goodes, Brett says it has always been a more positive thing than a negative. It's a sentiment echoed by Jake: "Of course there are more positives than negatives. I've never really thought about it too much, Adam's still just my brother to me."

But one thing the boys haven't done is play football together.

"With a bit of luck, one day when we will get to run around and don the guernsey together," Brett says. "We might go back to the local pub one year and have a year there playing together and hopefully win the flag . . . live the dream I guess."

From those timid beginnings in 1997, Adam has achieved much. "He's been such a great role for my other boys, for indigenous boys, and for all young men in the community," Lisa says. "I sometimes wonder if he really is my son . . . I'm so proud I can say he is."

The Sydney Morning Herald 16 September 2011

WORLDS APART

Peter Hanlon

SO OFTEN DO WE HEAR THAT A footballer or his club has been through a trying or difficult off-season, it can land as flat as a punctured Sherrin. In the case of Liam Jurrah, the summary has a truth and depth befitting this exceptional young man.

The backdrop to the first full pre-season Jurrah has completed in his three summers at Melbourne is so volatile, the threat to the only thing he values more than football—his family—so real that little can be said for fear of inflaming ongoing tensions. Those who spoke to *The Age* stressed only that the 22-year-old should not be seen to have taken sides in the violent dispute that engulfed his remote community of Yuendumu last September.

All agree on one thing: Jurrah's ability to reach an unprecedented level of fitness ahead of the new season in such a distracting climate is remarkable.

"People underestimate how intelligent Liam is; he's a very, very smart person," says Ian Flack, Melbourne's personal development coach who works closely with Jurrah and the five other indigenous players on the Demons' list.

"He deals with situations very well. He's just got great perspective— he can, to a certain extent, put things to one side. He still feels it, but he's just got a great way of dealing with situations and keeping his focus and perspective."

If his 17-game AFL career were somehow extended to 17 seasons, it is hard to imagine Jurrah having to deal with anything as heavy as this.

In short, a young man—a childhood friend and former Yuendumu Magpies teammate of Jurrah—was stabbed and killed in Alice Springs last September.

The victim's family sought to exact payback punishment under tribal law, but Northern Territory police intervened and charged a 20-year-old man with murder.

Civil unrest broke out in Yuendumu, and more than 100 Warlpiri people fled to Adelaide to escape the blood feud. They have since returned, only to encounter more violence, and many are now camping in parkland south of Adelaide, pleading for the Northern Territory government to provide mediation in the hope of finding a resolution that would allow them to go home.

Jurrah returned to Yuendumu, 300 kilometres north-west of Alice Springs, to begin his off-season break and landed in a community reeling from the death of his friend. His grief was interrupted by having to fly back to Melbourne to accept his 2010 Mark of the Year award at the All-Australian dinner.

"Here he is, he's got to suit up, put on a smiling face for the cameras, knowing one of his close friends has just died," says Bruce Hearn Mackinnon, a member of the Industrial Magpies group who first brought Jurrah to Melbourne in 2008, when he played with Collingwood's VFL team.

Hearn Mackinnon stresses that Jurrah was not targeted in the dispute, that all in Yuendumu know he had no role in it, and that his only wish is for a return to peace in his community. But he has family on both sides, and family is everything.

Melbourne was naturally concerned, but reassured of Jurrah's safety by Brett Badger, the operations manager of the Mt Theo Program, which facilitates development and leadership among Warlpiri youth as well as counselling young people at risk with issues such as substance abuse. "Brett keeps the club very much up to speed and informed on what's happening in Yuendumu," Demons chief executive Cameron Schwab says. "We got reassurance fairly quickly."

After spending time with his girlfriend, Shijara, in her native community of Hermannsburg, Jurrah returned to Melbourne and was on the track for day one of pre-season training. Then, in late November, the club was rocked by the death of Austin Wonaeamirri's father, Matthew, in a car accident on Melville Island.

"Liam has had his situation, but Aussie had just as big a trauma to deal with," says Flack. "And then Aussie had Maurice's [Rioli's] funeral as well. He's Maurice's brother."

The pain has been felt by all at Melbourne, yet the off-season has underscored how much the club has been enriched by the path it walks with Jurrah—who has arguably travelled further to reach the AFL than even the club's beloved Irishman Jim Stynes—with Tiwi Islander Wonaeamirri, and with all of its indigenous players.

Schwab thinks there is a story in the work Flack does with the players alone. He, Stynes and others at the club have visited Yuendumu multiple times, and Schwab says the involvement in the players' communities and their lives has become "a natural thing, it's done in a way that no one's trying".

They are conscious that an AFL career is the fulfilment of a dream—not only for the player but his people, too—but that it also robs a community of a young leader. Respecting the relationship is, says Schwab, the least Melbourne can do.

More than a dozen players and staff, including Jurrah and coach Dean Bailey, attended Matthew Wonaeamirri's funeral on Melville Island. The experience will stay with them forever, and was poignantly captured by Nathan Jones in a blog on his website.

Schwab feels the pull of Jurrah's country every time he looks at the painting by Liam's grandmother on his wall, which she gave to him and his wife Cecily [another hangs in Stynes' house]. "Liam's grandmother and great aunty are very well known Yuendumu artists," Schwab says. "My wife's Cecily, and Liam's grandmother is Cecily. My wife is American, and the only other Cecily she's met is an elder from Yuendumu."

Back on the training track in Melbourne, Jurrah's strides lengthened. Having arrived at the club in January 2009 with no pre-existing fitness base, his preparations last season were curtailed by a shoulder injury in the NAB Cup that required a reconstruction.

Perversely, says Demons fitness boss Joel Hocking, it proved a blessing for his overall fitness.

"We got to spend a lot more time with him, because rather than being one of 35 or 40 blokes doing the pre-season, he was one of five blokes in rehab," Hocking says, citing the benefits gained not just from exercises designed to build strength in Jurrah's naturally loose joints, but work tailored to increasing endurance. "This year, he gained more work ethic and understands the demands of the sport and how hard he has to work, and has probably found a few more levels of himself, learned to push himself a fair bit harder than he had previously. He's come out the other side really, really well."

Hearn Mackinnon, who with his wife Rea housed Jurrah when he first came to Melbourne and sees him often, says he is "glowing, he looks a million dollars".

He says Jurrah calls this "my first pre-season", and is very much aware of his new-found level of fitness.

He weighed 76 kilograms when he arrived at the club, and now nudges 85. Hocking says being a "fast-twitch" athlete has helped him to put on and hold the weight he will need to combat big-bodied defenders this season. The fitness department's challenge has been to tailor a program that enhances his "weapons" while making him more durable. "Still having his tricks and his X-factor was a big thing," Hocking says.

On the evidence of his efforts last Friday night, back on the Adelaide stage where he soared into football's all-time highlights reel last August, the building of a bigger, better Jurrah is on track. The scenes that followed in the Melbourne rooms were as captivating as his football.

More than 70 Warlpiri people, from toddlers barely on their feet to Jurrah's mother and grandmother, gathered to hail the young man they know as Jukurtayi.

Children with red- and blue-painted faces posed for photos with Stynes, as a beaming Jurrah moved quietly among his people.

The group had taken the wrong bus route and wound up in Port Adelaide that afternoon, with Flack making repeated calls to Shijara asking after their whereabouts, before discovering they were tackling the journey on foot. A fleet of taxis eventually ferried them to the ground.

This is nothing compared to the road they have already travelled. The ABC's AM program this week reported from the Adelaide parkland where Warlpiri people are camping as they await a resolution in Yuendumu. One woman spoke of being attacked during an aborted attempt to return home. "I got hit on the head and ended up in hospital for two hours," she said. "I lost a lot of blood." The woman was Cecily Granites, Liam Jurrah's grandmother.

Flack says Jurrah knows the esteem in which he is held. "He's respected by the whole community." He says Harry Nelson, a key Warlpiri elder who is with the group in Adelaide, has been another strong contact for Melbourne. "He's been very good with Liam, saying to Liam, 'You playing AFL footy for Melbourne is really important for the community, it gives the community a sense of pride, something positive to follow.'

"That's helped keep him on track, the fact that he knows he's got the support of his community. In a lot of ways he's playing for his people."

Jurrah is recognised as a future Warlpiri elder, but for now his focus is on being a footballer. His calm, professional approach to his third season in the big league does him enormous credit, and stems in part, says Hearn Mackinnon, from a "norm" few have known. "The sorts of family crises that kids in remote Aboriginal communities have to deal with growing up, we would be overwhelmed by dealing with just one of them, but in a sense it becomes almost part of life. From a very young age he's used to dealing with it, and just gets on.

"It's one of the reasons why, as much as he's a brilliant footballer, those of us who've been privileged to get to know him, we just think he's a brilliant human being. He's just ridden through everything."

No one knows this better than Badger, who speaks with Jurrah almost daily, and whose experience of big city and outback life gives him a keen appreciation of what Liam has done, the two worlds he balances, and all that he cares about. He describes Jurrah, who worked as a youth mentor on the Mt Theo Program before moving to Melbourne, as "an even better bloke than he is a footballer—which is really saying something".

Badger did not think it appropriate or beneficial to discuss the climate in Yuendumu, but was happy to talk about his friend, who he said seemed "especially happy, fit and raring to go this year".

All in the community are excited by what 2011 might bring. "All Warlpiri are proud of him and hoping for an injury-free year and his continued happiness down there, first and foremost," Badger said.

"I'm extremely proud to be close to him. Who he is, and not just talent, is a significant part of why he has succeeded on his unique journey. The Demons have been absolutely fantastic for, and with, him."

As he surely has for them.

The Age 19 February 2011

BLOOD BROTHERS

Chloe Saltau

There is a bond between Aboriginal AFL players that transcends allegiance to a jumper. To celebrate the positive influence of these men on and off the ground, The Sunday Age gathered them together for a series of photographs. John Donegan took the pictures and Chloe Saltau spoke to many of the players involved. The result is a fascinating insight into how they interact and how proud they are of each other.

LOOK CLOSELY DURING A MATCH, and you might see them wink at one another, or brush hands as they run by. "You sort of do it on the sly, but sometimes you get caught," says Chris Johnson.

Occasionally, Johnson's Brisbane teammates have looked at him quizzically after he has acknowledged an act of brilliance by an Aboriginal opponent and been caught, just as Sydney's Adam Goodes caught eyes with Aaron Davey after the Demons forward missed a shot after an electrifying chase during a fiercely contested match at the SCG last season.

As they jogged to their positions, Goodes subtly stuck his hand out near his thigh, Davey slapped it and they got lost in the game again.

"You don't try to do it so everyone can see, but if you watch closely you'll see a little 'low-five', if you can call it that, just to each other, or a pat on the back, or just a quick little wink," Johnson said.

When Johnson reluctantly moved from Melbourne to Brisbane in the wake of the Fitzroy merger in 1996, he took a while to warm to a new club and a new city. The presence of fellow indigenous players Darryl White and Michael

McLean made the adjustment easier, and he still hears their advice when young Aboriginal players land at the Lions.

When Anthony Corrie arrived from Darwin a few years ago, he moved in with Johnson and his wife, Vanessa, and their kids, and the 30-year-old feels more than the usual responsibility to help shape the careers of Ash McGrath and a more recent recruit, Rhan Hooper.

There is a brotherhood among indigenous players that transcends their teams and states, which has grown infinitely stronger since Johnson's AFL debut 12 years ago, and which is celebrated by a photograph of all the Aboriginal players in the AFL in *The Sunday Age* this week at a time when their influence on the game is perhaps greater than ever.

The Victorian-based players tumble into a photographic studio in St Kilda. They are quiet at first, and then Dean Rioli arrives with his Essendon crew. Instantly the noise rises, as Rioli goes to every player and touches his fist to theirs, slinging an arm around each of them.

Davey is a livewire in life as in football, and darts around winding the others up. But when it comes to talking about his moment with Goodes at the SCG, he is reserved.

"When we play against each other, we look after each other. We give each other a pat on the back," he shrugged, but explains later that when he watches footy on TV, he looks for the Aboriginal players and wants them to do well.

He loved watching Gavin Wanganeen, his older cousin, the most, until the former Essendon and Port Adelaide premiership champion retired on 300 games because of a chronic knee problem.

"I think it's how we've been brought up, to care for each other. There's about 50 of us playing in the AFL and we've got to stay together," Davey said.

In the past few years indigenous camps, started by the AFL Players' Association and held before the season in Melbourne, Uluru and Broome, have brought the Aboriginal players closer still, helped younger footballers adjust to the AFL lifestyle, manage their money and, according to Johnson, helped them "learn a bit more about our culture" by visiting Aboriginal communities in remote parts of Australia.

The Aboriginal All-Stars game, Davey says, is cherished above almost all else. "You don't get the chance to play with blokes like Jeff Farmer and Andrew McLeod very often, and we make the most of it and really enjoy it. We've got to go back to our normal clubs, but we do what we have to do and then after the game we catch up and have a chat."

Davey's father and the uncle of hard-working Melbourne defender Matthew Whelan grew up playing footy together in the Northern Territory, and it was Whelan who looked out for Davey when he was taken onto the Demons' rookie list.

"You know you're going to feel safe when you're playing with him, it's like playing with a brother," Davey said. "It's more about helping you enjoy it. He was there for a couple of years on his own after Jeff [Farmer] went over to the Dockers, and if I was the only one at my club I would find it real hard to fit in. He made me feel welcome and we ended up getting Shannon [Motlop] and Byron [Pickett]."

Every club has a similar support network. Jarrad Oakley-Nicholls, who made his debut for Richmond in the Dreamtime game at the MCG and floated through a late point that helped bury the Bombers, felt an instant connection with Andrew Krakouer, who had visited his school in Perth, and moved in with Richard Tambling for a month after he was drafted.

"I looked up to [Michael] Long and Chris Lewis as I was growing up, I would love to even get near the sort of career they had," Oakley-Nicholls said.

"I respect all the other indigenous players because they've had the will to get up and try to make a name for themselves. Hopefully that's what I can do."

In his nine years at Windy Hill, Rioli has frequently returned to the Territory and watched Tambling play. Nowadays, as he wills his creaky knee to get him 100 games, Rioli's breath is taken away by the pace and creativity of the Kangaroos' Daniel Wells.

"I'm waiting for Richie to mature and get games under his belt. It's going to be exciting. He's the one I'm waiting for most, but out of everyone here at the moment Daniel Wells is probably my favourite," said Rioli, who has talked of setting up a player management company for Aboriginal players after he retires.

Rioli's influence among the younger footballers at the studio is obvious, and when photographer John Donegan asks the 100-gamers, and those who are on the verge of 100 games, to stick around for another shot, the men on either side of him—Essendon's Nathan Lovett-Murray and former Bomber Cory McGrath, now with Carlton—each places a hand on his shoulder, a gentle acknowledgement of what the milestone would mean to him.

Rioli continued: "I've played a lot of footy on Matty Whelan, so I get to see first-hand how hard he is to play on.

"A lot of the times earlier on in my career, coaches liked to play Aboriginal players on each other because we know each other's game, we know we've got the flair and we'll take the risk. It's definitely hard, you always have a laugh and a joke when you're out on the field, but go hard at it when the ball's in your area. In the old days when I used to play against Che [Cockatoo-Collins] and Winston Abraham, we used to have a bit of fun on the field, but footy's gone a bit too serious, these days."

Still, it is common to see the Aboriginal players gather in the middle of the ground at game's end. "It's not quite that you go out of your way, it's just natural that you meet in the middle," Rioli said.

"Even though we all come from different states, we've all got the same sense of humour. When we get together, even if it's for a meeting to get something done, it's very hard to be serious. Everyone likes to clown around. It's a good vibe with these guys. You don't get to talk too much football."

In an age when football increasingly works to a plan, and team rules are sacred, the influence of the indigenous players becomes ever more important.

Thanks to the profound achievements of Long, Nicky Winmar, McLean and co in stamping out racial vilification in the AFL, Johnson believes they now get "a fair go" and are appreciated for the exhilarating gifts on show.

"The way the game has embraced us, they know we're electric and a pretty exciting bunch, they know if they can get two or three Aboriginals in their team, they know there's something special is going to happen," Johnson said.

Leon Davis, the first Aboriginal player to notch up 100 games for Collingwood, who has flourished for the Pies this season, is a quiet, private person who nonetheless felt it was important for him to insist on mediation when broadcaster Rex Hunt described him as being "black as a dog" last year, though he accepted Hunt's remark was not intended to be racist.

"It wasn't my intention to make it as big as it was, but it was good just to let the public know that it does happen," Davis said.

These days the maturing 24-year-old is an unofficial mentor to Chris Egan, the young Aboriginal player who came to the Magpies from Rumbalara, around Shepparton, who has been in the VFL this season. The older Magpie has impressed on Egan the importance of a solid work ethic to accompany his innate talents, and speaks from experience.

"I've always been on his back to make him improve, to let him know it's not all talent," Davis said.

As much as Davis will cherish his status as a 100-game Magpie for the rest of his life, he's now looking for "200, 250, see how we go". Naturally, all the players gathered in this photo would dearly love to emulate Wanganeen [a Brownlow medallist and the first Aborigine to play 300 AFL games], Pickett [a dual premiership player] and McLeod (a dual Norm Smith medallist). Equally, like brothers, they play for each other.

The Sunday Age 25 June 2006

DAVID SELWYN BURRALUNG MERRINGWUY GALARRWUY WYAL WIRRPANDA—AND DON'T YOU FORGET IT

Michael Gleeson

WE'VE KNOWN HIM AS DAVID WIRRPUNDA, but that's not the half of it. First, there are six [first] names, some of which even David occasionally forgets. But more importantly, we have been calling him the wrong name.

David Wirrpunda is not his name, it's David Wirrpanda. With an A not a U, and roll the Rs. Sure, it will be written Wirrpunda in the AFL Record today, and in the team lists in the newspapers and in just about every other place you see his name written. But they are wrong.

In a time when a player can get people to call him Jimmy, not James, in a week, David Wirrpanda has been trying for 10 years to get people to spell his name correctly. And they still don't, even at his own club.

"Everyone says my name wrong. It is Wirrpanda. It's spelt W-i-double-r and p-a-n-d-a. It would be good if you could put that in, I have tried to change it for 10 years but everyone says it the wrong way and they keep spelling it the wrong way," Wirrpanda said this week.

"It's from north-east Arnhem Land. I don't know how it came about that people spelt it the wrong way, it just happened when I got to the club and if I did a media thing, people would just write it down the way it sounded, I suppose. But they did it the wrong way and all these years I haven't been able to change it."

While he protests about the misspelling, his sister Aretha cheekily insists it was David who inserted the U in the name when he went to West Coast. After all, there are many David Wirrpandas in the north-west and David wanted to make his own name, she said.

David Wirrpanda was born in Carlton on August 3, 1979, to Margaret of the Dhulinyagon clan of the Yorta Yorta people of Ulupna in central Victoria and David of the Dhurdi-Djapu clan of Arnhem Land's Dhurbitjbi.

The couple moved back to David snr's tribal lands in Arnhem Land soon after young David was born but when the relationship faltered, Margaret and the kids retreated to family near Shepparton and then to Healesville, where his aunt Hyllus Maris had started the Worawa Aboriginal College.

Here, his precocious ability as a sportsman and leader was revealed. Aretha recalls him competing with and beating much older kids from the moment he could pick up a ball.

When he was five, he would do 100 push-ups—just to show he could. His mum's dad, Selwyn Briggs, was a talented footballer who tried out for Hawthorn but turned down the offer because of family commitments.

Growing up, contact with his father was limited to spasmodic phone calls and the occasional visit in the school holidays. His mother Margaret and her mother Geraldine Briggs were the dominant forces in his life.

Geraldine died four weeks ago. She was an extraordinary woman who was Victoria's first female Aboriginal activist, campaigning for Aboriginal citizenship and the establishment of the Aboriginal health and legal services, the Aboriginal Advancement League and many other Aboriginal groups.

It was work that won her an Order of Australia and work her daughter, Margaret, took up and which David now more gently champions.

Wirrpanda's mother's side was dominant when he was growing up, but in recent years he has reconnected with his father and is acutely aware of the responsibilities in both communities.

Dhakiyarr Wirrpanda was David's grandfather and in the footballer's words, he was "the king of all Arnhem Land. We are royal blood." The story of Dhakiyarr was recently told in an ABC documentary called *Dhakiyarr Versus The King*.

"Dhakiyarr was taken into custody by police for spearing a policeman and three Japanese," said Aretha. "The policeman had raped his wife, our grandmother, and when they took him into custody, he was on tribal land not Crown land, so it was a battle of jurisdiction. Dhakiyarr was killed by police when he was in custody."

Dhakiyarr's responsibilities will soon fall to David.

"Our culture is my first priority. Once I have completed what I am doing here, I will be straight home to address all my cultural needs and issues," Wirrpanda said. ". . . With the stance I have got to make for my family within our family groups, I have to be there for certain ceremonies and that is important for me and the community.

"Dad inherited my grandfather's position, and he has some responsibilities that my grandfather had after he died but I have to take over certain responsibilities as well.

"Footy is a walk in the park compared to the responsibilities I have as an indigenous person and family member of my own family, some of the tough calls and some of the things I am needed to be present at. What it comes down to is I am required to do a lot of things culturally and that plays a big part in my life.

"I had to do it two or three years ago to go up to a ceremony and I missed a game and obviously I missed the game against Geelong [when his grandmother Geraldine Briggs died], so it does jump up and it is very important you are present."

According to Aretha, those responsibilities are not restricted to one side of the family only, for within the Yorta Yorta and other Aboriginal communities, David has become a community leader of significance. "The elders have always groomed David. When he was about 10, the elders called mum over and said he has great responsibilities," Aretha said. "He is seen not just by the family clan as a leader but throughout Australia he is becoming very respected by the community."

Wirrpanda is forging his own path, establishing a foundation to assist not only Aboriginal kids but any disadvantaged youth. One he is mentoring through the foundation recently finished in the top few science students in Western Australia.

"That is a passion of mine—I am a very community-minded person. I want to meet and deal with issues in the communities that need to be addressed but my main priority is that I need to be a role model and inspiration for indigenous kids and also disadvantaged kids.

"I enjoy getting out there and sharing some of the things that have helped me through life—I never speak about footy, I don't want to tell kids how to be a footy player. To me, that is unethical, not everyone is going to be a sportsperson.

"It is a beautiful blend, my family background [his father's Arnhem Land tribal background and the political activism of his mother and grandmother]. But the main thing is I have a very good understanding of my responsibilities.

"That is all they ask for and I would like to think mum and my father and my family did their job of making sure that I grew up to be a responsible young man. I want to do the same thing they did for me for a lot of other kids."

The Age 24 September 2005

AFL CLUB "PREFERS WHITE PARENTS"

Michael Gleeson

A RECRUITER FOR AN AFL CLUB has privately admitted to the league that his club would be unlikely to draft an indigenous player unless at least one parent were white.

The recruiter is one of several recently approached by the AFL in response to rumours of unease at some clubs about recruiting indigenous players, and a drop in their numbers on club lists.

There are 80 Aborigines on AFL lists this year, down from 85 in each of the past two years.

Some clubs have told the AFL they are more reluctant than before about recruiting Aboriginal players because they are thought to provide a difficult management issue. Other clubs, however, remain firmly committed to recruiting Aborigines.

The issue was brought into focus by the arrest in the Northern Territory last week of Melbourne player Liam Jurrah for an alleged assault with a machete.

Jason Mifsud, the AFL's community engagement manager, confirmed there had been a hardening of attitudes against Aboriginal players at some clubs. "I have had direct conversations with a number of recruiting officers. A recruiter from one club told me that 'unless they have a white parent we are not going to draft an Aboriginal player and our club would not be alone in that'.

"That is a mind-set that is permeating back through parts of the industry. Fortunately, there are still many clubs that embrace Aboriginal talent," said Mifsud, whose role includes managing indigenous affairs.

Mifsud warned that if the attitude achieved a stronger foothold, the AFL would "turn 180 degrees and within five years we would have undone 15 years of hard work and progress.

"When people start talking about race as part of a recruiting decision, and then splitting that out to be a question of mixed race, fundamentally people are going into areas they have no idea about. It is ignorant and offensive," he said.

Mifsud said the attitude of some recruiters meant that "if you are too black you are not going to get drafted and in [places like] Warrnambool you are not black enough so you are not going to get drafted".

He said AFL football had been a rarity in Australian society for giving Aborigines a sense of identity and inclusiveness absent in other areas of life. "The one vehicle this country has had in the last 15 years to elevate, celebrate and recognise Aboriginal and Torres Strait Islander identity is football and if that door is going to start to get shut on us then we are going to fight and scratch to keep it open. Because if these prevailing mind-sets are as strong as we hear they are, we must fight to change them."

The Age 16 March 2012

THE CHANGING LANDSCAPE

Martin Flanagan

I'D HEARD THE WHISPERS BEFORE and, since Liam Jurrah's dramas of the past week, the whispers have grown louder—AFL clubs are starting to back away from recruiting indigenous players.

They're "too hard", it is said, "too much trouble". Recruiters are paid to deliver premierships, not racial harmony, the argument runs. Sponsors don't want their names associated with players breaking the law or offending community values.

Eddie McGuire, on his new show on Fox TV, made reference to the matter, although he put it in a larger context. He asked: "Is it becoming too hard not only for indigenous players but also for other kids without formal education?" He repeated the statistic that AFL players now have 15 contact hours of tuition a week—more, he claimed, than a commerce student at Melbourne University.

The AFL needs to act and it needs to act quickly. The game accrued a lot of moral authority during the 1990s and early 2000s by the lead it took in the area of indigenous relations, thereby cementing its status as the national game. Now we've entered another phase.

In my experience, when there are rising tensions between different groups, whether they be racial or religious, there is really only one remedy. Engagement. The alternative to engagement is a cycle of rumour and speculation that eventually finds expression through media types who mistake valuable opinion for saying the first thing that comes into their head, as opposed to arriving at a final judgment based on the best information available.

The AFL needs to get everyone together in a big room for what in international politics is called a summit. The clubs obviously need to be present—particularly as they now have so much power, the recruiters. But, no less, organisations such as AFL NT and AFL Central Australia also need to be represented.

The speakers should include former indigenous champions such as Andrew McLeod. McLeod addressed a forum of the United Nations in Geneva; he can address the AFL.

Past players such as the *Marngrook Footy Show*'s Chris Johnson should be invited. If necessary, discussions should be held behind closed doors so that people can speak frankly, but the aim of the discussions should be this—how do we work our way through this problem together?

There has been discussion recently over whether proposed changes to the interchange rule will disadvantage indigenous players. As with all proposed rule changes, the people whose views I'm most interested in are the players. But I also want to hear from the indigenous players.

Sydney's Adam Goodes is entitled to be seen as a major figure in the game. I want to hear what he thinks. I have heard Hawthorn's Shaun Burgoyne speak—in the quietest of ways, he was firm and utterly clear in his opinions. I want to know what he thinks.

McGuire's estimation of the game's trajectory and current whereabouts is, I believe, correct. It seems a sad but inevitable consequence of modern professional sport that the wealthier sports become, the more people are employed in specialist and coaching capacities and the more technical the games become.

It doesn't mean the games become any better or more enjoyable to watch. Indeed, I would argue the main thrust of all this applied thought to Australian football has been essentially negative. Basically, the changes of the past decade have amounted to borrowing tactics from other sports, notably soccer and basketball, that frustrate or block the passage of the ball from one end of the ground to the other. Compare that with the contribution of the person who came up with the idea of the high mark.

As the game becomes more about systems of play, more about programmed plays and cramming players' heads with information before the match, I always go back to a remark of Nathan Buckley's: "Footy's like a tune. The indigenous players never forget it—the rest of us struggle to remember it at times."

In terms of material wealth, footy's bigger than ever but those with a responsibility to the game would have to be drunk with power to forget for a single moment that our code is locked in a race to survive with soccer and the two rugby codes. If Melbourne Victory disappoints this season, it can recruit a couple of Brazilians for next year. If Melbourne Storm disappoints this season, it can go to New Zealand or scour the Pacific Islands for likely replacements.

In the Irish language there is a phrase, "sinn fein", which translates as "ourselves alone"—that is the position of Australian football. We have no ready supply of players outside these shores. Furthermore, when I went to school, everyone played sport and everyone played football and cricket. Now only those who are good at sport play sport and footy has to compete with a smorgasbord of activities for their affections.

Can anyone seriously suggest Australian football would have been a better, more enjoyable game without the talents of Farmer, Jackson, Rioli, the Krakouer brothers, Long, McLeod, Wanganeen etc? Yes, relations across the cultural divide at the heart of this country are hard, but every weekend coaches demand what is hard from players. It's time for those running the game to step up.

The argument can be summarised simply. In 2012, the face of the game is an indigenous player, Hawthorn's Buddy Franklin. Richmond passed him up in the draft because they thought he was trouble.

The Age 13 March 2012

THE SUITS

Football has always been big business, with the egos off the field often as big as those on it. Squabbling between club presidents was once the norm, but that changed as the decade unfolded. "As surely as 2000 was the year of the Bomber, and the year of the Colonial Stadium shemozzle off the field, 2001 is increasingly the year of the president," columnist Jake Niall wrote. "They are blueing and suing, attacking and defending. They have become a circus to rival the World Wrestling Federation."

Those in the boardroom do have an important role to play and, like any forward worth his salt, must kick goals for their clubs to prosper. Former Carlton president John Elliott did that for years, but his reign would eventually go up in smoke. "His forced departure after 20 years as Carlton president continues a spectacular decline in the fortunes of a man once counted among Australia's most powerful business tycoons, and touted as a future Liberal prime minister," Caroline Wilson penned in 2002.

Eddie McGuire, meanwhile, has transformed Collingwood into a powerhouse, while AFL chief executive Andrew Demetriou has done the same for the league as a whole. Demetriou's influence extended to establishing the Gold Coast Suns and Greater Western Sydney, forming part of the AFL's vision for a truly national competition.

FOOTBALL BOSSES STEP INTO LIMELIGHT

Jake Niall

CLINTON CASEY AND DAVID SMORGON did all but choose their weapons and fire from 30 paces. Joe Gutnick is forever waging war on his enemies, the AFL and Demon dissidents on the board. Eddie is defending his entangled interests, while Big Jack, Carlton's cultural attache, is never far from a headline.

As surely as 2000 was the year of the Bomber, and the year of the Colonial Stadium shemozzle off the field, 2001 is increasingly the year of the president. They are blueing and suing, attacking and defending. They have become a circus to rival the World Wrestling Federation.

It was Russell Robertson's misfortune to take a hanger while Gutnick was mingling with the Melbourne masses. Joe was the real show last Sunday. Talk to the presidents and they'll agree that the focus should be on players, coaches and, indeed, football. They're only acting in the interests of their members and if the media hangs on every word, what can they do about it?

"I don't want to see officials' involvement affecting what we're trying to do on the field," said Richmond president Casey, reflecting on his role. "But there does come a time when someone has to show some leadership and say 'this is our position'." Casey says the members demand this of their president.

Geelong president Frank Costa thinks the presidential focus hurts the game. "I don't think that's good for football."

How did president politics end up like this? It's been brewing for a decade or more. John Elliott, Allan "Pie Chief Hits Out" McAlister and Footscray's Peter Gordon were pioneers in the art of AFL-bashing. But their efforts then seem tame compared to Joe's full-frontal attacks, and the skirmishes of those days didn't quite have the venomous intensity of the Casey–Smorgon spat.

But the presidents wouldn't be followed by the media if there was no story. So what is it?

Compare the profiles and occupations of the Victorian presidents of 10 years ago to now.

No less than five were ex-players—Ron Evans (Essendon), Ron Hovey (Geelong), Stuart Spencer (Melbourne), Neville Crowe (Richmond) and Travis Payze (St Kilda). McAlister (Collingwood) was a publican, Gordon a lawyer. Hawthorn's Trevor Coote was a builder. Fitzroy's Leon Wiegard was a radio personality, but far from the Eddie league. Only Big Jack and the late Ron Casey (North Melbourne), a Channel Seven executive, had profiles beyond football.

Elliott and Evans were the only big business figures and the latter was better known for topping the VFL goalkicking in 1959 and 1960 than for running the Spotless Group.

Now, virtually every Victorian president is a multi-millionaire. Most revealingly, NOT one is a former league player, unless you count the handful of reserves games that Rod Butterss played for the Saints back in the seventies.

Gutnick's mining companies and role in Israeli politics are news. Geelong's Frank Costa owns the largest fruit and vegetable wholesale company in the country. Ian Dicker (Hawthorn) ran condom and rubber product giant Ansell and now chairs Costa's board.

Bulldog president Smorgon is a Smorgon. Casey owns an extensive aged care business. Essendon's Graeme McMahon used to manage Ansett Airlines. Butterss sold his IT employment business for plenty. Kangaroo chairman Andrew Carter, a computer man, is the newest and least known president, but give him time.

If Eddie McGuire does not (yet) have the wealth of Smorgon, Costa, Gutnick or Elliott, he more than compensates by giving Collingwood the oxygen of publicity.

Note that it is the Victorian presidents with the big names and bucks. Their interstate counterparts are as invisible as player 38 on Fremantle's list. Few people would even know that the West Coast chairman is Michael Smith, or that Brisbane is now headed by Graeme Downie.

These new clubs are run more like corporations than those in Victoria.

Their chief executives are the bosses and actually have higher profiles than their anonymous chairmen. But the real difference, as Casey and Smorgon readily admit, is that Victorian clubs need presidents with serious business connections to survive or get a sponsorship edge in a super-competitive 10-team market.

Where would Melbourne be without Joe, or someone of his generous ilk? Would the Dogs be alive if not for Smorgon's networking? The Cats were blessed that Costa had such close connections with the management of Bank of Bendigo, which agreed to a deal that greatly reduced Geelong's debt, at one stage hurtling towards $8 million (now $2.5 million, thanks to Frank and the bank).

Unlike the chairmen of the rich interstate franchises, the Victorian presidents owe their position not to state football commissions and AFL board appointments, but to the whimsical will of the members. They are politicians.

When publicans, ex-players and small business people were presidents, clubs were much smaller operations. They now turn over $15 million to $25 million. Costa says just as footy gets quicker and more physically taxing each year, the demands are escalating off the field.

"What tends to get lost as the business gets bigger," said Casey, "is footy. That's the part that we need to temper."

The Age 5 May 2001

FINAL SIREN FOR ELLIOTT AS BLUES EJECT THE OLD GUARD

Caroline Wilson

JOHN ELLIOTT, THE AFL's MOST enduring and controversial president, last night quit the Carlton football club board just 24 hours before he was to be voted out by his members.

His forced departure after 20 years as Carlton president continues a spectacular decline in the fortunes of a man once counted among Australia's most powerful business tycoons, and touted as a future Liberal prime minister.

A moist-eyed Mr Elliott, 61, announced his departure in the premiership room of the grandstand named in his honor at Optus Oval.

He was flanked by long-standing powerbrokers Wes Lofts, Barry Armstrong and Peter Kerr, who also quit the board and had been pushing him to resign since Friday.

Handing over the reins to one-time friend and former Carlton chief executive Ian Collins, Mr Elliott said: "The ordinary member has spoken. We accept the decision. We will now close ranks and move forward."

Mr Elliott and fellow outgoing directors then headed to the Carlton hotel owned by another premiership ruckman, Peter "Percy" Jones.

They were joined by the only surviving members of the Elliott ticket, former premiership players Stephen Kernahan and Greg Williams, who by Sunday had received enough support from the Carlton members to be voted on to the new Collins-led board tonight.

Mr Elliott's inevitable defeat—he had received only about 600 members' proxies, compared with Mr Collins' 2100—came one day earlier than expected.

He quit only hours after the AFL revealed it had charged the Blues with two breaches of the salary cap for the 2000 season.

The league did not rule out banning the club from the national draft on November 24, in which Carlton currently holds the first two choices from the most talented young footballers in Australia.

"I think they will be pleased to see the last of me," said Mr Elliott, a long-time critic of the AFL. "The stuff that came out today, the timing was too coincidental and it didn't tell us anything anyway."

Mr Collins, who worked as Mr Elliott's chief executive at Carlton for a decade until 1993, will tonight be voted president at an extraordinary general meeting at Crown Casino.

Mr Collins, who celebrated with fellow Carlton One ticket holders in his Telstra Dome boardroom last night, will have held office for only six days when he meets the AFL Commission on November 19 to answer the player payment charges.

The AFL probe is continuing with Mr Collins' new board colleague and club champion Stephen Silvagni already under investigation.

Mr Collins yesterday accused Mr Elliott of hypocrisy in criticising other clubs such as Essendon and Melbourne for cheating the salary cap in the past. He said he would plead "mitigating circumstances" on behalf of the new board. The two men, who spoke briefly last night, were scheduled to meet early today.

"I think John's had an extremely long period of office and I think a lot of that's been good," said Mr Collins. "But in recent years we've seen a downturn in the club's fortunes and now we are at the lowest ebb in the club's history.

"If you stay in any job too long you get lazy and you don't think as clearly as you should."

Asked whether he thought Mr Collins was the right man to replace him, Mr Elliott said: "Well, he is the man who is going to do it."

He said he would continue supporting Carlton, which he described as "the greatest sporting club" in Australia. "I'm immensely proud of what the club has achieved in being consistently competitive, in winning premierships and in developing and nurturing the calibre of young men who have played in the famous Carlton guernsey."

Mr Elliott's admission of defeat yesterday came after a disastrous year for himself and the club. Apart from the salary cap charges, Carlton finished last on the league ladder for the first time in its history, and is facing a big trading loss for 2002.

Mr Elliott has endured persisting turmoil in his personal life and in business.

Amid the court drama surrounding allegations of trading while insolvent as a director of the failed Water Wheel Holdings, Mr Elliott's second marriage collapsed. He has also left his famous Toorak mansion for an apartment in Carlton, and sold his clifftop home in Flinders.

The Age 12 November 2002

AFL PLANS TWO NEW CLUBS IN FOUR YEARS

Caroline Wilson

THE AFL WILL BECOME AN 18-TEAM competition within four years, with plans to establish a Gold Coast team by 2011 and a team in western Sydney by 2012.

In an exclusive interview with *The Age*, AFL chairman Mike Fitzpatrick has revealed the league has begun packaging a nine-game per round, home-and-away season to be sold as the linchpin of AFL broadcast rights beyond 2011. It is set to announce a tender process for two new club licences before the start of this season.

Conceding that it would prove "virtually impossible" to tempt even the most struggling Victorian club to move, Mr Fitzpatrick said he had spoken to all three AFL TV broadcasters, and the Nine Network, about the league's intention to expand by 2012. "We've spoken to the networks and they are very keen to get more content. It's quite clear the Melbourne clubs have emotional attachments and infrastructures they are not prepared to relinquish."

The AFL had done much work last year trying to persuade North Melbourne to move to the Gold Coast, and was disappointed when it chose not to. "If you can't get a team to relocate on the basis that North was offered, then I don't think it's ever going to happen. In a sense it has solved a problem for us. If we are looking at establishing a 17th team on the Gold Coast by 2010–11, the 18th team out of Sydney could follow within a year."

Mr Fitzpatrick will outline his expansion plans to the 16 existing clubs next week. The plans include building a 10,000-seat stadium, with administrative, training and social facilities, at Blacktown in Sydney's west.

Mr Fitzpatrick and league chief executive Andrew Demetriou outlined the expanded competition plans to channels Seven, Nine, Ten and Foxtel in Sydney before Christmas.

Nine executive Jeff Browne, whose network plans to bid with Foxtel for the media rights beyond 2011, said: "I have a policy of not discussing any talks we might have with the AFL."

The new Queensland team is expected to be offered similar inducements to the $100 million package put to North Melbourne.

Mr Fitzpatrick did not rule out shortening the premiership season to 17 rounds by 2012 to ensure each team played each other once. "It's obviously something we'd look at."

By building the Blacktown stadium, Mr Demetriou's aim to schedule a weekly game in Sydney by 2015 has been brought forward by three years.

Mr Fitzpatrick, who became AFL chairman a year ago, said: "One of the issues I had when I came in was that we didn't have the relationship with government that we should have and other codes were organising themselves quite successfully around us."

The Blacktown stadium should be completed in time for an NAB Cup pre-season fixture in March next year. The two-oval complex will be home for the second Sydney team, to play most of its home games at Telstra Stadium at Homebush.

The league's plan is certain to antagonise the Sydney Swans, which have long insisted the Sydney market is nowhere near ready for another team.

Mr Fitzpatrick also revealed that the AFL was considering drug testing footballers by taking hair or saliva samples. "We are reviewing our illicit drugs policy and these new technologies we are investigating, of hair and oral testing, could detect drug use going back three months."

The Age 16 February 2008

FROM HEADSTRONG TO HARMONIOUS, FOOTBALL BOSS HAS REINVENTED HIMSELF AND WON RESPECT

Caroline Wilson

ANDREW DEMETRIOU'S PUBLIC IMAGE HAS journeyed from the opinionated mover and shaker who six years ago this week launched his tenure as the new AFL chief executive with a poorly judged address to one of grand final week's more traditional events.

Speaking at the post-Brownlow Carbine Club lunch, Demetriou was perhaps trying to be funny when he dismissed rugby league and a popular NRL guest. Kevin Sheedy said several days later that Demetriou had better lift his game.

Back then Demetriou tended to divide people. Now he rightly prides himself upon having brought them together—this week in the case of the 16 AFL clubs, who two days ago vowed to continue to harmonise with the league and reap significant financial rewards as a result.

A traditionalist who has declared Good Friday a football "no-go" zone, he has repeatedly thwarted moves for a night grand final and in his first public pronouncement on taking over the league's football operation promised to retain the centre bounce.

Demetriou was much kinder about the NRL this week. "I don't think anyone takes any joy out of what they have been through this year," he said of the rival code's off-field scandals. "We've been there and I do believe [NRL chief executive] David Gallop's strong stance has been consistent.

"I do agree with him that front-page news of that type is not helpful, despite the publicity. Look at what's happened to Kyle Sandilands. It hasn't helped him."

Next May, Demetriou will have worked at the AFL for a decade, having said initially he might not be in the industry for long. Watching him ham up his sixth Brownlow count on Monday night, the sense was he would not be leaving the top job any time soon. The prevailing view is that AFL chairman Mike Fitzpatrick and Demetriou may not have written their commitment in blood but as a two-man team have broadly agreed to remain at the helm of the competition until at least the end of 2012 after the introduction of the 18th club—currently known as Greater Western Sydney.

Demetriou appears far better equipped to steer the competition through the coming years. The football boss who early in his AFL tenure wrote a scathing report on Fremantle, took on Brisbane Lions chief executive Michael Bowers over a sponsorship conflict, exchanged verbal blows with St Kilda coach Grant Thomas and threw up his hands repeatedly over past administrations at Carlton and Melbourne, admits cautiously that certain matters could have been better handled.

Five years ago the AFL put television before clubs and scheduled two night preliminary finals, handing Brisbane a major disadvantage. Demetriou and several commissioners left before the first bounce to attend the opera. The AFL boss would not repeat that error of judgment now.

He rarely takes the bait these days to spar with provocative Hawthorn president Jeff Kennett and when he does erupt with rapid-fire abuse of a critic, he does so in private.

Demetriou believes he has developed a better understanding of what it takes to run a football club, pointing out that the clubs are also performing better. "The manner in which they have responded to and in many cases defied the global financial crisis is a great example of that," he said.

Outgoing Essendon chief executive Peter Jackson agreed there had been a serious shift for the better in the AFL's relationships with its clubs. Jackson took over at the Bombers in 1996 and pinpointed the league's failure between 1998 and 2002 to take its clubs with them in the creation of the new stadium at Docklands, along with the developing framework that accompanied the national competition.

"They didn't think they needed to take the clubs with them and they didn't respect them," he said. "I'm not saying that was entirely their fault, but the AFL was a little bit arrogant and there was animosity between them and the clubs, and specifically this club."

Jackson said there had been a change for the better in Demetriou also. "He was a bit headstrong, is a nice way of putting it," he said. "When he first came in he probably knew all the answers.

"He's much more confident and much more relaxed in the job now and as a result he's grown in the role. Like many at the AFL he didn't necessarily respect the clubs but the clubs have been there since the 1800s and . . . the depth of talent at the clubs has improved along with the talent at the AFL.

"I can't say why he is more relaxed or why he was headstrong before. I didn't know him well enough. Maybe it's because he's got a family. Kids do that to people, they bring you back to earth.

"All I know is he's a better operator because of it."

Demetriou was widowed and in his late 30s when he replaced Ian Collins as the AFL's football operations boss in 2000, having lost his wife and long-time partner, the celebrated war historian Jan Bassett, to cancer eight months earlier.

Appointed to the AFL chief executive's role some three years later, he was by then an expectant father of twins with the AFL's corporate accounts manager, Symone Richards. The couple married soon afterwards and the Demetrious now have three girls, with the 48-year-old having moved from Kew to Hawthorn to Toorak since joining the AFL. He remains independently wealthy with an impressive property portfolio.

"Not a lot of people who get to high levels remember those they knew on the way up," said player agent and long-time confidant Ricky Nixon. "He's mixing with the big boys now but he still keeps up with his old friends and the guys he went to [Newlands High] school with.

"Probably because he's been through his own troubles he's sensitive to others. He was one of the first to call me earlier this year and check if I was OK."

Nixon was one of a group who helped launch Demetriou's return to the AFL via his pivotal role at the AFL Players' Association. "Back in the days he was running the AFLPA his headstrong ways served him well," said Nixon. "But like some coaches who adapt and change their ways to succeed as opposed to those who bitch and whinge and moan, he has publicly reinvented himself.

"He can engage you, take himself down to your level and then actually take your opinion into account. He is very bright. Mind you he can still ring me up and tell me to go and get stuffed and we'll still be fine in a matter of days.

"But he's not perfect. If I have to be negative I'd say he's possibly the worst chairman of selectors ever to preside over the All-Australian team, and if he doesn't sack himself he is deluded."

The Age 23 September 2009

BAGGING EDDIE IS NOT ALL BLACK AND WHITE

Martin Flanagan

LAST YEAR, WHEN THE BEN COUSINS story was running hot and West Coast was burning with him, the idea was mooted that poor player behaviour be punished by the clubs involved losing draft picks and premiership points.

I wrote a column objecting to what was being proposed. The tradition in Australian football has always been that the game was open to all, that everyone was given a go. What was being proposed, I said, would lead to clubs censoring themselves as to the type of people they recruited. There'd be no more players like Jimmy Krakouer and Gary Ablett snr, both of whom were in serious trouble before beginning their AFL careers, but it would actually cut a lot deeper than that.

The person who responded most energetically to what I wrote was Eddie McGuire. I received one enthusiastic text after another on the subject. In recent times, he told me, Collingwood had in its team one player who was completing a master's degree and another who couldn't read. Like all clubs, it had kids from broken homes. The AFL has former street kids basically rescued by footy. If you open your door to all comers, as has been the tradition of our game, there is inevitably going to be trouble. The way football is dealt with by the media, each incident of trouble is portrayed as a crisis for the club and the game.

I originally got to know Eddie McGuire through having a difference with him. I sided with Tim Lane against Eddie calling Collingwood games on Channel Nine. About six months later he tracked me down and an animated discussion ensued. We didn't agree on that, but there was something we did

318

agree on to do with reporting. Like all people who experience fame, he was finding that things he was alleged to have said or done were then being used as the basis for follow-up stories without anyone asking him for his version of the event. He was being fictionalised. I agreed to ring and get his side of any argument from him and not from the media.

Since then I have got to know him reasonably well. I don't understand the ins and outs of his career with the Nine network. I have no idea what his outside business interests are. He burns with a bright flame and I imagine working near him could be wearing. But I would also describe him as a naturally political person. Most people when they talk about politics are really talking about the political game. Eddie's like Michael Long. When they talk about politics, they're talking about what ought to be done, what can be done, to make a difference.

Not knowing him in 1999 when he went to John Howard's convention on the republic in Canberra, I silently agreed with those who said he'd be out of his depth. Now he's someone whose political views I listen to with interest. He was in America last month and what he saw was an economy grinding into recession, or worse. Eddie thinks big changes are coming, and they're not going to be kind.

This week, in the city of Melbourne, two Collingwood footballers featured more prominently in the news than the Olympics. Eddie and I agree on why Collingwood is such a major personality in Australian sport. The 1930s is to Australian sporting culture what the 1960s is to popular music. The world was then in an economic depression. Europe was flirting with fascism. Australians adored a cricketer and a horse, Bradman and Phar Lap. The football club which dominated the decade was Collingwood. Eddie knows a lot about the 1930s. He talks about people like Syd Coventry who captained Collingwood to four premierships, won a Brownlow Medal and was later president of the club. "No one talks about him now," he muses, "but his achievements are greater than Michael Voss's."

He also talks about the soup kitchen set up in front of the old Ryder Stand to feed the poor and the homeless; the grandstand built by local tradesmen out of work. He tells me the unemployed got in free to Collingwood games during the Depression.

If you ask Eddie what Collingwood Football Club is about, he says it's about its relationship with the community. The club has a formal "community policy" and is involved in numerous community initiatives.

In the area about which I know most, relations between indigenous and non-indigenous Australians, I rate Kevin Sheedy and Michael Long as the major agents of change over the past 20 years. But Eddie's on the list. When he took over Collingwood, it had the reputation of being the worst club in terms of racial abuse. It was part of a culture that I thought couldn't be changed. Eddie changed it. He had key people who understood what he was attempting, like coach Mick Malthouse and captain Nathan Buckley, but nonetheless the change came from the top.

Of course, you could argue that the change was in Collingwood's interest. Young Aboriginal talent didn't want to go to Collingwood; they were terrified of the place. You can argue the change initiated by Eddie was an example of what is called enlightened selfishness, but I think it goes deeper than that. Under Eddie's presidency, Collingwood has a history of helping other clubs. Each year, Melbourne Football Club's biggest fixture is its Queen's Birthday match against Collingwood. Each year, Collingwood allows Melbourne to take the gate.

Western Bulldogs president David Smorgon says: "Without Eddie, we wouldn't have landed Lease Plan, our major sponsor for the past six years." Smorgon describes Eddie as "a very genuine person who does what he says he's going to do". When the AFL ignored the claims of the Moyston Willaura Football Club to be involved in the 150th celebrations (Tom Wills grew up at Moyston), I rang Eddie. Collingwood, along with Essendon, are now among the sponsors of the Tom Wills night being held at the Moyston footy ground on August 18.

Everyone pays a high price for fame. The price Eddie pays is that everyone thinks they know him and what makes him tick. I don't believe they do. As I read football politics, Eddie is now in a spot of bother. Politics at any level are in part about perception. His comment to the players about his commitment to Collingwood having cost him four gold Logies—which he insists was a joke—has taken off.

The old Celtic chieftains were judged in part by the prosperity they brought their people. For 10 years, Collingwood has had great prosperity, but this year, while Eddie says the club will have an operating profit of around $2.5 million, it will have a loss of around $2 million after the sale of two hotels.

And then there's Alan Didak, the club's best player and, in that sense, most valuable asset. As I see it, whichever way Eddie goes on that, he loses. In terms of their careers within the game, a whole lot rests on tonight's match and the rest of the season for Eddie and Mick Malthouse.

Journalists say Eddie is hyper-sensitive to criticism. He may be, but look at the volume of criticism that has come his way in the past week. This paper even ran a full-length editorial critical of him. But if, as Eddie fears, much tougher economic times are just around the corner, I expect Collingwood to step forward and play a part. If that happens, it's in part because Eddie McGuire hasn't let Collingwood Football Club forget where it comes from.

The Age 9 August 2008

OUTSIDE THE (CENTRE) SQUARE

While a team's form, ladder placings and injuries are the nuts and bolts of reporting on football, there is much more to the sport than this. Rohan Connolly spent a week at the Western Bulldogs in 2008 and takes us behind the scenes. Danny Southern was a quirky character during his playing days with the Bulldogs, and has remained so in his life post-football, as Samantha Lane explained.

The passing of some of the game's greats always sparks heartfelt emotion. Martin Blake attended the funeral of legendary Richmond footballer and media performer Jack Dyer in 2003, and wrote: "Football is full of myths, legends, misconceptions and half-truths—and one of them is that Jack Dyer, or 'Captain Blood' to the masses, was more hard-man than great player."

"Sirengate" in 2006 reinforced that even the simplest things, such as hearing the siren, can go awry. "It is amateur hour," Blake wrote in a first-person reflection of what happened when umpires officiating at the clash between St Kilda and Fremantle at Launceston's Aurora Stadium failed to hear the siren. Play continued for a further 20 seconds, allowing the Saints to score a point to tie the match. Days later, the AFL would rule the match should have ended when the first siren sounded. The Saints were stripped of the two points for a draw, and the Dockers given the full four points.

Another major issue was the drugs-in-football debate which reared its head again in 2007 when a television network opted to report the contents of stolen medical records. "For footballers, the AFL and all who love our game, these are testing times," senior *Age* reporter Dan Silkstone wrote.

Columnist Peter Hanlon has the wit and craft to make light of football's serious side, and that came to the fore again in his "Tagger' A-Z column of the 2011 grand final.

INSIDE THE KENNEL:
THE CONNOLLY REPORT

Rohan Connolly

The Age *spends a week in the Western Bulldogs' inner sanctum as coach Rodney Eade prepares for a season with plenty on the line.*

MONDAY

Pre-season for the Western Bulldogs began earlier than for any other AFL club, all the way back to October 15. There's been plenty of gut-busting fitness work, hour upon hour of skills, drills and lectures.

But now the point of it all is within touching distance, the first game of the new season just six days away, against Adelaide, and you can see the real spring in the step of the Bulldogs' senior list as it drifts in to Whitten Oval from 8am to prepare for a 10am training session.

There's the eager kids, highly rated draftees Jarrad Grant and Callan Ward, and Josh Hill, who has played one game for the Bulldogs but, after a sparkling pre-season, is a real chance to earn his second this weekend.

There's former Adelaide pair Ben Hudson and Scott Welsh, who are ready to make their debuts for their new club, and whose inside knowledge of their old teammates is going to come in particularly handy this week.

But the old stagers, like skipper Brad Johnson—set to play his 300th game tomorrow—Scott West and Jason Akermanis look no less toey. The reason for it all is at hand.

Perhaps, too, it's because as the club's new training and administrative headquarters come nearer to completion, the players can finally shower and change in their new facility and get the hell out of the dilapidated old visitors' rooms in the John Gent stand that they've been forced to use for months.

There's still some practical hurdles to jump, however, none the least the lights hanging down from the indoor training-area roof, which are yet to be covered by protective netting and are at the mercy of any errant kick.

That and the raging heat. It's pushing 40 degrees outside already, and inside, with the air-conditioning still a couple of weeks away, it's like a sauna. The pre-session warm-up is almost redundant, but when it's done, senior coach Rodney Eade launches straight into an important focus area for tomorrow.

The coach doesn't usually jump in so quickly, notes one seasoned observer. He's fired up, too.

The session itself is spirited despite the heat, a 10-minute warm-up with the balls, a kicking drill, some full-on match practice, two different handball drills, one involving ground balls, the other tackling, before finishing off with some goalkicking on the run.

Assistant coaches Leon Cameron (stoppages), Wayne Campbell (forwards), Peter Dean (defence), John Barnes (rucks) and Brad Gotch and Simon Dalrymple (development) are all heavily involved, liaising closely with fitness head Cameron Falloon.

It wraps up after an hour or so, but then it's straight into a meeting room for a short video lecture on the Crows, done by highlighting several passages from Adelaide's NAB Cup grand final against St Kilda.

That's it for now for most of the list, who'll be back a little later on in the afternoon for a weights session, some for physio. The rubdown tables become a sanctuary and counselling service of sorts for the players as physios Simon Macaulay, Sue Cautley and Sam Rosengarten do their stuff. Club doctor Gary Zimmerman laps up the latest tales of love and loss and offers some world-weary advice.

"It's all right for you, you're a porn star," a player tells the moustachioed doc. And there is, it has to be said, a resemblance to adult film actor Ron Jeremy. Facial resemblance, that is.

There's no respite for the leadership group, though. Skipper Brad Johnson and Daniel Cross have other commitments, but Scott West, Robert Murphy, Daniel Giansiracusa, Matthew Boyd and Dale Morris have been summoned to a match committee meeting for the first time.

"We just want to talk to you about the way we're thinking," Eade tells the group assembled along with Cameron, Campbell and Dean, before running through the basic philosophy being adopted for the all-important first game and the questions being considered.

A second ruckman to support Hudson or an extra runner? Young Dylan Addison or Stephen Tiller? A possible late inclusion depending on who the Crows fly over from Adelaide?

The relative fitness levels and injury situations of both the Dogs and their opponent are spelt out. The importance of Adelaide's champion Andrew McLeod restated. The Crows' style analysed again.

The senior group is comfortable throwing its two bobs' worth in, with seven-time best-and-fairest West looking well and truly at home sitting in Eade's regular seat, his feet swung up on the desk. "I was just taking him off," West laughs, later on.

"It gives you a really good understanding of how they're thinking," he continues. "They don't have to justify to anyone who they pick and why, but I think it's great that they're open enough and can trust us enough to talk about why someone might be getting a game or not."

TUESDAY

It's a day off for the players, sort of, a number continuing to file in for physio, massage, one-on-one sessions or just a chat with their particular line coach.

For the coaches, this morning is probably the big session of the week, with a lengthy match committee meeting to thrash out just how to handle Adelaide, and just who will be doing the handling.

Eade, Cameron, Campbell, Dean and new football manager James Fantasia, another ex-Adelaide pick-up, cram into Eade's office around a whiteboard, which has the Crows' players already up there in their expected positions. Campbell places the most likely Bulldogs match-ups for them.

Eade has already had several extensive briefings from Falloon about who is definitely unavailable, who might make it and who is a touch underdone. He sums it up for the group.

There's a debate about how many ruckmen to take into the game. Hudson is the No. 1 man, Peter Street is potential support. Cameron notes that in St Kilda's NAB Cup grand final victory over the Crows, the Saints were well beaten for hit-outs, yet still managed to win the clearance count.

The discussion moves to the all-important midfield. The assistants are asked for their engine-room match-ups, and a consensus emerges. Forward coach Campbell argues a convincing case for one of his key forwards to remain in attack rather than be played elsewhere.

"Is there any chance of you leaving any of my forwards alone?" Campbell jokes to Cameron. "We have a forwards meeting and it's just me and Will (Minson)!"

The team for the first game is all but settled. Exciting young pair Tom Williams and Andrejs Everitt are injured and out. So is Farren Ray. But Giansiracusa and Lindsay Gilbee have both got through their VFL hit-out last weekend and will play.

Hudson will handle the bulk of the ruckwork, with support from manufactured key forward Minson. Hill will play his second AFL game. There's only one spot up for grabs, between Addison and Tiller.

The focus moves to Adelaide. The Crows' pattern of play. Their intent to kick higher scores and move the ball quicker. Adelaide dangermen Simon Goodwin and McLeod are discussed in depth and contingency plans are made for their shifts to various positions.

That's the game taken care of. Now there's some housekeeping. Fantasia hands out a guide to assess the quality of AFL lists, from category one players through to category five. The coaches will do the Bulldogs. He and recruiting manager Scott Clayton will take care of the other clubs.

It's a big task and makes for plenty of paperwork. The coaching panel already has to wade through exam papers that the players completed last week. The paper consisted of 36 questions covering game plan, options and terminology.

With the match committee meeting over, it's time for the really big one; the football department troops into another meeting room for a lesson on how to use the new phone system. Campbell is less than enthused. "Don't you just dial zero before the number?"

It's still bloody hot, and everyone begins to sweat as the intricacies of transferring, forwarding, conferencing, station speed dial and voicemail are absorbed. A door is opened for some air. Unfortunately, there's a hydraulic crane right outside installing the netting. The crane beeps loudly when it goes up or down.

As the voicemail instructions are issued, Eade's eyes glaze over. "What if I just want to make a call?"

Finally, phone school's out. Now the Dogs get ready for tonight's function for players and partners in the new rooms. Guests will be shown around, and shown a visual summary of the players' pre-season that has been prepared by video man Paul Newport, accompanied by music. "For Reasons Unknown", by American band The Killers, has been proudly chosen by Campbell.

As the Bulldogs started training so early, there's a lot of ground to cover. Figures are superimposed on the footage of kilometres run, punches thrown and weights lifted.

There's comedy, too. Gilbee is left very flat-footed in a reflex contest with Nathan Eagleton. Youngster Josh Hill leaves himself far too open in a spar with boxing coach Tim Smith and is duly bopped on the nose.

A huge laugh erupts right next to me as that piece of footage is screened. It's Hill. "He got me a beauty," he chuckles.

WEDNESDAY

Today is a particularly early start for Eade. He and Campbell are required to be at Telstra Dome by 7am for a coach's breakfast sponsored by WorkSafe. The players start arriving from 9am for this morning's 11am training session. There's to be a bit of match practice, but the focus today is on kick-ins and zones.

Set plays from the kick-in are rehearsed over and over. Players repeat the task of standing in those all-important holes to stop the opposition launching an easy attack from a stoppage. Then they break up into groups for line work. Forwards work with Campbell, midfielders with Cameron, defenders with Dean.

A tick after midday, as the list drifts off the track, Eade and imminent 300-gamer Johnson conduct a press conference outside the rooms. Then the squad for Sunday's game and the coaching panel cram into a meeting room for a thorough briefing.

Opposition analyst Nick Austin kicks things off as the video and big screen are cranked up again. There's a rundown on Adelaide's strengths and weaknesses. The Crows' talent for stoppages and fast starts is duly noted.

A series of edits from Adelaide's NAB Cup games against Hawthorn and St Kilda is shown and key focus areas are reinforced.

Cameron talks the Bulldogs players through the stoppage strategies and those Crows who deserve close attention. Some St Kilda kick-ins from the NAB Cup grand final are run, and Dean chimes in with some advice about the patience required for the set plays to work.

Bullet points on the whiteboard are summarised. Then Eade calls the rest of the senior list to join the throng. He has a copy of a video played at last week's AFL season launch. He's been raving about it and he hopes it will have a similar impact on his players.

"It really hit home why we play football," he tells the group. "You can take your money, you can take your All-Australian stuff . . . this is what it's about."

Austin hits the "play" button. It's an eight-minute diary about grand final day last year. As a rousing classical music score booms out, the story unfolds.

Expectant supporters waiting for the moment of truth. Nervous Geelong and Port Adelaide players getting ready in the rooms. The first bounce. The big plays. The bone-jarring bumps. The emotion of the Cats as the final siren sounds and their 44-year premiership drought is broken.

But the biggest impact comes with the shots taken hours after the finish. Geelong's bus is waiting to take the Cats to a post-game function, but the players stop, walk back up the race and lean on the boundary fence, absorbing what they have just achieved.

Joel Corey sums up those quiet moments in the dark at the MCG beautifully. "It's not often in life you get to a point where you're truly peaceful. To actually share a point in time like that [with his teammates] was unbelievable. Just walking back down the race on to the bus, I knew we were forever linked to each other."

It's gripping and moving stuff, and Dean, who knew that premiership moment as a defender with Carlton in 1995, admits to more than a little emotion.

You can hear a pin drop, and Eade says nothing more. He opens the door for the group to file out. "Right, guys."

A short time later, veteran West, he of seven best-and-fairests, 320 games, but still no premiership, sits quietly on a bench in the weights area, gazing into space.

"Bit pensive, Westy?"

"Just taking it all in," he says.

It's fair to say the video has had an impact.

THURSDAY

Today, the players will break up into groups with their respective line coaches for specialised skill work.

Cameron's group works on decision-making. Gotch and midfield general West oversee some ground ball drills. Dean works with his men on bodywork and spoiling. Skipper Johnson takes a group for marking practice, Campbell has half-a-dozen players working on quick hands, and Dalrymple takes the kids through kicking exercises.

Biomechanist Kevin Ball is in to give his academic bent on players' kicking actions and styles. There's a machine being set up to monitor the efficiency and accuracy of that simple swing of a leg on to leather.

Gotch, who will also coach the Bulldogs' new VFL affiliate Williamstown, and Dalrymple go about their work with the Bulldogs' development group, a squad of 18 players in their first, second or third years in the AFL.

And in their new training home, soon the Bulldogs will be able to set up a drill in which a pre-recorded video, shot from centre half-forward and projected against a wall, shows several different versions of forwards and defenders making position for a pass into goal. The player with the ball will be asked to pick the right option and deliver accordingly.

All very high-tech, and a far cry from what this club has known. "You grin and bear it," says West of the temporary digs under the old stand, "but I can tell you, the players were starting to get a bit narky about it. It's great to be able to get in here and have a bit of swinging room."

Team manager Mark Kimpton, or "Klippo" as he is known, can testify to the state of the old digs. He was head trainer when the Doggies went on a road trip to Perth, and he and his colleagues decided to do something about the John Gent stand's rat problem.

"We exploded a few of those really powerful rat bait bombs before we left," he recalls. "We came in early on the Monday to clean up, we opened up, and there were dead rats, sprawled everywhere, lying on their backs with their feet in the air, some as big as bloody cats. It was like the killing fields!"

Ben Hudson wouldn't have known about stuff like that playing for the resource-rich Adelaide, but the boy from Werribee is grateful to be back on home turf, playing his first game for his new club against his old one. Welsh will also play his first game for his new club against the old one.

Hudson's brain has been picked for information on the Crows. "If you gave me a list, I'd be able to point out their positives and negatives . . . I don't know if they'd all be about footy, though," he laughs.

"There's certainly a bit of added incentive to perform well. You know once you're traded that you're going to have to face up to them one day or other, and I suppose it's good to have it first-up, so you're not looking at the calendar thinking, 'When do we play them?' You could say it's like every other game, but you'd be lying."

There's another recruit of sorts, too—Jason Akermanis. Last year's debut season with the Bulldogs wasn't a gem, but he's had a big pre-season, and that Aka swagger has returned.

"I'm actually running properly for the first time in two years," he says. "Once you get to a really fit level, the body's right, and you know you can do all those things you've been able to do, within reason, it should be only a matter of time before you start playing the footy you knew you could.

"I've always thought maybe next year would be my last one, but suddenly, I don't feel like that at all now my confidence is back."

FRIDAY

Just over 48 hours until D-Day, and you can tell the game is close the second the players hit the training track at 10am. The intensity is high, the movement of the ball is quicker and cleaner. Voices call much, much louder.

Theories on training change frequently, and this year, the Bulldogs have a new strategy: to have their biggest session two days out from game day. What's the point in doing the bulk of the work early in the week when players are still feeling the bumps and bruises from their last hit-out and can't extend themselves fully?

While there might be some risk during match practice work, at least everyone's up and going when it counts.

The last spot in the team has been decided, by natural attrition as it turns out. Tiller has come down with a nasty bout of food poisoning, and is on a drip. Addison gets the nod.

After about an hour-and-a-half, the session ends and an impromptu reunion begins as the players leave the track to be greeted by retired club legends Chris Grant and Rohan Smith.

The 300-game pair are here to pay their respects to the exclusive club's latest inductee Johnson, and both look like they could put on their gear and step straight back into the action.

As players warm down inside, a quick Easter raffle is held, then it's into the meeting room for a quick recap on plans for Sunday.

Campbell starts it off by reminding his forward group of their responsibilities and zones for Adelaide's kick-ins. Dean reminds the defenders of the kick-out plays. Cameron throws up the "what ifs?"

Eade takes over and restates the plans for the Crows' key men. Mitch Hahn gets some words of encouragement, while Ryan Hargrave is reminded that "we need a big game from you, Shaggy". "We've got to run hard," says the coach. "If you're stuffed, come off. The bench has got to be mindful of that."

Attention then shifts to Johnson. Eade reminds the team that the milestone shouldn't be what's required to motivate them, but points to the words written on the whiteboard. They read: "Work ethic, courage, focus, consistency, desire".

"Those things really embody his career," says the coach. "If ever a guy embodied what we stand for, it's Brad Johnson."

Grant, Johnson's predecessor as captain, then addresses the group. To reach such a landmark, he says, isn't just about skill and talent, but the effort to keep fronting up, to structure not just your football but your lifestyle around the needs of the team.

He lauds his former teammate's willingness to continue to learn, and to listen to teammates, no matter how junior. Grant then recalls his own 300th game, coincidentally also against Adelaide.

It's a favourite memory, he says, mainly because the Bulldogs won that Saturday evening. That helps him recall the detail, the come-from-behind victory over the Crows, with Dale Morris, now a team leader, making his senior debut. Grant wants his teammate of 14 seasons to be able to have a similarly crystal-clear recollection of his big day.

The lights are dimmed, and a video package of Johnson's best is played, set to Elton John's "Your Song". The images begin back in 1994, but come 2007, the look is just the same. The passion, the pumping of fists, hugging of teammates, and that trademark beaming smile.

The players file out, and start heading home for what remains of the Good Friday holiday. They'll each do their own short warm-ups in private tomorrow, then it's just a matter of waiting for Sunday's 1.10pm start.

The mood is buoyant, positive, but—most notably—determined. Six months of hard work are about to be put to the test, and the Doggies can't wait. "It's not about a sense of atonement, making up for last year," Eade says. "It's more about just getting back to where we think we should be."

Which in this tight-knit club is somewhere considerably higher than the bulk of a sceptical football world believes. The Bulldogs are ready, not for the first time, to prove more than a few wrong.

ANALYSIS

"You're only as good as your last game," goes one of AFL football's favourite cliches. Or in the case of the Western Bulldogs, your last seven.

After 15 rounds last season, the Bulldogs were 9–6, seventh on the ladder, and seemingly destined for a second successive finals appearance. Then it all fell apart. Six losses and a lucky draw pushed a popular pre-season tip for the top four all the way down to thirteenth.

Tough questions were asked, particularly of coach Rodney Eade. The club ordered a review of its football department, and there were significant changes to off-field personnel.

Assistant coaches Chris Bond, Sean Wellman and department head Matthew Drain all left. New to the "kennel" in 2008 are Peter Dean, as defensive coach, Brad Gotch as development manager and VFL coach, and Simon Dalrymple, also in development.

There's now a full-time football manager in James Fantasia. And two more assistant coaches have switched roles, Leon Cameron from defence to midfield and stoppages, Wayne Campbell from stoppages to forwards.

The senior list has had a big makeover as well, veterans Chris Grant, Luke Darcy, Matthew Robbins and Brett Montgomery retired, Jordan McMahon and Sam Power traded. In came former Adelaide pair Ben Hudson and Scott Welsh, along with Geelong's Tim Callan.

It's some shake-up. But a football world with a short attention span isn't in a forgiving mood.

After the success of 2006, the Bulldogs were supposed to be the next big thing. Instead, they disappointed. And the critics have turned nasty.

Five of eight tipsters in last week's "Footy 2008" guide in *The Age* had the Doggies pencilled in for the bottom four.

Eade is sitting second favourite in the annual "first coach to be sacked" market.

That tag would make many AFL coaches embarrassed and angry. Eade instead laughs it off. "The bookies and punters aren't going to be making the decision," he chuckles.

But the apparent bravado might also be because he and the Western Bull-dogs see a very different story developing. One which *The Age* had a glimpse of this week when we were invited inside the inner sanctum at the redeveloped Whitten Oval, for training, team meetings and the generally Pentagon-like security of the match committee.

Tomorrow's season-opening clash with Adelaide is a big day for the club on a number of levels. There's respected captain Brad Johnson's 300th game. And the dismal finish to 2007 demands some sort of rebuttal to the doomsayers.

A win also would not only provide a boost for a smaller Victorian club's always critical membership levels, but keep the baying hordes away from Eade's door for a while.

But the mood coming out of the kennel this week wasn't the slightly tedious "David and Goliath"-type gritting of teeth against the odds. More one of quiet confidence that the fundamentals required by a serious AFL challenger are there, and that the necessary fine-tuning has been done.

It's confidence enough to survive more critical savaging. And at the same time, should the results start coming again, resist the urge to thumb the nose at a football community that can remember the events of last July and August vividly, but apparently not the two and a half years that preceded them.

The Age 22 March 2008

AGENT FOR CHANGE: DANNY SOUTHERN

Samantha Lane

DANIEL SOUTHERN DOUBTS HIS DECISION to convert to Islam—a commitment the retired Western Bulldog made only after he moved to Egypt—would have been supported by an AFL community he found to be closed and sometimes discriminatory.

The guest of honour at an AFL Players' Association breakfast today, Southern, now aged 36, married and a father, will feel comfortable discussing why he has taken the Arabic name Mustafa.

He would have been far less inclined to be so open before he left Melbourne for Cairo, which is the unstable city he now calls home.

Football, in Southern's experience, was not a scene that tended to celebrate difference. In fact, over his career, from 1994 to 2000, sometimes it rejected difference outright.

Unsurprised that an AFL player is yet to publicly declare his homosexuality, Southern yesterday recalled a vivid memory of a former teammate's blatant racism in front of one of his few close friends from the game—Torres Strait Islander Mark West.

Southern did not want to name the Bulldog responsible, preferring to let sleeping dogs lie.

But despite such off-putting experiences—Southern also recalled yesterday how he'd feel sick at some of the derogatory talk about women in change rooms—he believes that football is perhaps Australia's best agent for important social change.

"You go to the MCG and there's 90,000 people there and it's similar to being at a mosque in Cairo on a Friday," he said. "You've got every single race, every single nationality sitting right next to each other and all with the same love and passion and interest.

"It's one of those rare things that bring people together here. And if it's done right, I think it should be one of the forums that unites people more than anything else here, because it's such a powerful thing."

Southern is visiting Melbourne with his Egyptian wife of two years, Reham, and his 10-week-old son Zakaria Daniel Mark Southern.

The family has left Cairo in the midst of a revolution in order to attend today's breakfast.

Southern felt obliged to accept the AFLPA's invitation given he found professional fulfilment post-football in the tourism industry after an AFLPA-run transition program.

For most of Southern's life, football was everything. He loved playing the game, and though he hasn't watched a match for seven years, still loves it. It was some of the things he saw within football that he did not approve of.

"I remember the day very clearly when I was sitting in a car with my teammate Mark West, a Torres Strait Islander guy. It was me, Mark West, and I won't use the name of one player, and we were in a car together driving through Footscray.

"This other player said, 'Look at all these Asians, what are they doing here?'

"We dropped him off and Mark said, 'I wonder what he says about me. I'm black, I'm different, if he's saying something racist about Asians, what is he saying about me?'

"I don't know what the AFL has been working on, but obviously there has been a big thing with the Aboriginal players and they've tried to create awareness and tried to get racism out of the game and that's a great thing."

Being a mullet-haired, tough defender for the Bulldogs, Southern felt wrongly typecast.

A regrettable on-field incident that led to former Eagle Peter Sumich blacking out while in his grasp did not exactly help dispel the picture of a wild child with thuggish tendencies.

In his spare time, however, Southern was not in pubs but in his local library in Flemington.

A nearby cafe run by a Somali Muslim by the name of Muhammad Ali was where he was first introduced to the religion to which he would later convert.

Would football have been accepting of that? "I don't think so," Southern said yesterday. "I don't think it was too open.

"I'm sure it wouldn't have been good for my career, certainly if I'd still been playing and converted in 2002 [after September 11]."

While Southern thinks it is inevitable an AFL player will announce himself as gay one day, his sense is that it will not be soon.

"I think it takes people long enough outside the public eye, let alone inside the hurly-burly world of AFL football where everyone is macho and masculine.

"When they finish playing football, those same guys go through a really bad stage because they're yesterday's heroes. It's like, 'Nobody loves me any more, I'm fat and I'm bald, what am I going to do now?', and they struggle with it. It's a shallow existence, it was rife in the industry and I'm sure a lot of people are still driven by that."

The Age 14 April 2011

INSIDE A HORROR WEEK FOR CARLTON

Caroline Wilson

JOHN ELLIOTT STRODE DEFIANTLY INTO Percy Jones' Carlton pub two nights ago and announced he was writing a book. The disgraced football club president had been drinking and he was unrepentant and angry.

Elliott blamed Carlton's loss one week ago of the AFL's valuable two opening picks in the national draft on former club champions Craig Bradley and Stephen Silvagni, who disclosed their roles in the Blues' salary cap cheating earlier this month.

Carlton, declared Elliott, would not have been so savagely punished by the AFL if "Silvagni and Bradley had not ratted on us". He then turned his anger upon prominent Queen's Counsel Colin Lovitt, the president of the Carlton Cricket Club and a director of the Carlton social club.

Elliott told Lovitt that he was a traitor and called him a lot of other names as well. "You'll be in the book," he threatened. Another former director, Peter Kerr, took Lovitt aside and suggested that Elliott's successor Ian Collins should call a meeting and a truce of the old and new boards. Otherwise, said Kerr, a lot of former directors might feel uncomfortable attending the football next year.

But the wrath of Elliott is the least of the club's concerns—Carlton is facing the biggest threat to its playing future in its 105-year history. The independent auditors BDO officially moved into the club on Monday and will not complete their work for at least another week.

Already the trading loss—estimated at $180,000 by Elliott upon his departure—looks closer to $2 million once the complicated deals between Carlton's three arms (football, cricket and social clubs) are uncovered.

Not only did the new board at Tuesday night's meeting raise the prospect of reducing new coach Denis Pagan's $1.9 million, three-year contract, but the club's cash flow problems have been so poor that Pagan, who read about his pay cut in the newspapers, has seen some of his wages arrive late.

And former coach Wayne Brittain, whom Elliott sacked in September, has taken the Blues to court for contractual demands worth an estimated $200,000. Brittain still had a year remaining on his contract but was told the club simply did not have the funds to settle with him.

Apart from losing their first four picks from last Sunday's draft, the Blues have also lost picks No. 1 and 2 from 2003 and were fined $930,000 for evasion of the AFL rules. They have also lost their first pick from next month's pre-season draft although the club could be banned from taking part in it anyway, because it is $1.2 million over the salary cap going into 2003.

Unless the Carlton players accept relatively radical pay cuts, the club faces another $3 million AFL fine next month. So drastic is the Blues playing list situation that the AFL yesterday extended its club player payment estimates deadline by a week to December 13.

The Elliott outburst took place at a 60th birthday dinner for Wes Lofts, the self-made multi-millionaire who played for Carlton in defence for a decade before becoming chairman of selectors and Elliott's right-hand man on the board.

Lofts, along with a group of other directors, are looking at buying a corporate box to watch Carlton's nine home games at Optus Oval given that they are unlikely to be spending much time in their old position at the official lunch.

As his private, business and football worlds continue to crash down around him, even Elliott's closest friends fear he may have reached the emotional point of no return. Even the proprietor of his regular city lunchtime haunt, Caterina's Cucina in Queen Street, is worried about him.

Geoff Lord, the former Hawthorn Football Club president and fellow Elders' director owns the Elgin Street apartment building where Elliott lives. Lord mentioned on Thursday night that he was unsure as to whether Elliott had actually paid any rent. But if Elliott is a mess, consider the state in which he left his football club after 20 years as president.

Collins, who was already working overtime attempting to fix the problems at Telstra Dome, received a congratulatory telephone call on winning the presidency on Wednesday from John Tribe, chief executive of Delaware North, which holds the catering contract at the stadium.

Tribe also reminded Collins that Carlton owed his company $140,000 for unpaid meals served at Blues' functions at the Docklands stadium during 2002. "Join the queue," said Collins. The auditors have not yet resolved how much money is owed to the Blues' other caterers, including AFL chairman Ron Evans' Spotless group.

Yet when Tribe asked the clearly overworked Collins how he was enjoying the job, he replied: "I'm loving it." This despite the threat of insolvency.

On player payments, Collins has pinpointed nine players—led by captain Brett Ratten, Anthony Koutoufides and 2002 club champion Corey McKernan—largely because those were the ones seen by the new board to be the most overpaid. Koutoufides was due to earn more than $1.1 million in 2003 and also in 2004, making him the AFL's highest paid player.

Although Elliott took charge of the biggest contracts, the new board is also casting judgment on officials including football operations general manager Colin Kinnear, recruiting boss Shane O'Sullivan and chief executive Don Hanly.

Said former Carlton captain John Nicholls: "We've replaced one president who needed to be replaced with another one who's equally tough and autocratic. Like John [Elliott] he is not liked by [AFL chief executive] Wayne Jackson but I think he is the man for the job.

"I've known Collo for years and he is a friend but he really is tough and ruthless. He will enter with a big stick and demand 25 per cent pay cuts and negotiate his way down. I liken the situation now to the example of an alcoholic or a drug addict or chronic gambler. To really fix the problem you need to hit rock bottom to realise you need help."

The only board members Elliott remains in contact with are two other former champion players Stephen Kernahan and Greg Williams, who survived the Carlton One takeover on November 12. Elliott has urged the pair to remain on the board and fight some of the proposed changes. Five nights ago, Kernahan and Williams managed to defer for a week a motion to rename the Elliott stand, the second newest stand at the club and one which shares, with the Legends stand, a debt of at least $9 million. They want to remain on the club's selection committee and argued strongly on Tuesday night against vice-president Graham Smorgon's push to reduce Carlton's player payments to 92.5 per cent of the salary cap.

Although Collins has an unofficial agreement in place with another former premiership captain, Mike Fitzpatrick, that the latter will take over the presidency when his business commitments allow it (around 2005 or 2006), Smorgon is seen as harboring presidential ambitions.

And while Kernahan and Williams remain determined to stay on the club's match committee they feel unwelcome on the board. They have been joined on the new football sub-committee by long-time Elliott critic David McKay, Silvagni and Ken Hunter. Hunter, who played in two Carlton premiership teams and is now also the AFL and CUB's national relationship manager, was never allowed by the previous regime to have any say in the areas of football or marketing. He was the first director to quit the Elliott board back in August.

Hunter's wife, Mandy Donnini, is now working at Optus Oval as the club's membership liaison officer. Collins' big fear is that the Blues' members, like their playing list, are ageing.

Nicholls and Alex Jesaulenko along with former premiership player and coach Robert Walls have offered to lead a club membership drive but Collins has bigger problems on his mind. He has scoffed at suggestions that wealthy supporters like Richard Pratt will come to the party with five-figure offers of funds.

Two days ago Pratt said that Carlton would survive but that it sat roughly 10th on his list of priorities. A generous benefactor in terms of employment and sponsorship at the club, Pratt has never been in the business of big donations. And yet commissioner Graeme Samuel made it clear to Collins after last weekend's punishment was handed down that the AFL was not concerned about the Blues' financial future.

It wouldn't want to be. No one, even the club's biggest detractors, want Carlton to go under. AFL crowds in Victoria were down by 10 per cent in 2002, and the Blues' poor performances provided a significant contribution.

"The supporters will make sure—and there's enough influential people there—to keep the club afloat," said Jesaulenko. "I told Jack [Elliott] at the '72 reunion that he'd had his time. The AFL set the rules now, not the clubs and you've got to play the game on and off the field."

The Age 30 November 2002

A STREET NAMED DESIRE

Emma Quayle

CHRIS YARRAN AND MICHAEL WALTERS are in Nick Naitanui's living room, sitting squeezed into a two-seater couch. They are trying to remember the first time they met, and it's hard; they can't remember not knowing each other.

Chris can still see Nick's big afro hairstyle, and recall the day he jumped onto the PA system at primary school and called a Melbourne Cup. Michael can remember how quiet Chris used to be, how he never used to speak until someone spoke to him, and Nick can't remember Michael being anything but a chatty, cheeky, energetic kid. "Look at him!" he laughs, pointing at a junior basketball photo in which Walters leans towards the camera with a big, goofy grin. Walters doesn't even bother objecting, or even just rolling his eyes: there's another photo, on another wall, where he's hamming it up even more.

Walters was the first to move into Bushby Street—a long, wide road in Midvale, in Perth's outer-eastern suburbs—and nobody ever called him Michael. As a baby, he travelled from Perth to Adelaide with his parents and big brother, to see his father's family for the first time. As the train rattled along, and the sky turned dark outside, he refused to fall asleep, so his father made up a lullaby, calling him "my son son". It caught on: his brother, Colin, wouldn't let anyone call him anything but "Son Son" after he did, finally, drift off to sleep. These days, he'll settle for Sonny as well.

Walters was four when "Nicko" Naitanui moved in, six houses down the street, his fraternal twin brother Mark in tow. Next door to them was Yarran, who was living with his mother at her parents' place.

The 17-year-old has lived in many houses and in many streets over the years; at times, he wasn't entirely sure where he would be sleeping the next night. But Bushby was the street Yarran kept coming back to, and Midvale the suburb that most felt like home. The three boys started primary school together and—except for a few years when Yarran moved an hour away to Northam, still dropping by some weekends—they have lived within a few minutes of each other. The draft will make their long-shared dream come true, but separate them for the first real time in their lives.

Football connected the boys, from the very start. Yarran can remember the three of them clumping down the bitumen road together, to the oval at the end of it, already wearing their footy boots. They would drag a bin out onto the road in front of Nicko's place, lining it up alongside a mail box, a tree and a concrete pole—cheap, easy goalposts. Between the Naitanuis' cousins, Yarran's cousins, Walters' brother and the other kids in their street, there would be up to 30 boys on the road at once, tackling each other to the asphalt, scampering to the side when a car tore past, scoring bonus points for hitting the bin or the tree, and never craving company. "All you had to do if you were bored," said Naitanui, "was go and knock next door."

Yarran was the kid who always hit the target; the one with the sharp, instinctive skills. He only ever wanted to be one thing: an AFL footballer.

"Son Son" was the little one, who went to bed each night with his footy and would scurry around after the bigger, older kids, all energy.

At school, Naitanui could do anything he turned either his mind or body to: he was the class accountant, counting the money when his class went off on excursions, and winning almost everything on athletics day. His mother, Atetha, thought he would end up becoming a basketballer; he started kicking the football only because the other kids did, and it was actually the least of his talents.

"I was just a skinny kid and I couldn't even kick properly.

"I'm still struggling now with it," he said, smiling. "But most of the kids in Midvale, that's just how we played. We didn't really practice or train all our skills like some other kids, we just ran around on the street. We'd have little scratch matches, four on four, and all we did was play."

Still, he could tell even then that Yarran's plans were sensible ones. "You just knew," he said.

"Some kids are just better than the rest. Chris was the best one of us all."

Life hasn't exactly been easy, for the boys or those around them. Naitanui's parents, Atetha and Bola, moved to Sydney almost 19 years ago, from the Fijian village near Suva where Nick's older brother and sister still live. He has never lived there himself, but when he goes there, each year, he feels at home. His parents moved away because they wanted opportunity, said Atetha, but the twins were just one when Bola found out he had cancer and only a few months to live.

Alone, Atetha moved the boys to Perth, simply because she had a brother there and wasn't sure where else she should go. She still sometimes wonders how she made it through, how she kept from collapsing, but she knows her boys kept her going, that they gave her no choice. "If I'd given up . . ." she said, pausing. "I couldn't give up."

Atetha, who married again three years ago, always resisted signing on for a pension—she never wanted to be given anything and she always wanted to work, even if it meant things were a little bit trickier to pay for. For the past 14 years she has worked for Homewest, helping to find housing for homeless people in the eastern suburbs and working with some of the kids who grew up playing kick-to-kick with her own boys. Some seem too embarrassed to look her in the eye.

"It's like the kids here are in hiding, they turn the other way when they see that I am coming," she said. "I say to Nick and Mark always, when you see these boys, talk to them, don't even think they have been in jail. It's sad, it's very sad. Some of these young indigenous boys that played with my boys, I thought that they were going to make it. They had so much talent, so much skill. But drugs and bashings and assaults . . . that's the way of life here. That's how these kids survive."

As he was growing up, Walters knew that his mum and dad struggled some months to pay the rent; that even filling the petrol tank to take him to a training session was sometimes a stretch. "It wasn't something you ever really thought about," he said. "You just sort of knew, that we had it a bit harder than most people."

He can only ever remember being a happy child, although this year has been a wrenching one. Walters' parents separated earlier this year and his father, Mick, moved home to Adelaide.

He came back to Perth mid-year, but left again in September, two days before Walters played for the Swan District's under-19 team in a grand final. His grandfather flew straight from Adelaide to watch him play, but Walters was emotional, deflated and, said his mother, Martha, forced for the first time to reassess his biggest idol.

"It was devastating. It really hurt 'Son Son' and it's been a real struggle for all of us," she said. "He looked up to his father, I think 'Son Son' really just wanted to make dad proud, and thought what he was doing was the right way to do that. He's an emotional boy, he's a fiery boy—the only time he isn't fiery is when he's playing on the football field—but he's worked through it now.

"He knows he has some exciting times coming up and that he has a lot of support and that a lot of people love him. He loves dad, but dad has to be put at the back for a while, and that's hard."

It's something Yarran had to grapple with a lot longer back. He was eight when his father, Malcolm, was jailed; he still sees him, and talks to him on the phone, and his most vivid memories are of walking home with him from footy training, hand-in-hand. He can't remember feeling ashamed of where his dad was, and will be for a while yet, but when other kids asked him about it, he didn't want to talk.

"I just took it as life, as the way life goes," he said. "I never said much about it and it's still hard now, to think about it. But I just think of the good times with him, and I saw my mum and how she didn't let it bring her down. She didn't want it in my head, she wanted me to feel proud. With where I am, I sort of owe it to her. She's the one who kept me playing football."

Yarran had a grandfather willing to take him wherever he had to be, any time. He had neighbours willing to chip in with petrol money when they could. He had footy—and there was never a choice to skip training, he said, because Naitanui would be banging on his door, telling him to hurry.

But more than anything, he had his mother, Deb, who didn't want any of her five children—Chris is the youngest—to carry someone else's burden. Even if it meant she had to, or felt that she did. "It was hard but I adjusted. I had to," she said. "If I was to let things slip, I think the whole family would have fallen apart. I just stayed strong and did the best I could. I always said to Chris, never feel ashamed of where dad is, you have to go and live your own life."

As he grew up, Naitanui began to notice newspaper articles saying Midvale had the highest break-in rate in Perth. Men would return home to Bushby Street after stints in jail and while he was conscious of where they had been, he couldn't quite reconcile that with with how happy and safe he had always seemed to feel. Later, he had friends go off to jail; like Atetha, he'd grown up thinking they were the ones who had the best chance to go far.

"It's kind of sad to see and to even think, that you've got mates and they're locked up now. But you see them, some of them get out of jail, and they seem so happy for you. Even as a kid, you knew it was a tough place we lived in, that people were in trouble with the police, but they were always good to you. They were always looking out for you."

More recently, all three boys have felt keenly that people judge other people according to their postcode. Two years ago, Naitanui had no reason to believe he could play in the AFL; when he made the under-16 West Australian squad, he told the coaches he didn't want to play. His reluctance was internal; he didn't think he was good enough. But after he was talked into taking his place in the under-16 team and met other, more fortunate kids who also assumed he wouldn't get there, his mind began to change.

"You'd meet kids who go to private schools, and they sort of looked down on you and asked where you were from and laughed at you," he said. "Looking back, I know it was a bad place we came from, but we didn't know any different, we just knew it as home. Some other kids thought they were better and I think that gave me a desire to make it even more, to show it doesn't matter where you come from, that you can still do as well as any other kid can."

Yarran agrees. "It's sort of good for the community," he said. "I reckon we could help a bit, with where we are now."

Yesterday, in Perth, three mothers and their teenage sons had lunch together. It was a kind of farewell; their last chance to spend time together before "Son Son", Nicko and Chris are potentially drafted to three different teams, to three different states. They felt apprehensive, but, more than anything, excited. They wished they had thought to take some photos back in the Bushby Street days, to have somehow known what was going to happen—but then again, why would they have? "They were just three little boys, whoever would have thought that this was where they would be?" said Atetha, proud of what the boys have overcome and achieved, but equally proud of herself, Martha and Deb. "We didn't do too bad, did we?"

The Age 22 November 2008

JACK DYER: A FINAL ROAR FOR A FALLEN TIGER

Martin Blake

FOOTBALL IS FULL OF MYTHS, legends, misconceptions and half-truths—and one of them is that Jack Dyer, or "Captain Blood" to the masses, was more hard-man than great player.

So when his old mate Bob Davis stood up to deliver his part of the eulogy to Dyer at St Ignatius in Richmond yesterday, he set the record straight immediately.

Davis pointed out that of about 11,000 men to have played league football, Dyer made the 21 who were chosen in the AFL's team of the century a couple of years ago, perhaps as one of the first picked.

Kevin Bartlett, Richmond's other most famous son, also spoke at the requiem mass yesterday, and made the same point.

"What is true is that Dyer is the greatest player in the history of the Richmond Football Club, arguably the greatest player of all time," said Bartlett. "He has been the icon of the club, he has been the symbol of the Richmond Football Club, he has been the inspiration of the club, he's been the motivator of the club, the force behind the club. He's been the spirit of the yellow and black."

It was an emotional day for the Tigers and, indeed, for all the football community. Dyer's death last Saturday at age 89 gave Richmond people no time to prepare a proper tribute to its greatest son by the time its players ran on to the ground on Sunday.

But about 1000 people attended yesterday's requiem mass, held at the church where Dyer was an altar boy, where he was married in 1939, and where his own two children, Jack and Jill, were married. Yesterday his grandchildren led the prayers. The Richmond players and students from St Ignatius school, where he was a pupil, formed the guard of honour as the club theme song was played over the loudspeakers.

Later, back at Punt Road Oval beneath the Jack Dyer stand, the Tiger faithful gathered around an emblem of his No. 17 guernsey etched into the turf as his family released 312 yellow and black balloons, one for each game he played for the club. Together they gave another rousing version of "The Yellow and Black".

The tributes will continue when Richmond meets Hawthorn in its final game of the season on Sunday.

Bartlett said Dyer "played 312 games for the Tigers, kicked 443 goals and broke 364 collarbones". He said Dyer inspired people throughout the Great Depression and a world war.

"He gave the masses something to cheer about, he gave the masses something to smile about, something to talk about. He even gave them something to boo about," he said.

Bartlett recalled his first meeting with Dyer, as a 16-year-old Richmond under-19s player in 1963. He had been seriously injured at the first bounce of a final and was awaiting an ambulance in the dressing rooms when the legendary figure appeared at his side. Dyer stayed 15 minutes talking to a lad he had never met, not to know that a couple of decades on the boy would overtake his club games record.

Bartlett said he had ribbed Dyer years later about his assurance that day that the pain would be gone by the next day. Bartlett was to spend the next fortnight in hospital with a hip injury. "He [Dyer] said: 'I didn't know much about hips. I only know about collarbones.'"

Davis, the straight man to Dyer and Lou Richards on *League Teams* and *World of Sport*, recalled their time on TV. "Dyer specialised in mangling the English language and droll humour," Davis reminisced. "The more serious he was, the funnier he was."

Once, said Davis, he and Richards hoodwinked Dyer into believing that his interview subject, a new Hawthorn player by the name of Bohdan Jaworskyj, spoke little English.

"He patted him on the chest and said: 'Me Jack Dyer. What your name?' The kid said: 'Bohdan Jaworskyj, Jack. What are you on about?'"

Bartlett did not attend the supporters' function at Punt Road yesterday, maintaining his estrangement from the club that sacked him as coach more than a decade ago. But his voice was breaking as he closed his tribute at St Ignatius. "Jack played at a time when the players played for the love of the game. And the game loved Jack Dyer."

JOHN RAYMOND DYER	
Born	November 13, 1913
Died	August 23, 2003
Richmond player	1931–49
Richmond coach	1941–52
Played	312 games, 7 grand finals, 2 premierships (1934, 1943)
Member	Sports Hall of Fame Team of the Century

The Age 28 August 2003

WHEN THE SIREN BLEW, IT WAS AMATEUR HOUR

Martin Blake

I DIDN'T HEAR THE SIREN. Sitting high up in the press box in the grandstand, and behind glass, I don't believe any of the journalists covering the game heard it.

To begin with, it was too quiet, so pathetically inaudible that comment was passed in the box earlier in the day about the danger of a close finish. Aside from that, the crowd was making a din, as you would expect at the end of a close game.

The problem was caused by the siren, which is clearly inadequate. That the authorities in Launceston were told by the AFL some time back that it was inadequate, as now emerges, will scarcely please Grant Thomas or Chris Connolly and does not reflect well on anyone involved. It is amateur hour.

What we did see immediately was that the Fremantle players were celebrating as umpire Mathew Nicholls prepared to effect a ball-up in the forward pocket at the 29-minute mark. The assumption was that they had heard something, even if we could not hear it behind the glass of the press box.

But when umpire Nicholls appeared to be engaging in debate with Byron Schammer and Des Headland, I knew that he had not heard the siren. Instinctively, I looked to my left to see if any of the other umpires were approaching, perhaps having heard it.

And as I looked, I saw Hayden Kennedy, the non-controlling umpire and one of the best in the business, running at close to full tilt from centre half-back towards the centre. Going by body language, it appeared to me that Kennedy had heard something and was about to stop the game.

But Kennedy stopped in the centre, looked towards the timekeepers' box and cupped a hand to his ear. It was as though he was unsure if he had in fact heard the siren, and was looking for confirmation from the timekeepers. In other words, another blast on the siren. But again, I couldn't hear any siren.

The scenes that ensued were among the most shambolic I have seen in football. Fremantle players gathered around Nicholls imploring him to stop. Ideally at this point, he would have been calm enough to stop play for a moment and check with one of the other umpires. Common sense would have suggested this. But under pressure, Nicholls ploughed on with the bounce, St Kilda cobbled a behind and the rest is a piece of history.

We descended on St Kilda's rooms first, by arrangement with the clubs. The Saints had the earlier flight out, and hence wanted to complete media commitments quickly. This would prove to be important, for when the half-a-dozen journalists bailed up Thomas in the dressing rooms, he had no idea that Fremantle was planning to protest. None of us knew, because we had not sought any reaction from the Dockers at that point.

Thomas was supercilious and unstatesmanlike, canning the umpires for losing control, shrugging his shoulders and saying that he had given up trying to work them out. This would come across as churlish, for everyone who watched the game knew that in scraping a draw, St Kilda had been lucky. When Malcolm Conn of *The Australian* asked him if he believed St Kilda had actually drawn the game, Thomas laughed out loud. The result, said Thomas, was one thing that was obvious.

Yet he must have known at that point there was a chance of a protest. Any football person would have known. The St Kilda coach is under intense pressure, and he showed it at this moment, for it is hardly a good look for the players—let alone the supporters—to see their coach laughing and shrugging his shoulders at a difficult situation. It's his job to deal with the cards presented.

Connolly, of course, is under the pump as well. Like Thomas, he is a coach without the team success that gives you money in the bank in the pressure stakes. His every move is scrutinised in Perth. And he was filthy, to say the least, about what had happened.

When the journalists found him in an ante-chamber in the Fremantle rooms, he began by asking us what we thought of the finish. Two journalists said they felt the club had been wronged. I wasn't one of those. I was aware of the rule that states that the game is not over until the umpire acknowledges the siren, as I'd come across it before. I still think that is a big barrier for the Dockers to overcome as they fight to extract the victory, even if the moral aspect is another story.

Connolly spoke his mind in an articulate way. But again under pressure, he was silly when he claimed that in St Kilda's shoes, he would hand over the points. He ought to have stuck to what he and Fremantle felt about it. It's not for him to second-guess St Kilda's attitude.

At these times football people can say odd things. Cameron Schwab, the Dockers' chief executive, tried to link the finish with the Jim Stynes incident in the 1987 preliminary final, when it has no parallel. Schwab was asked if he could recall a similar situation, and he immediately said that yes, he was at Melbourne when Stynes' run across the mark, and 15-metre penalty after the siren, cost the Demons a spot in the grand final. But there was no dispute on that day about the timing of the siren, which is the whole issue here.

No reaction was available from the players. By the time the journalists covered the press conferences of both coaches, the St Kilda players had disappeared to their bus and back to Launceston airport. Fremantle would not allow any players to comment, although there was one interview done by Josh Carr in bizarre circumstances. The Dockers allowed Carr to talk, but would not permit him to canvass the end of the game.

Hence three reporters spoke to Carr knowing that he was at the heart of the story but with no chance of extracting his views. Such is the level of control exerted by clubs nowadays.

So what was expected to be a quiet game in the southern state—two games in Melbourne would surely assume more importance on the day—turned into a tumult. By the time the journalists finished filing copious words on the events of the day, virtually all the security guards had gone and darkness had well and truly fallen. Lock the doors on your way out, they told us.

For what it's worth, I don't see how the result can be changed unless umpire Hayden Kennedy heard the siren, which I suspect he did. The siren at Aurora Stadium—and possibly at other grounds—needs to be replaced. Either that, or the umpires need to be wired up so that they know exactly when time runs out. Wouldn't that make some sense?

The Age 2 May 2006

OUT OF BOUNDS?

Dan Silkstone

FOR FOOTBALLERS, THE AFL AND all who love our game these are testing times. Two men pee in a cup and, months later, QCs trade precedents in an oak-panelled court room. Players are not talking to the network that effectively pays their salaries, police raid a newsroom and a club is swamped by a public relations crisis about which it is not entitled to know full details. Amid it all, the AFL must have wondered this week what the hell was going on.

It all started with a phone call and it could have ended minutes later the same way. The woman told the reporter she had found documents in the gutter outside an Ivanhoe rehabilitation centre. Confidential medical records of two well-known players with little-known drug problems. She couldn't return them because the gate was locked. And so she sold them to the Seven network for $3000. They published and were damned.

As an injunction descended like a clattering drawbridge, precious little could be reported about the biggest story in town. Instead, journalists turned to reporting on themselves. In Janet Malcolm's classic book *The Journalist and the Murderer*, a jailed killer sues a journalist after receiving some dodgy ethical treatment during an interview. During the resulting case, public sympathy swings behind the honest killer and against the supposedly deceitful hack. The story of the journalist and the drug users has gone much the same way.

Reporter Dylan Howard has maintained all week that he simply took the woman at her word. But the furious responses of the doctor whose records had disappeared, as well as AFL chief Andrew Demetriou, Police Commissioner

Christine Nixon and Players' Association chief executive Brendan Gale heaped scorn on that notion.

What, if any, obligation Howard and his news chief had to investigate the legitimacy of the documents is a matter of ethics and debate. It wouldn't have been hard to do. A simple telephone call to the hospital or the doctor in question would have established that the records should never have been in possession of the woman, however she got them. But the call was never made.

A call was made to the club, just minutes before the story went to air. Ten minutes before the item was to lead the 6pm news, the network was advised that an injunction was being sought by the aggrieved doctor. Surely, by this stage, they must have known that there was opposition to the broadcast of the documents from their owner?

They broadcast anyway, leading the bulletin and beating the injunction by some 40 minutes. Within days the woman was charged with theft, the records seized and the reporter was also facing police investigation as the station became public enemy No. 1 for AFL players.

Eight minutes after the story aired, Howard was interviewed on radio 3AW, where he also works on weekends. Asked if he was convinced by the woman's story—that she had found the documents in the gutter—and had ruled out that they were stolen, he answered: "Absolutely."

Reporter and station's motives were simple, lust for a scoop in the competitive world of TV news. It was, therefore, interesting to hear the network's line of argument in the Supreme Court on Thursday as it sought to escape the injunction and republish details from the confidential medical records.

Seven was not the first to publish this information, the station's barrister pointed out. Other networks, alerted to the impending scoop by Seven's own promotional crowing, had figured out the identity of the club in question and rushed to air. And so the most salacious footy scoop this year was publicly disowned by those who'd risked everything to deliver it.

All up, the details were reported 44 times by various media organisations before the injunction landed at 6.42pm. Millions saw it and, for those that didn't, details are just a click away on the internet. How, Seven's lawyers asked the court, could you possibly put that genie back into the bottle?

It's easy to understand why the players involved wanted their identities protected, but the events of this week and the hysteria surrounding the issue have been about much more than just the reputations of two young men.

Drugs in football this year have been not so much a hot button topic as one requiring nuclear launch codes.

The AFL found itself effectively wedged between its three most important constituencies with a problem it surely wishes would just go away. Players signed up to a recreational-drug testing regime in 2005 that no other major sport required from its athletes, after they were convinced that the AFL policy would focus on education, intervention and rehabilitation—offering those caught by the tests confidential medical treatment.

The resulting "three strikes" policy has been controversial in some quarters but has had strong support from the Players' Association. Under the system, club officials are not notified until a player has tested positive three times. After the second positive test, the club doctor is notified and the player sent for counselling and rehabilitation, but the club remains oblivious. As a furious Andrew Demetriou wrote this week: "We don't want them to hide their problem. We want them to deal with it and to receive the support they need."

That system has been understandably unpopular with those charged with running AFL clubs. Imagine piloting a $30 million a year business embroiled in a media scandal and not knowing who had committed the indiscretion being reported on. Or try being a club doctor, knowing the truth about drug use in the team, but unable to tell those running the club. AFL presidents had feared this scenario all year. Some, such as Hawthorn's Jeff Kennett and Geelong's Frank Costa, have spoken out against the policy. One club's fear is now reality.

The events of this week, coupled with those last year when news of three other drug-taking players leaked from testing agency ASADA, have left the players without faith in the system's ability to guarantee their privacy and prompted threats that they will withdraw from it. The federal government, bent on delivering a tough-on-drugs stance, has repeatedly castigated the AFL policy as "sending the wrong message" and pressed the league to toughen it up.

All year these issues have smouldered. This week, Seven added a handful of documents and the whole lot went up in flames, a week before the start of the finals showpiece. You could almost hear the groans at AFL headquarters.

Any doubt about what was at stake was dispelled on Thursday by the barrister acting for the AFL and the Players' Association: "The protection of that material is critically important to the future of the illicit drugs policy in the AFL and to those who would be subject to it going forward," he told the court. "If confidentiality cannot be obtained then the AFL and the Players'

Association have issues." The whole drug policy was in jeopardy. "The destruction of a regime that has a lot of good to do in the community."

Seven fought its corner bravely. Howard appeared everywhere, chastising the media for missing the real story—the claims of drug use by a number of players at a Melbourne club. That message was compounded when Andrew Johns—rugby league's greatest modern player—was caught in London in possession of ecstasy. Johns admitted he had taken the drug for more than a decade and had regularly "played roulette" with NRL drug testers. It had, he explained, helped him to deal with the pressures of performing.

Surely then, it is worth asking the question: are elite footballers more likely to take drugs than anybody else?

Not really, say the experts. Pippa Grange, the AFL Players' Association psychologist, sees hundreds of players each year for a variety of social problems. Some of them struggle with drug issues, she says, but not to any greater extent than other young men.

Professor Nick Crofts, from the drug and alcohol research organisation Turning Point, says all the available research shows AFL players abuse drugs less than other groups of young men. "The rate of use of illicit drugs in the cohort of AFL footballers is substantially lower than their matched cohort in the general population," he says.

There are several reasons. AFL players are given far more drug education than the average young man, are generally more concerned with diet, fitness and other issues that affect their performance, and are also aware that they will be tested.

Crofts says he has been disgusted by the reporting this week around the drug issue in football and found the criticism of the AFL policy hard to understand. "Why are we treating the AFL as if it is an arm of law enforcement?" he asks. "When did we cross that line? That's what police are for."

So furious is the drug expert that he and Bill Stronach—CEO of the Australian Drug Foundation and a past adviser to the AFL on drugs—will spend the weekend gathering signatures from eminent Australians to an open letter that will express concern at criticism of the league's policy and will be placed in major newspapers. "It won't be just health professionals," he says. "We will go wider than that. There are a lot of people who think this is a good policy."

Clearly the players and their representatives have been stung. Asked this week if there had been a breach of trust that would never be forgiven,

Richmond's Joel Bowden said the anger would take a long time to subside. "We know we are public figures and that brings a certain scrutiny," he said. "But there was something sickening about this that was just wrong. It's just too much."

Players have boycotted Channel Seven reporters all week and are refusing to co-operate with the network's coverage of games this weekend. But it's not easy these days separating just who and who is not media. The days of reporters on one side of the fence and players on the other are gone. Seven's "boundary rider" is Ricky Olarenshaw, a former player and now agent to leading players. Would they talk to him?

The football world is a small one; the football media smaller. Witness Seven's Howard—the day after the story broke—interviewing Magpies president and Channel Nine man Eddie McGuire on behalf of 3AW. Days later, McGuire backed a decision by senior Collingwood players to refuse to talk to Seven while admitting that as a reporter himself he would have covered the story—though perhaps a little differently. On radio station SEN they wondered aloud about whether Essendon player Jobe Watson was talking to his father, SEN and Seven presenter Tim Watson. Later Watson excused himself from SEN interviews with players in case they felt "uncomfortable".

By week's end Howard had been cut off from the AFL's media notification list, barred from Players' Association news conferences and shelved from game day duties at 3AW while the storm subsides. For him and his station it has been some week. He is, ironically enough, the first person ever to be publicly sanctioned by the AFL in relation to breaches of its illicit drugs policy.

The Age 1 September 2007

IN TIMES OF TREBLE

Linda Pearce

IN 1955, FOOTBALLERS IN THE best team in the land were paid about £8 a game in cash and provident fund money. Their bonus came when the hat was passed around the MCG members' bars and dining rooms on the last Saturday night in September, collecting enough to present each of Melbourne's 20 premiership players with close to £100 extra.

The next year, after a second consecutive grand final win over Collingwood, defender Trevor Johnson estimates the bonus was about £60. And when the Demons of 1957 became just the fourth group in VFL history to claim three successive flags, the reward had shrunk by a further third.

"They certainly weren't reaching as deep into their pockets," recalled Johnson, now a successful Perth mushroom farmer and explosives manufacturer, with a chuckle. "We'd worn out our welcome!"

As more recent premiers, Brisbane, Essendon and the Kangaroos can attest that modern success has had a rather more inflationary effect, and that new-fangled device, the salary cap, has compounded the difficulty of keeping flag-winning squads together. No longer, though, is there a reliance on supporters to augment the part-timers' wages symbolic of a time well past.

And yet, in the 45 completed seasons since what would now be called a three-peat, no team has replicated what Melbourne last achieved with a team of bank tellers, teachers, tyre salesmen and milk bar owners, one of whom, Geoff Tunbridge, asked only for the petrol money to cover his drive from Ballarat, and would arrive 20 minutes before the first bounce munching on a meat pie.

Back then, in what was supposed to be a rebuilding year after the retirements of captain Noel McMahen, his deputy Ken Melville, Denis Cordner, Stuart Spencer, Ralph Lane and Geoff McGivern from the 1956 team generally acknowledged as the best of a golden era, the peerless Norm Smith managed to galvanise his less experienced troops for what would be the third of five premierships in six years.

The only blot was the famous grand final upset against loathed rival Collingwood in 1958, but that's a story for another day. "Going into '57 we didn't think that we'd have a team good enough to win the premiership, so that's really what made '57 so special, the fact that Norm Smith was able to get us up for three in a row," said former rover Ian Ridley. "We were more worried about four in a row; we thought we'd get four. And that's when we came unstuck."

But not before the hat-trick was completed. In 1957, Melbourne finished the 18 home-and-away rounds six points clear on top of the ladder, but was upset by Essendon in the second semi-final after trailing by 48 at half-time, at which time captain John Beckwith had climbed on to the locker-room bench to lead a rallying rendition of "The Grand Old Flag".

His team fell 16 points short that day, but the recovery was in motion, and, after a 68-point preliminary final towelling of Hawthorn, a 10-goal revenge beating was inflicted on the Bombers before 100,324 grand final spectators. While Beckwith could barely jog around the Albert Ground during a secret 10am "fitness test" on match day, best-afield was his 21-year-old deputy, Ron Barassi jnr, who had kicked four goals by half-time.

Gathering first in the clubrooms under the members' stand, the players and their partners celebrated at a low-key dinner at the MCG where, two years earlier, the most outrageous event was the serving of red and blue ice-cream.

"It went on until one or two in the morning, and, by and large, that was it," recalled Dick Fenton-Smith, a first-year player from the amateurs with the appropriately cliched hyphenated name. "A few of us went back to the ground the next day for a Pleasant Sunday Morning, but that was the extent of it, because we all had jobs to go to. We were getting £8 a week, so you had to have a job beside it."

Football-wise, Melbourne's was a job very well done. The injection of youth and unfulfilled ambition helped to spark the older players facing the challenges of such a long stay at the top, challenges that were more mental than physical. "It does affect your mind quite a bit," said Beckwith. "When you get close to it, you know that one slip and you're gone."

Five-time premiership midfielder Laurie Mithen adds: "The other teams try harder. We used to say to ourselves in the middle of the season to expect them to throw everything at us because they have everything to gain if they can beat the premiers, and it got a little bit harder for us to keep turning them back.

"When you're on the rise, for the first year or two, it's all still fairly exhilarating and you don't have to talk yourself into getting motivated; it's late in the second year and the third year and into the fourth where you've got to force yourself to keep up the high standard. You know you've got to hold the rest of them off. It would make an interesting psychological study."

The Lions would probably acknowledge as much privately, although defender Chris Johnson said at the Gabba last week that it is only the media and, occasionally, supporters, who talk about the possibility of a historic treble that may be as few as 17 games away. Having lost only Des Headland from last year's premiership 22, the players will admit only to more immediate goals, such as Saturday night's fixture against Melbourne.

"Brisbane are the chopping block now, aren't they? Every game is going to be really hard for them," said dual premiership half-back Keith Carroll. "It's a great challenge, isn't it?" agreed Ian Thorogood, a first-year player in '57 who played in the 1959–60 flags and later coached Carlton. "They've got the task in front of them. Anything can happen and the real key is injuries."

Last Monday at the Gabba, Brisbane coach Leigh Matthews said that part of his team's problem this season had been that each week about six players from his chosen 22 had "struggled to be reasonable contributors". Interestingly, Beckwith had some weeks earlier admitted that the signs of Melbourne's occasional complacency had manifested similarly.

"You don't approach the game with the same fierceness that you should every week," he said. "We found it was six players would play well, and six players would play average, and six players would play ordinary, but it wouldn't be the same six every week, and I think that does apply to Brisbane. There's a pretty fine line. It doesn't take much for your ability or your attitude to drop. It is hard to keep up for the whole year."

Even so, no member of the 1957 team would have imagined that their achievement would still be awaiting repetition in mid-2003. After all, it had last been done just 16 years earlier, and by the all-conquering Magpies little more than a decade before that. "If you'd asked me, I would have said it would have been done again in the next 20 years or something, but it's been a while, hasn't it?" Barassi said. "Nearly half a century."

Should Brisbane achieve such a feat this year, Matthews' men would rightly be hailed as immortals, yet, at the time, less was made of what Barassi calls the "triple" than the fact that it was yet another flag for the power club of the decade.

"In those days the other 11 clubs weren't that keen on Melbourne, because we kept on winning," said Johnson. "We were not that popular."

Mithen believes the Demons' reaction to their success reflected a more relaxed, but no less popular, football age. "We enjoyed the moment, but then when it was over we got on with the rest of our lives, and waited until the next season rolled round in February–March, so we had this different perspective on what we were doing," he said. "It was a relief to get the third one done, and an attitude of 'let's go and enjoy it like we did the others'."

Yet the club's darkest grand final day was just a year away, with Collingwood destined to upset the raging favourites and protect its record as the only team to win four successive pennants. It was a truly bitter pill, for even though the Demons dominated again in 1959–60, and won five of the seven successive grand finals they played in from 1954 to 1960, too much success, it seems, is never enough.

"There were a few players there like [Brian] Dixon, [Frank] Adams and myself, just to name a couple, who were greedy, greedy, greedy," admitted Barassi, an immortal himself all these years later. "We wouldn't have cared if we'd won 10 in a row, we'd still want the 11th."

Melbourne's 1955–57 treble may come into sharper focus in grand final week, should the Brisbane Lions make it through for another tilt at the flag. On the Wednesday before the grand final, the 1950s Demons players will gather for a reunion in the club rooms under the members' stand—the last such gathering before the building is demolished to make way for a new stand.

PREMIERSHIP HAT-TRICKS	
Carlton	
1906	Carlton 15.4 (94) d Fitzroy 6.9 (45)
1907	Carlton 6.14 (50) d South Melbourne 6.9 (45)
1908	Carlton 5.5 (35) d Essendon 3.8 (26)

PREMIERSHIP HAT-TRICKS	
Melbourne	
1939	Melbourne 21.22 (148) d Collingwood 14.11 (95)
1940	Melbourne 15.17 (107) d Richmond 10.8 (68)
1941	Melbourne 19.13 (127) d Essendon 13.20 (98)
Melbourne	
1955	Melbourne 8.16 (64) d Collingwood 5.6 (36)
1956	Melbourne 17.19 (121) d Collingwood 6.12 (48)
1957	Melbourne 17. 14 (116) d Essendon 7.13 (55)
Collingwood's awesome foursome	
1927	Collingwood 2.13 (25) d Richmond 1.7 (13)
1928	Collingwood 13.18 (96) d Richmond 9.9 (63)
1929	Collingwood 11.13 (79) d Richmond 7.8 (50)
1930	Collingwood 14.16 (100) d Geelong 9.16 (70)

THE PLAYERS
Melbourne 1955–57

Even though these were the days of 18 players and two reserves, the Demons had only nine players—Frank Adams, Ron Barassi, John Beckwith, Bob Johnson, Trevor Johnson, Peter Marquis, Laurie Mithen, Ian Ridley and Don Williams—who completed the hat-trick of flags.

Brisbane Lions 2001–03

There are 20 players in with a chance of completing the hat-trick this season. They are: Jason Akermanis, Marcus Ashcroft, Simon Black, Jonathan Brown, Shaun Hart, Chris Johnson, Clark Keating, Nigel Lappin, Justin Leppitsch, Alastair Lynch, Beau McDonald, Craig McRae, Mal Michael, Tim Notting, Martin Pike, Luke Power, Brad Scott, Chris Scott, Michael Voss and Darryl White.

Other Lions premiership players were Robert Copeland and Daniel Bradshaw in 2001, and Des Headland and Aaron Shattock in 2002.

THE COACHES
Norm Smith
The Melbourne icon played in four premierships (1939–41, 1948) and coached the Demons to six flags (1955–57, 1959–60, 1964) from eight grand finals.

Leigh Matthews
The Hawthorn great played in seven grand finals, winning four of them (1971, 1974, 1976, 1983). He has never lost a grand final as a coach (Collingwood 1990, Brisbane Lions 2002–03).

THE HEROES OF 1957
John Beckwith (captain, back pocket): "I'm very proud of playing in an era like that. If Brisbane do it, good luck to 'em, because it's a very difficult achievement."

Peter Marquis (full-back): "It was a defensive game of football back then. I'd kick it to Johnny Beckwith and he'd kick it out of bounds, and we did that for 100 minutes."

Dick Fenton-Smith (back pocket): "It just personifies the excellence of Norm Smith that he was able to take 13 brand new players into a side in 1957 and in one year mould them into a premiership side."

Keith Carroll (half-back): "I think we expected to do it, that was the trouble. I think we just thought we'd win each week. Being defeated was always a shock."

Laurie Mithen (centre): "It wasn't as thrilling in '57; it was just sort of a relief that we'd held them all off again for another year, so let's go celebrate."

Brian Dixon (wing): "I was conscious of at least equalling what had been achieved in '39–40–41 and I think most of my teammates were."

Trevor Johnson (centre half-forward): "I'm sure people didn't appreciate how hard it was to win three in a row. And I don't think we would have if we hadn't had Norm Smith."

Geoff Tunbridge (half-forward): "There was a good feeling about winning three in a row; there was a terrible feeling about losing the next one."

Ian Ridley (forward pocket): "When you look back at it now, it's incredible that it hasn't been done again in almost 50 years. It just shows you how hard it is."

Ron Barassi Jnr (forward pocket): "Quite a few senior players retired, so the youngsters were pretty chuffed to come up with the goodies. We took a lot of pride in that particular win."

Frank Adams (rover): "There's so much more scrutiny on the club, the team and the individual player now. In our day in '57, television had only been in a year."

Ian Thorogood (reserve): "It was the first premiership for me, and that in itself was special; whether it was two in a row or three in a row really didn't matter."

Unavailable: Geoff Case (half-forward), John Lord (centre half-back), Athol Webb (full-forward), Colin Wilson (ruck-rover)

Deceased: Peter Brenchley (reserve), Bob Johnson (ruck), Ian Mclean (wing), Don Williams (half-back),

The Sunday Age 25 May 2003

BAT OUTTA BARTEL

Peter Hanlon

WOULD YOU DO ANYTHING FOR LING? Have you seen paradise by the Malcolm Blight? Stick out your guts and let your voice break awkwardly, it's Tagger's A–Z guide to the grand final.

A is for Andrew Krakouer, who flitted and floated and might have been the finale's fairytale. And for Andrew Mackie, who is so smooth you could refrigerate him and he'd still spread on cheap bread. And for Allen Christensen, whose 19th game may be the happiest of his life, even if he plays a thousand. A is also for A Sham, A Disgrace, and A Big, Fat Waste of Money. It seems sad to spoil the moment by bringing up Meat Loaf, but we'll do it just the once.

B is for Bartel, Jimmy. What a player. So brave. So assured. So admirable. So timeless. So clearly the best performer on grand final day 2011. Unlike someone else we could mention, but we've said far too much about Meat Loaf already.

C is for Cloke, Travis, a mountain of a man who gave hope to the masses that he might again throw them on the back of his chopper and roar off to the gates of heaven, where all the tattooed sinners could come crawling on back to you. Sadly, in time he came to realise it's no longer 2010. If only Mr Loaf would be similarly awakened to the fact that it's not 1977 any more either.

D is for Dids, who didn't. Also for Dane, who was down. And Dale, who did his darndest but couldn't tame the tabbies. And for Dawson, too, as in Simpson,

366

who presumably won his place in the half-time sprint final in a raffle. D is also for dickhead. And my, the AFL's pre-game entertainment committee is going to be hard-pressed next year to find a bigger one.

E is for envy, which we're annually told is felt by every last man, child and amoeba on planet Earth and beyond as they put their sad-sack existences on hold and sit trance-like before our grand final. Oh, how they must have wished they were here, communing with lucky us, having their naive, innocent football questions answered. "Why isn't Tomahawk on daytime TV?" "Isn't what the red man's doing to that tattooed guy considered taboo in your culture?" And, "Who the $#@! thought Meat Loaf was a good idea?"

F is for Footyhead, Tagger's friendly barman who'll always keep a spare stool for Stevie J. Despite a busy day, Footyhead found time to ponder how neat it was that Meat Loaf played at the Superbowl, although maybe they could have got him to hand out the Bat Out of Hell Medal to that Jimmy bloke, which may have been better use of the lyric.

G is for Greatness, This Is. And what a simply great theme that was for another great September. It even passed the test of time by still sounding just great in early October. Whoever came up with such a great catchphrase is just great. And it would be no great surprise to learn they also thought Meat Loaf was a great idea.

H is for Hawkins, Tom, who has two premiership medals and his best days before him. Unlike someone whose name temporarily escapes us.

I is for idiots, and in a football crowd there's plenty of them, especially the people who hold up signs reading "Goal" after someone kicks a goal. "I" is also the first word in the Meat Loaf song "For Crying Out Loud", which contains the memorable line, "And can't you see my faded Levis, bursting apart . . ." Ah, they don't make idiots like they used to.

J is for a couple of Joels, a Josh and a J-Pod. Corey was cool, calm and creative, Hunt got a handle on those pesky little Pies, and Podsiadly is a premiership player, so feels no pain. Which leaves Selwood. Some misery-guts will no doubt be moaning that he got a couple of free kicks for high contact, again. He's got a head. If you tackle it, he gets a free kick. It can't be that hard. Come to mention it, neither can getting someone for the pre-match who doesn't cost HUNDREDS OF THOUSANDS OF DOLLARS, and who CAN ACTU-ALLY SING.

K is for Kimba, a town of 600 or so on South Australia's Eyre Peninsula, which in good years is blessed by the birth of a handful of fresh little Kimba bubs. To the eternal gratitude of Geelong folk, 1981 was a very good year, as one of the new arrivals was Corey Enright, a footballer of understated magnificence. Kimba is also home to an eight-metre high objet d'art known as the Big Galah. When Enright sits down to watch the replay, he's sure to be heartened to see another Big Galah headlining the pre-game entertainment.

L is for Love, as in "I Would Do Anything For (But I Won't Do That)". Like all beaten grand finalists, the Magpies are left to ponder that sometimes doing anything for love—except "That"—isn't enough, and if you don't do "That" as well, you don't get to go the whole nine yards. Or to the big dance. Or something. Maybe Meat Loaf could take that job Mick doesn't want any more and fill in the blanks.

M is for mistakes, and they weren't confined to the pre-game. Umpire Ryan would be grateful that paying dropping the ball against Corey Enright when he kicked it a millisecond after being tackled wasn't the biggest of the day. And the goal umpire who waved Sharrod Wellingham's poster through would be relieved the Pies didn't get up by a kick, or he might have been run out of town faster than Meat Loaf.

N is for Nathan, as in Buckley, and it wouldn't have been fair to him to have Mick looking over his shoulder next season. Just as it wouldn't be fair to keep banging on about how crap Meat Loaf was on Saturday. But it sure is fun.

O is for Ordinary. Sometimes you have an ordinary game, but you've still got something to offer. Other times, you need to face the possibility that the game might have passed you by. Cameron Mooney and Darren Milburn have done it, even though it's ripped them apart inside. Over to you, Meat.

P is for Paul, as in Kelly. He is an Australian singer-songwriter whose music touches the soul of this land and its people. One of his songs even starts with a line about the MCG. He has been making people happy and proud to be Australian in a nice, leave-your-Southern-Cross-tattoo-and-flag-cape-at-home kind of way for more than 30 years. One of these days, even the AFL might hear of him. Not that he'd be as good as Meat Loaf, mind you.

Q is for Quarter, Third. And Quarter, Fourth. That's when the Tomahawk had the time of his life. Unlike Meat Loaf, who had his in the front seat of a car in 1977.

R is for ranga, and isn't he a beautiful sight, especially with a broken nose. The only thing at the MCG on Saturday that was redder than Cameron Ling's head was that stupid hanky Meat Loaf carries around. Perhaps it's like tying string around your finger, and he uses it to try and remember how to sing.

S is for Steele, and is Sidebottom, who has a funny name but a serious liking for the biggest stage. And for Scott, as in Pendlebury. See Sidebottom, minus the bit about the funny name, and plus "and a serious liking for the small- and medium-sized stages too". S is also for Stevie J, who could entertain a crowd sitting on an empty stage singing "I'm a little teapot" with a saucepan on his head. Which is worth considering as a pre-game alternative to Meat Loaf.

T is for Travis, as in Varcoe, who in 11 seconds made many people so much happier than someone else we might already have mentioned could manage in 11 minutes, plus time-on and motorbikes.

U is for underdone, which Ben Reid and Darren Jolly may have been. Meat Loaf, on the other hand, was so far past his use-by date it's a wonder there wasn't a repeat of last year's granny when the MCG toilets backed up and there was a river of effluent running through the change rooms.

V is for Vanessa, as in Amorosi. And she should be thanked for giving us a glimpse of what Josh Hunt would look like if he turned up to Mad Monday this morning wearing an orange wig and a black tu-tu. She is also a performer blessed with empathy, as she demonstrated by turning the conclusion of "Advance Australia Fair" into an unfathomable growl that did Meat Loaf proud.

W is for Worth Every Cent, and even the fattest corporate cats who wouldn't know Jimmy Bartel from Jiminy Cricket would have to agree Saturday's grand final was just that, especially as they probably got their ticket for nix. As for the entertainment, there's probably no need to call in the ACCC to figure out that someone got ripped off.

X is for Ex, as in no longer being something that you used to be. On stage on Saturday were Michael Long, Alex Jesaulenko and Doug Wade, who are all ex-footballers. And a bloke named Meat Loaf, who is an ex-entertainer.

Y is for Why?, the lament of the broken-hearted. Why didn't Travis keep kicking goals from half a suburb away? Why didn't Krak and Taz and Leon make their dreams come true? Why did the Tomahawk come of age against us? Why in bat-less hell did they pay all that money for Meat Loaf?

Z is for zzzzzzzz, or as Jack Thompson said, "Now we can all get some sleep." And if you're as old and broken down as Meat Loaf, you'll need it.

The Age 3 October 2011